Richard W. Hull
New York University

MODERN AFRICA
Change and Continuity

P9-EDA-150

PRENTICE-HALL, INC., ENGLEWOOD CLIFFS, N.J. 07632

Library of Congress Cataloguing in Publication Data

Hull, Richard W (date).
  Modern Africa.

  Bibliography: p.
  Includes index.
  1. Africa, Sub-Saharan. I. Title.
DT351.H83   967   79–13130
ISBN 0–13–586305–8

Printed in the United States of America

10 9 8 7 6 5 4 3 2 1

Editorial/production supervision by Marina Harrison
Interior design by Serena Hoffman
Photographs by Richard Hull
Cover design by Wanda Lubelska
Manufacturing buyer: Ed Leone

PRENTICE-HALL INTERNATIONAL, INC., *London*
PRENTICE-HALL OF AUSTRALIA PTY. LIMITED, *Sydney*
PRENTICE-HALL OF CANADA, LTD., *Toronto*
PRENTICE-HALL OF INDIA PRIVATE LIMITED, *New Delhi*
PRENTICE-HALL OF JAPAN, INC., *Tokyo*
PRENTICE-HALL OF SOUTHEAST ASIA PTE. LTD., *Singapore*
WHITEHALL BOOKS LIMITED, *Wellington, New Zealand*

TO THE LATE REVEREND JAMES H. ROBINSON
(1907–1973)
Founder of Operation Crossroads Africa

Contents

chapter **9**

Patterns of Culture *233*

Preface

This book explores the fabric of sub-Saharan African civilizations, from the early nineteenth century to the present, but emphasizes the period after 1875. It is essentially a descriptive and analytical survey of elements of change and continuity in Africa's political, economic, social, and cultural institutions through three historical eras—precolonial, colonial, and independence. It revels that extent to which those institutions were shaped by changing African circumstances, brought on in part by the impact of the West.

Students and laymen are aware of the major dilemmas facing contemporary Africa: neocolonialism, dictatorships, ethnic and racial conflicts, explosive population growth and urbanization, malnutrition and disease, and the search for social justice and cultural identity. While we sway to musical vibrations of Afro-Beat and marvel at beautifully designed contemporary fabrics and sculptures, we express horror over Idi Amin's genocidal acts in Uganda and the blatant racism inherent in South African apartheid. Although we have come to know the surface events of contemporary Africa through the mass media, we are left confused and frustrated, largely because these events are not set within an historical/institutional context.

African civilizations are undergoing a process of constant change and upheaval. It is essential to appreciate that this has always been so. Preindependence institutions in Africa were not static and rigid. Many elements of contemporary African civilizations originated in the colonial and precolonial eras. For example, modern South African apartheid is the culmination of patterns of racial discrimination originating nearly three centuries earlier. Such highly democratic and egalitarian governments as Botswana, the Gambia, and Tanzania are partially the outgrowth of precolonial political systems based on free and open interaction. Bethwell Ogot of Nairobi University commented ". . . we are not likely to understand the nature and role of the military in postindependence Africa unless we also study the nature and role of the military in precolonial as well as in colonial Africa."* The same holds for most other institutions.

*B.A. Ogot, ed., *War and Society in Africa* (London: Frank Cass & Co., 1972), p. 5.

Thus, in trying to explain how Africa has come to be what it is today, I have gathered the threads of specific phenomena and institutions and woven them through three periods (precolonial, colonial, and independence) to form a complete tapestry. Readers in search of a comprehensive encyclopedic survey of African history will not find it here. For brevity and clarity, some ethnic groups and leaders have been touched upon lightly or not at all. I have sought to identify groups and leaders that influenced the course of recent African history or that provided the best examples of specific processes.

Regions in sub-Saharan Africa differ in importance in terms of population, resources, recorded data, cultural achievements, and so on. While more attention may be given to West or Central Africa in discussing urbanization or the plastic arts, greater emphasis may fall on southern Africa when dealing with questions of land alienation, migratory labor, and industrialization, or on East Africa when the spotlight shifts to agricultural development, socialism, or problems of economic integration.

In the past, most survey texts have focused on specific regions and were geared to serve a given academic discipline. They were narrowly directed to students of either history, art history, politics, anthropology, or sociology. Since the late 1960s, African civilizations have been incorporated into general courses in world civilizations required of students in various disciplines. A growing number of colleges have developed interdisciplinary, multiregional survey courses on African civilizations. This book attempts to fill the needs of such courses. It grew out of my desire to expose New York University students not only to the political history of Africa, but also to its artistic, architectural, religious, social, cultural, legal, and economic history, and to provide insights into their interaction. Formal lectures were enriched by artifacts, musical instruments, and color slides. The success of that approach led in 1974/75 to the presentation of a forty-seven-part series on "African Civilizations," telecast nationwide over the CBS network.

This book is also the culmination of seventeen years of reading and research in the United States, Western Europe, and Africa. However, much of the information is based on the specialized books, articles, and unpublished theses of fellow Africanists. I am particularly indebted to the following: Kwame Daaku, Samuel Decalo, Omoniyi Adewoye, Michael Crowder, Robert Collins, Susan Hall, A.G. Hopkins, Robert S. Jordan, Basil Davidson, Bethwell Ogot, John S. Mbiti, Margaret Peil, Reon Meij, T.O. Ranger, Robert S. Smith, Leslie Rubin, Leonard M. Thompson, Immanuel Wallerstein, and J.F.A. Ajayi. I am especially grateful for the valuable suggestions made by Graham W. Irwin and Kenneth Wylie. However, to Brian Walker, formerly History Editor at Prentice-Hall, must go the credit for bringing this book to fruition. After three years of hot pursuit, he finally persuaded me to commit my ideas to writing.

THE PRECOLONIAL ERA

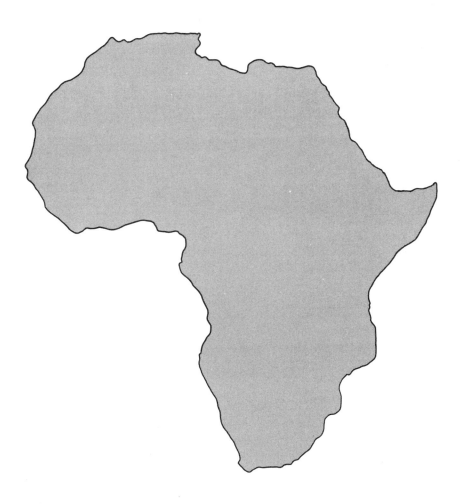

chapter 1

Patterns of Authority

EXPANSION OF AUTHORITY

In many regions of Africa the late nineteenth century both culminated in and led to the disintegration of the process of administrative centralization in the African states. The origins of this process reach back several centuries. From the late seventeenth century or earlier, a number of African kingdoms with homogeneous populations began to expand into territorial empires and embraced peoples of differing cultural traditions, religious beliefs, systems of authority, and ethnic backgrounds. This was the start of a new era of imperial expansion and exploitation, on a scale unprecedented since the golden eras of the empires of Ghana, Mali, Songhay, and Mwenemutapa many centuries earlier.

Beginning in the early eighteenth century in West Africa's grasslands, Muslim clerics of the Fulani ethnic group declared *jihads,* or holy wars, which led to the formation of the theocratic states of Futa Jallon (1725) in the central part of the modern Republic of Guinea and of Futa Toro (1776) along the southern bank of the Senegal River. This Muslim reformist movement reached its climax between 1804 and 1810 with the great Fulani jihad in the ancient Hausa-ruled kingdoms in what is today northern Nigeria. There, the ethnic Hausa ruling dynasties were overthrown one by one and replaced by Fulani revolutionaries. The various autonomous kingdoms, or emirates as they were subsequently called, were joined under the charismatic leadership of the cleric and teacher, Usuman dan Fodio, into the newly formed caliphates of Sokoto and Gwandu.

Southward, near the beginning of the rainforest, the Yoruba kingdom of Oyo expanded into an empire under the spiritual leadership of the Oni, who resided in the sacred city of Ifé, and under the secular leadership of the Alafin, whose palace lay in the city of old Oyo. To the West, the interior kingdom of Dahomey swept down to the coast and engulfed a series of small democratic city-states. Farther west, in the forest behind the Gold Coast, various Twi-speaking kingdoms formed a confederacy called Asante, with Kumasi city as its center and with an Asantehene as its monarch. It, too, expanded and pressed hard against the small autonomous Fante coastal states, whose only protection was the nearby British presence.

Similar trends appeared in East Africa in what is today Uganda. The compact and homogeneous kingdom of Buganda on the northwest shore of Lake Victoria had seceded from the unwieldy Bunyoro empire and had begun to expand territorially, everywhere challenging Bunyoro's hegemony. In southern Africa, small clans under the military leader Dingiswayo, and later Shaka, exploded into the lands of their peaceful Sotho-speaking neighbors. Many politically segmentary systems were destroyed and their inhabitants scattered, although by the mid-nineteenth century new states had been created by the refugees, notably Swaziland, Basutoland, and Matabeleland.

The above are but a few of the rapid political changes occurring across the continent. Many were in response to the threat and challenge of the growing influence of Europeans and Arabs in the political and economic lives of the traditional Africans. By the early nineteenth century, numerous African societies had developed centralized monarchies and had vastly enlarged the scale of their political units. Many of the better organized peoples were raiding and exploiting their neighbors, absorbing smaller principalities and placing them in a tributary position. The less politically organized societies affected by these trends were forced to restructure their patterns of authority on the basis of territorial chieftaincy rather than on the old basis of ritual and clan or lineage leadership. Initially, royal power tended to be strengthened through the process of centralization and the appointment of chiefs over the newly conquered lands. The original clans and traditional hereditary authorities sometimes were suppressed.

In many areas, the second half of the nineteenth century was a time of political consolidation. Centralized and largely appointive bureaucracies gradually emerged at the expense of the old hereditary aristocracy. Hereditary lineage systems and ritual priests and their orders were being challenged, as monarchs developed the criterion of merit in the appointment of administrative officials and assistants. In some cases, individuals of servile origin were given important titles and positions of considerable political power and economic wealth. In East, West, and Central Africa, increasing opportunities for war, trade, and commercial and agricultural enterprise generated new wealth and power for commoners, now challenging the political establishment. The political establishment had to cope with new external challenges—the infusion of foreign religious systems, especially Islam and Christianity, the latter with its conflicting denominations and Western values of individualism and egalitarianism. This was compounded by the accelerating penetration of capitalism and the opportunity for private and individual accumulation of wealth. In addition, the expansion in scale of kingdoms into territorial empires of an ethnically plural nature demanded fundamental constitutional changes, as well as radical restructuring of the system of government administration. Unfortunately, most African states could not make the adjustment quickly enough. Over

much of the continent, the last quarter of the nineteenth century was characterized by protracted civil wars and constitutional crises in which elites were
enmeshed in popular revolts by commercial entrepreneurs and military and
provincial chiefs. These conflicts were exacerbated by the growing presence of
official and nonofficial Europeans, in the capacity of missionaries, traders,

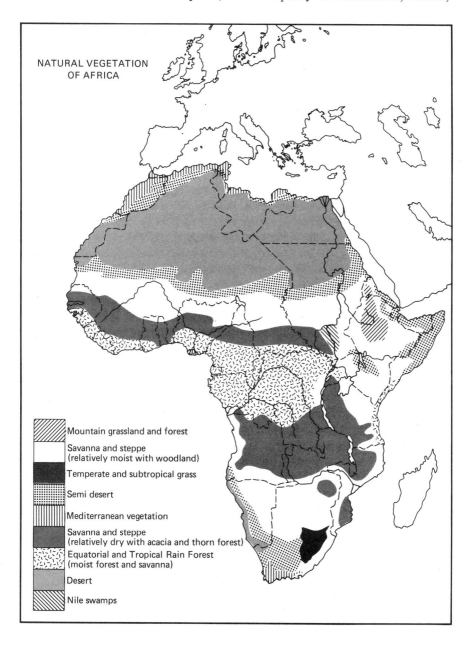

NATURAL VEGETATION
OF AFRICA

Mountain grassland and forest

Savanna and steppe
(relatively moist with woodland)

Temperate and subtropical grass

Semi desert

Mediterranean vegetation

Savanna and steppe
(relatively dry with acacia and thorn forest)

Equatorial and Tropical Rain Forest
(moist forest and savanna)

Desert

Nile swamps

hunters, and consuls, not only on the periphery of coastal enclaves, but increasingly within the political boundaries of African states. All of these trends can be better understood through case studies; it should be made clear that the following illustrations are by no means comprehensive. They are merely examples.

The Sokoto Caliphate, formed between 1804 and 1810 and administratively consolidated by 1837, may be seen as one of the most ambitious attempts at large-scale political integration in modern African history. It included several

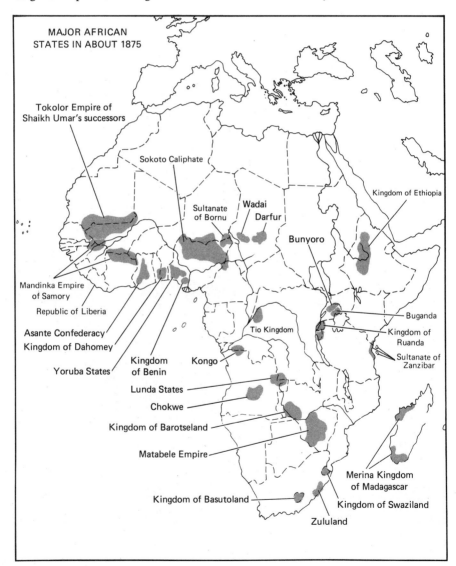

MAJOR AFRICAN
STATES IN ABOUT 1875

Tokolor Empire of
Shaikh Umar's successors

Sokoto Caliphate

Kingdom of Ethiopia

Sultanate
of Bornu

Wadai

Darfur

Bunyoro

Mandinka Empire
of Samory

Republic of Liberia

Asante Confederacy

Kingdom of Dahomey

Yoruba States

Kingdom
of Benin

Kongo

Tio Kingdom

Buganda

Kingdom of
Ruanda

Sultanate of
Zanzibar

Lunda States

Chokwe

Kingdom of Barotseland

Matabele Empire

Merina Kingdom
of Madagascar

Kingdom of Basutoland

Kingdom of Swaziland

Zululand

million people living in expansive emirates. Our examination will focus on Katsina, one of the major emirates in the caliphate.

It must first be emphasized that the Hausa were among the earliest settlers in northern Nigeria and that the Fulani were relative newcomers, having begun to filter in from the west in the mid-fifteenth century. The Fulani revolutionaries of the early nineteenth century were not members of the old Katsina Fulani establishment that had for centuries coexisted with the Hausa rulers. Rather, they were fairly new to the area and were only part Fulani, with strains of Arab, Mande, and other ancestry. Arriving later, they had to compete with Hausa agriculturalists for the dwindling reserve of fertile lands. These proud Fulani pastoralists despised peasant society, believing it to be inferior to their own. The jihad in Katsina may therefore be seen, in part, as a struggle between quasi-Fulani rural pastoralists and sedentary Hausa agriculturalists.

From oral testimonies, it would appear that the jihad in Katsina was fought largely by Fulani and that their primary motive was political—the overthrow of Hausa rule at every level of government. However, the clash between the rich, landed Fulani establishment and their poorer, though perhaps more politically ambitious, cousins indicates that there was a degree of class rivalry besides the ethnic competition between the Fulani and Hausa. Fulani newcomers, some of them nouveau riche, undoubtedly wanted political status commensurate with their roles as advisers and teachers; it is likely that the rural Fulani poor sought more grazing land and a more equitable tax system.

For the Fulani Muslim reformers, the holy war was a great success for they now controlled the former Hausa fiefs and therefore possessed great wealth and influence. Even though it was looked down upon socially by some of the older prewar elites, a new class had emerged. In the case of the Hausa aristocracy, the holy war had been a disaster. In nearly every instance, they lost political control and were driven into exile. The Hausa therefore lost political representation in Katsina and enjoyed few civil rights in the Sokoto Caliphate.

The Shaikh (sheik) Usuman dan Fodio established his base at Sokoto city and through his flag-bearing lieutenants was able to join the formerly independent Hausa kingdoms into a mighty and expansive Fulani empire. He assumed the title of Sarkin Musulmi, which literally means "King of the Muslims."

The title had dual significance, for the Sarkin Musulmi was both the political and spiritual overlord of the kingdoms in his immense empire. After dan Fodio died, successive rulers of the Caliphate (empire) assumed this title. Katsina's monarch, like those of other emirates in the Sokoto Caliphate, recognized the superiority of the Sarkin Musulmi and sent gifts to him from time to time as a token of their respect and allegiance. Within a few decades, this tribute became an annual payment of a portion of Katsina's revenue. The Sarkin Musulmi also had the privilege of deposing and confirming the appointments of not only the ruler of Katsina but the major hereditary nobles and kingmakers as well.

Since it would have been impossible for the Sarkin Musulmi to oversee the administration of every dependent kingdom, he appointed a representative to each. These agents spent several months each year in the dependent emirates and saw to it that Sokoto's share of the revenue was collected and transferred to the treasury of the Sarkin Musulmi.

During the nineteenth century, Katsina's emirs were preoccupied with wars of liberation waged by the old Hausa elites that had been driven into exile. These wars were costly and required that the emir be as strong as possible. From the 1840s on, successive Katsina emirs tried to bolster their power by centralizing their governments. Titled fiefholders were henceforth required to spend a portion of each year at the capital under the watchful eye of the emir and his court. Over time, this residency requirement was extended to the point at which the fiefholders rarely visited their constituencies and became, in effect, absentee landlords without direct political control over their fiefdoms. The responsibility for tax collection and general administrative supervision was now entrusted by them to their slaves, who were given the title of *jakada*. This transfer of responsibility was highly significant, for it resulted in a new class of government officials—a wealthy and powerful slave hierarchy without social status but with varying degrees of control over local administration. It furthermore led to the increasing urbanization and stabilization of the Fulani aristocracy.

Emir Belo and his successors may have brought the Fulani aristocracy more tightly under control, but it is doubtful that this led to any sweeping extension of authority over the major fiefs. In fact, those fiefholders who received their titles directly from Sokoto and who remitted their taxes to the Sarkin Musulmi resisted these attempts to force them to reside at the emirate's capital. The special relationship with Sokoto, which some of them had enjoyed since the days of the jihad, enabled them to maintain a certain degree of independence and made it difficult for the emir to encroach on their prerogatives.

Katsina's emirs sought to overcome the authority of the weaker landed aristocrats in several ways. First, they enlarged the palace staff, gave them new titles, created new forms of taxation, and entrusted them with the responsibility for collecting those taxes. Consequently, there were two sets of tax collectors: those responsible directly to the emir and those who were employed by the fiefholders. Second, some of the palace staff were given fiefs to govern and were made directly responsible to the emir. Katsina's emirs thus gave the slaves a large measure of political control over local administration and tax collection, and in so doing hoped to short-circuit the power of the hereditary aristocrats, who had quite naturally tried to block any aggrandizement of power by the office of the emir.

Katsina's incessant wars with the Hausa exiles in Maradi to the north are important because they reveal the continuing weakness of the Katsina regime. Most of the battles were defensive. Katsina—despite its numerical superiority— was not united enough to prevent the Hausa exiles from probing deep within its frontiers. For Katsina's emirs, the connection with its overlord, Sokoto, was

Mud palace of the Emir of Maradi, Republic of Niger, West Africa.

a mixed blessing. Shaikh Usuman dan Fodio and his successors had imposed on the emirate an effective system of checks and balances. The powers of the successive Katsina emirs were circumscribed not only by the ultimate authority, the Sarkin Musulmi, but through those aristocrats who had received their commissions directly from Sokoto. This assured dependence and helped to ensure continuing loyalty and cordial relations between the two political entities. Successive emirs of Katsina also received their commissions of office from the Sarkin Musulmi, who lent legitimacy and strength to their position vis-à-vis certain titled local aristocrats. By the same token, those latter officials cherished their own special relationship with Sokoto and used it to shield against attempts by emirs to whittle away their authority and prerogatives. The tragedy for Katsina was that the Fulani Muslim reformers had failed to give the Hausa a role in the governance of the new, post-jihadic regime. The Fulani wanted the total destruction of Hausa authority, regardless of whether a given Hausa chief happened to have professed Islam. By failing to win the unequivocal support of the Hausa peasantry (especially the Hausa townsfolk) and some of their overlords, the Fulani had to cope with neutral or hostile elements within Katsina throughout the century. Finally, the Fulani reformers avoided any substantive land reform and held the non-Islamic, non-Hausa, and non-Fulani peasants in subjection. Thus, the great jihadic victories in Katsina and in other emirates of the Sokoto Caliphate were somewhat hollow. In the long run, a sharing of power between Fulani and Hausa Muslims might have ensured peace and greater popular representation in government.

The financial demands of war forced emirs to constantly raise taxes and broaden the base of taxation. In about 1845 in Katsina, all important male craftsmen became liable to tax payment, and the cattle tax was raised periodically. By the 1880s, taxes had begun to fall heavily upon the upper-middle-class traders, the peasants, and the nomadic pastoralists. The urban Fulani, especially the government bureaucrats, usually were exempt from taxation.

On the eve of the British conquest in 1903, Katsina's emir ruled an emirate more centralized than it had been since the jihad of 1804–10 or earlier. But there was a price for this. The political maneuverings of successive emirs produced the very situation they wished to avoid: that of being a captive of their own advisers. During their search for power, they succeeded in freeing themselves from the traditional restraints placed upon their office by the Fulani aristocracy, especially the kingmakers. In so doing they became increasingly reliant upon the chief palace slaves and their own appointees for critical decisions and for administration. This naturally was disturbing to the titled aristocracy. Local subordinate traditional officials were becoming alarmed, insecure, and demoralized by the emir's frequent and arbitrary depositions and appointments. This resulted in intense rivalry for local administrative posts and a concomitant decline in the power and prestige of these positions. Those fiefholders residing in the capital of Katsina seemed to care little about the standard of administrative efficiency in their distant fiefs as long as taxes were collected punctually. Thus, their subordinate slave tax collectors had much leeway. They, in turn, frequently intimidated local village chiefs, and this led to a cleavage between the two sets of authority.

Emir Abubakr (r. 1887–1904) had forged a more centralized state than had existed before he came to power, but in so doing he created severe internal strains and set into motion centrifugal forces which, if it had not been for the subsequent British conquest, eventually might have had the opposite effect— political fragmentation.

A variation on the themes just discussed may be seen in western Nigeria. The old Oyo empire was centered near the Niger River on the edge of the savanna and near the caravan routes running between the coast and the Hausa markets in the northern savanna. Oyo, one of the Yoruba-speaking kingdoms, reached its zenith in the mid-eighteenth century. It encompassed many Yoruba kingdoms, all of which recognized the city of Ifé as the origin of their ancient civilization and its spiritual center. The *Oni* of Ifé has been considered by all

Yoruba as their spiritual overlord. But over the centuries the office of Oni became politically subordinate to the *Alafin* of Oyo. The Alafin was considered the most powerful political figure and was at once king and priest to his people. Though he had considerable power, he had to share it with others—primarily with the Oni, on the one hand, and a council of hereditary nobles called the Oyo Mesi, on the other. This was a body of seven major chiefs selected from among members of the leading descent groups. All of them held titles hereditary in their own families; consequently, the Alafin could not choose them, nor could he dispose of them. They therefore enjoyed a degree of independence.

The major member of the Oyo Mesi was the *Basorun,* who was like a prime minister. He was the principal kingmaker, and along with the other members of the Oyo Mesi chose successors to the Alafinship. The Basorun was also considered the interpreter of the Alafin's own spirit. As high priest of almost all the major cults, he could proclaim that the ancestors and heaven had lost confidence in the Alafin and could therefore demand that the Alafin commit suicide. The Basorun would exclaim, "The gods reject you, the earth rejects you, the people reject you." Following this pronouncement, one member of the Oyo Mesi was required to die with the Alafin. The Oyo Mesi also had to obtain the permission of another important body, the Ogboni Society. The Ogboni Society consisted of influential men and a few elderly women who commanded great respect; it was devoted to the cult of the earth, but it also

Installation ceremony of the new Emir of Daura, northern Nigeria 1966. Emir is riding Arabian stallion under a royal umbrella and holding the legendary silver dagger of Bayagida, the 10th century founder of the Hausa states.

had judicial and political functions. In addition, the society acted as a mediator between the Alafin and his staff, on the one hand, and the Oyo Mesi, on the other. At installation rites, they played the crucial role of giving the Alafin the power of his ancestors.

Let us return again to the office of Alafin. The Alafin had an enormous palace staff. Directly under him was the *Aremo,* his eldest son. In the early days of the Oyo empire, he was the heir apparent. He assisted his father in the performance of the rituals. There were also three graded palace eunuchs: one acted as chief judge; the second as administrative head of the cult of Shango, a cult worshipping the Alafin's deified ancestors; and the third eunuch was responsible for fiscal affairs and for the central intelligence agency. After the eunuchs were the titled royal slaves, called *Ilari.* They were sent out into the distant provinces to collect tribute and to oversee administration. Also connected to the palace were eight titled ladies, led by an official queen mother. The Alafin's real mother was put to death upon his accession to office. In the provinces were associations of town chiefs, or *obas.* Most of them were figureheads, tightly controlled by local Ogboni Societies. It should be noted that the "town" was the basic political unit on which Yoruba local government was based. Towns were groups of lineages made up of families. The first lineage to settle in a given town usually dominated the rest.

Government in Yorubaland had a complex system of checks and balances. For centuries its unwritten constitution gave the country unprecedented peace and prosperity. Alafins were bound by tradition, precedent, and these countervailing bodies. The Oni and Alafin were regarded as men who could do no wrong and commanded tremendous respect from everyone. They held the nation together and gave it its moral, political, and cultural mission.

BREAKDOWN OF AUTHORITY

This remarkably democratic and dynamic system of governance worked very well for many centuries. Then, in the seventeenth century the Oyo kingdom began a policy of imperialism, of territorial expansion. Oyo became an empire and with the conquest of different societies and the acquisition of war booty, the Alafin and his palace bureaucracy grew in wealth, power, and numbers. The executive branch became fat, unwieldy, and overconfident. By 1750, the executive staff numbered over fifteen thousand, most of whom were of servile origin and were, therefore, directly responsible to and dependent upon the Alafin for their tenure. By the late eighteenth century, tension had begun to build up between the Alafin and the Oyo Mesi. Alafins began to step beyond their constitutional bounds, and the Basorun and Oyo Mesi forced more and more of them to commit suicide.

In the 1790s, the Alafin attacked a town belonging to Ifé. This act was unprecedented and sacrilegious, and the Alafin had to commit suicide. People now began to lose faith in the office of Alafin. Subsequent Alafins were weak and had to contend with ambitious and unscrupulous Basoruns. Succession to the Alafinship no longer passed automatically to the ruler's eldest son. Basoruns, as kingmakers, began deliberately to select weak Alafins to office and soon overshadowed them. Concurrently, the Oyo empire was being threatened militarily by Muslim Fulani from the north. Eventually the whole structure of the empire collapsed. The nation had lost confidence in its leaders and in its once-outstanding system of government. In 1837, the magnificent capital, Oyo city, was destroyed by the Fulani onslaught, and the Alafin was forced to flee. The disintegration of the Oyo empire upset the delicate balance of power and created a political vacuum. Subordinate kingdoms seceded and competed for power. Yorubaland was plunged into almost complete anarchy, law and order breaking down everywhere.

The collapse of the old Oyo empire resulted in a southward demographic shift, from savanna to forest, and in political rivalries and wars among successor states. The need for security led many communities to unite in order to survive and to allow themselves to be amalgamated into larger towns under strong military leaders. Out of the ashes of the Oyo empire rose powerful city-states, notably Ibadan. Power and glory fell into the hands of the military, for only they could save Yorubaland from social and cultural obliteration. In Ibadan, chieftaincy titles became open to men of talent with military prowess. Throughout Yorubaland, the war chiefs played a greater role in the governments of the towns. In the process the principle of hereditary kingship receded.

The Fulani invasion eventually was repulsed, and the civil wars also ended. But the Yoruba were weakened and disspirited by all this and were rendered extremely vulnerable to still another invader—the British. The Yoruba people had failed to create an effective new political order in place of the one that had flourished in old Oyo. The British, after contributing to the disintegration through the arms trade, in 1893 became peacemakers and the power that filled the vacuum left by old Oyo's demise.

The Asante Confederacy, in what is today the forest zone of central Ghana, had a similar history. The confederacy emerged in the late seventeenth century through the ascendancy of Kumasi, a small city-state lying along a major intersection of trade routes between the coast and savanna. According to legend a golden stool fell from the sky onto the knees of the Kumasi chief, who henceforth became the Asante chief, or *Asantehene*. The stool came to be regarded by the people of Kumasi and the neighboring city-states as symbolizing the spiritual unity of the Asante nation. All Asante, as the people came to call themselves, acquired a dual allegiance: to their own chiefs and lineage heads, and to the Golden Stool and its possessor, the Asantehene. The people were further linked together by an annual national event, the Odwira festival. Osei Tutu, the first Asantehene, solved the problem of provincial administration by incorporating all the kingdoms, or city-states, lying within a twenty-to-thirty-mile radius of Kumasi into the Asante Confederacy and extending Asante membership to their people. Each kingdom retained a large measure of administrative autonomy. Their leaders shared power in the national assembly with the Asantehene, the queen mother, and the royally appointed military chiefs of Kumasi.

All worked well until Asantehene Opoku Ware (c. 1721-50) decided to expand. The confederacy's armies fanned out in a north-south direction, and by the late eighteenth century the confederacy, with its swelled army, had established its hegemony from the Gold Coast through the high forest and far into Muslim lands in the northern savanna. Asante had been transformed into a territorial empire consisting of Kumasi and the original metropolitan kingdoms, all voluntarily held together by the Golden Stool, plus the outlying conquered territories, welded together by a combination of military force and the diplomacy of the Asantehene. The conquered peoples were denied Asante citizenship and were excluded from the conferation's councils and assembly. Increasingly, the power and very survival of the Asante empire came to depend almost entirely upon military force.

By the end of the eighteenth century, literate Muslims from the north were attracted by the Asantehene to Kumasi to serve in the central administration as treasurers and scribes. Eventually, the Muslim presence resulted in a clash between Islam and the traditional religious system. The Asantehene, Osei Kwame, was deposed for his pro-Muslim sympathies and for his efforts to introduce Qur'anic law in place of traditional legal precedents.

Beginning in the early nineteenth century, successive Asantehenes concluded that the empire could be consolidated administratively only by weakening the authority of the confederation chiefs. They did this by trying to reduce the metropolitan kingdoms to the same status as the more distant conquered territories. By the 1820s Asante was moving towards a bureaucratic system in which many administrative positions were appointive rather than hereditary. Unlike the older aristocracy, dating back to pre-Asante times, the new bureaucracy was made subservient to the king, or Asantehene. Outside of Kumasi, the traditional rulers tried to resist and were initially held in check by an intelligence unit created by the Asantehene. The democratic national assembly was gradually expanded through royal appointments and ultimately lost its ability constitutionally to check the Asantehene's power.

This centralizing policy failed to achieve the objective of unity, in part because of Asante's persistent wars with the British on the coast after 1824. These wars weakened the army and emptied the central government's treasury. The Asantehene's ability to control the provinces was diminished, and the peripheral southern states in the confederacy were therefore able to rebel and to reassert their independence under British "protection." After each invasion the British withdrew, rather than incurring the cost of bringing Asante under their administration. Following the British burning of Kumasi in 1874, the prestige of the Asantehene fell further and centrifugal tendencies began in the north as well. Throughout most of the last quarter of the nineteenth century, Asante was beset by constant civil warfare, succession disputes, palace coups, attempted assassinations, and economic stagnation. The Asantehenes had to preoccupy themselves with struggles with the federated kingdoms and the imperialistic activities of the meddlesome British. They also had to cope with a rising class of African and mulatto traders and commercial farmers who protested against the ruinous war taxes and economic uncertainty. Finally, in 1896 the British de-stooled and exiled the Asantehene. After some military resistance led by the powerful queen mother, Asante in 1901 became an administrative unit of the British Gold Coast.

CENTRALIZATION AND BUREAUCRATIZATION

By the mid-seventeenth century in East Africa, the small, compact kingdom of Buganda on the northwest shore of Lake Victoria had become independent from the archaic and unwieldy Bunyoro empire. Bunyoro had been weakened by its constant raids on its neighbors and enabled Buganda to gain strength. Over the next century and a half, Buganda more than doubled in size, largely at the expense of Bunyoro. The various Ganda clans were bound together by allegiance to the king, or *kabaka,* whose position was hereditary. He was advised by a legislative council, called the *lukiko.* Within the lukiko sat the prime minister, or *katikiro,* who, as the most powerful commoner in Buganda, was directly responsible to the king. Under the katikiro was a long line of administrators, including the powerful county chiefs. At the close of the eighteenth century, the Buganda government was moving from a feudal hereditary structure to a bureaucratic framework based on meritocracy. Successive kabakas strengthened their positions by centralizing the administration. This was achieved by weakening the hereditary clan leaders and replacing them with royal appointees. By the last decade of the eighteenth century, seven of the ten county chiefs were appointed by the kabaka, rather than inheriting office.

Buganda continued to expand territorially, and by 1875 it was one of the most powerful states in East Africa. With firearms furnished by Arab traders, the kabaka's powerful army raided its neighbors, especially Bunyoro, Toro, Ankole, and island principalities near Lake Victoria. As Buganda grew in territory, the kabaka expanded the number of chiefs. The acquisition of new territories necessitated an expansion of the administration and gave greater power to the kabaka and his military chiefs. But the people in the tributary states were not assimilated, as long as they paid taxes and sent gifts to the central administration.

In the last quarter of the nineteenth century, firearms became more widely

Reconstruction of a precolonial reed palace of a kabaka, or king, of Buganda. Kampala, Uganda, 1970.

available and Buganda was confronted with rebellious tributary states. The closure of the Zanzibar slave market by the British in 1873 also deprived Buganda of a major portion of its trade. The kabakaship was weakened further by the introduction of foreign religious elements—the Muslim Arabs after 1844, the Protestant Church Missionary Society (CMS) in 1877, and the Roman Catholic White Fathers a year later. Muslims, Christians, and traditional religious leaders competed for power and influence at the kabaka's court. The kabaka constantly shifted his support among them, depending on their ability to furnish trade goods and on their knowledge of the outside world. Meanwhile, the three rival politico-religious groups vied for local converts. This led to excessive Christian influence over the youths at the court, to the execution of thirty converts in 1886, and to open civil war two years later between the kabaka and the converts to the three foreign religions. Kabaka Mwanga lost the war, and the hereditary chiefs seized the opportunity to reassert a large measure of their authority. By then, chieftaincy in Buganda was in the ascendancy over monarchy. Central government was debilitated further and was divided by the imperialist ambitions of the French, Germans, and British, all seeking control over the Nile's headwaters and the East African interior. In 1890 the Germans recognized what is today Uganda, as a British sphere of influence. Four years later a formal protectorate was established over the area. After an unsuccessful attempt to rebel in 1897, the Kabaka Mwanga fled and, along with the king of Bunyoro, was deported by the British to the Seychelles Islands in the Indian Ocean.

Southern Africa had a similar history. After the disintegration of the Rozwi Mwenemutapa empire in the mid-sixteenth century in what is today Zimbabwe, the ancient Shona people lost political unity and a centralized authority. They were scattered thinly over a wide area and lived within a very loose Rozwi confederation. Other than a proud history, their major bond was the Mwari cult and its spirit mediums.

In the 1830s, these peaceful Shona endured successive waves of Ngoni invaders, many of whom were fugitives of the Zulu kingdom in South Africa. The last wave was in 1837, led by the militant Ndebele, who were the elite of Shaka's Zulu army. Within a decade the Ndebele had imposed a highly centralized militaristic government on the almost defenseless Shona. The two ethnic groups had fundamentally different interests. The Shona had earned their livelihood from long-distance trade and gold mining, while the Ndebele raised cattle, raided, and farmed. The Ndebeles' stress on disciplined, tightly controlled troops enabled them to overthrow easily the Shona's relatively more complex and sophisticated social and political system. The Ndebeles' power came to rest on military force and coercion, as well as on the control of captives and cattle. The basis of the Shonas' social and political organization had been land and religion.

The Ndebele quickly established a small and highly centralized military state centered on the capital at Bulawayo. It was initially ruled by a warrior, Mzilikazi, who acted as absolute monarch. He was succeeded at his death in 1868 by Lobengula. The latter occasionally sought the advice of three major councilors from two councils. Matabeleland, as the empire came to be called, was always a meritocracy, even to the extent that males in the royal families were excluded from government in order to prevent nepotism. What mattered most was an individual's military acumen and his ability to elicit blind obedience. Not everyone had free access to this meritocracy. Beneath Mzilikazi and his successor, Lobengula, was an aristocracy, called the *zansi*, consisting of pure Ndebele who as fugitives had accompanied Mzilikazi on the long trek from Zululand. They held nearly all the important positions in the administration and army and controlled the regiments.

Matabeleland was divided into four provinces, corresponding to the four army divisions. Each province was under an *induna,* or war chief. The provinces were in turn subdivided into regimental communities (*buto*), each under a lesser induna. Only the king could create or dismantle a buto. Unlike the traditional Shona leaders, the indunas had no ritual or hereditary claim to office, for all positions were in the hands of the king.

Militarism became the basis of Ndebele solidarity and Matabele nationalism. The king had no private army or palace guard but did have effective control over the entire military structure. While some of the conquered Shona were incorporated and assimilated into the Matabele empire and its regiments, most remained in a tributary relationship and frequently were raided for crops, cattle, and able-bodied men. The proud Ndebele had little respect for the Shona, whom they considered effete and cowardly. Yet they did adopt their religious system and became faithful followers of the Mwari cult. The unwillingness of the Ndebele to share political power with the Shona may have been their undoing. Matabeleland was conquered and colonized by Rhodes' British South Africa Company in 1893 partly because the oppressed Shona refused to join the Ndebele in their resistance. The Ndebele rebelled against the settlers three years later when Rhodes' forces were tied down in the abortive Jameson Raid against the Boers in the Transvaal. In the second Matabele War of 1896–97 the Shona united with the Ndebele but by then it was too late.

THE ZULU IMPACT

Many polities that arose in the vast area between the Limpopo River and the southern end of Lake Tanganyika were inspired by the Zulu kingdom. The father of the Zulu nation was Shaka, who from 1818 to 1828 created a powerful, centralized, militaristic kingdom held together by a standing army of over 40,000 warriors. Shaka was a military dictator. He determined his own policy, unlike Nguni chiefs of the past, who had always ruled in consultation with their headmen and councilors.

By the 1870s the Zulu kingdom had become the most powerful African State south of the Zambesi River. The dominant values of Zulu life were those of the strong warrior. A Zulu was called "war-shield of the king" and vowed strict obedience to Shaka and his successors. All youths were subject to the draft, much as they were in the West African kingdom of Dahomey. All power was concentrated in the army, in which a man could realize his full potential. Zulu men and women were organized into age regiments, placed in segregated military settlements, and, like the women's Amazon Corps of Dahomey, took vows of celibacy. The children and older members in society were responsible for producing crops and raising stock in the civilian villages, while the army devastated hundreds of square miles of territory far beyond the Zulu heartland. Shaka's violent imperialist ventures touched off a northern Nguni diaspora. Some Nguni refugees formed their own military bands and established conquest states in southern Mozambique, Swaziland, Malawi and, in the case of Mzilikazi, in what is today Zimbabwe. Most of these were modeled after the Zulu state.

Zululand lay along the strategically vital South African coastland, adjacent to the British colony of Natal. British policy since the 1840s had been to prevent the landlocked white Afrikaner republics from expanding to the sea and securing an independent port. It was inevitable that the entire coast of South Africa would fall under British control. They had begun to annex portions of Zululand in 1877; two years later the Zulu army under King Cetswayo gave the British their greatest defeat since the Crimean War. It was a devastating blow to Victorian sensibilities. Months later the British returned and, with superior weaponry, totally destroyed the 30,000-man Zulu army. The short stabbing spear was simply no match against heavy British cannons and rapid-firing rifles. After 1879, Cetswayo was deposed, and Zululand was divided into thirteen separate territories under thirteen rival chiefs. It was a Machiavellian tactic to divide Zulus against themselves. The process of national disintegration began and accelerated in 1887 when the British annexed the remainder of Zululand, dividing it into districts and placing each under a European magistrate.

BOERS AND BRITONS

By the last quarter of the nineteenth century, blacks in southern Africa were rapidly losing control over their political destiny. Between 1852 and 1854, two Afrikaner republics, the Orange Free State and the Transvaal, were established north of the Orange River on the vast open grassland plateau that was formerly under Sotho control. These republics were the culmination of an Afrikaner diaspora out of the British-controlled Cape Colony. They wrote constitutions expressly forbidding any nonwhite participation in their republican governments. Africans were denied citizenship, even though they made up the majority of the population. Both states had a strong presidency and a representative legislature, called a *volksraad*. Though the almost bankrupt Transvaal was proclaimed a British Crown Colony in 1877, it regained its self-government four years later after the first Anglo-Boer War. By then, Afrikaners, spurred on by British interference in their affairs, had acquired a national consciousness. In 1880 they formed a political organization, called the Afrikaner Bond, which was pan-Afrikaner in objective and sought to mobilize Afrikaans voters throughout South Africa.

The Cape Colony, under firm British control since 1805, was granted representative self-government in 1853. Its constitution provided for a parliament consisting of two houses, both wholly elected by men, regardless of race. In 1872, the Cape was given control over the executive, subject only to veto by the British parliament in London. While the Cape constitution may have been color-blind, the property and education qualifications for voting were so high as to exclude nearly all nonwhites. Indeed, no colored or African ever sat in the Cape parliament.

A parliament was also created in Natal in 1856 and the colony received control over its executive in 1893. A complex web of laws virtually excluded Africans and Asians from the franchise. Between 1899 and 1902, the imperial British armies again went to war with the Afrikaner republics in the second Anglo-Boer War, this time fully incorporating them into the British Empire. In 1910 the former colonies of the Transvaal, Orange Free State, Natal, and the Cape were joined to form the Union of South Africa. The political consolidation of South Africa had thus been achieved, but at the cost of a bloody war and at the expense of the black majority.

THE DEMOCRATIC IMPERATIVE

It would be inaccurate to view sub-Saharan Africa in the late nineteenth century as everywhere under the governance of centralized regimes ruled by powerful monarchs. Local authorities struggled to retain their prerogatives and stoutly resisted centralizing tendencies. In fact, Africans in many regions continued to live under somewhat democratic, politically segmentary systems in which power rarely extended beyond local chiefs, hereditary clan elders, ritual priests, and rainmakers. Chiefs almost everywhere remained custodians of the ancestral lands and allocated them to deserving subjects. In turn, they were given a share of trade, crops, and livestock. Chiefs were expected to be the most generous men in the country, winning loyalty through patronage and engaging the population in mutual gift-giving.

The Igbo of eastern Nigeria provide an outstanding example of direct democracy. Despite centralizing tendencies in neighboring states, the Igbo adhered to a form of respresentative democracy, based at the village-group level. The largest unit of Igbo political organization was usually a collection of villages whose inhabitants believed they descended from a common founding father. Village government consisted of two institutions: the village assembly of citizens, made up of all adult males and lineage heads, and the council of elders. Every citizen was entitled to participate in the assembly, and all decisions had to be unanimous. Age groups and secret societies assisted in the enforcement of the assembly's decisions. By the 1880s some Igbo villages had an *Obi,* or presidential monarch, who ruled through the council of elders and the village assembly. Yet individual achievement rather than heredity continued to be emphasized. Every Igbo, no matter how humble his birth, could aspire to economic and political leadership.

Similarly democratic forms of government existed in the lightly populated areas of East, Central, and southern Africa, where people lived at a bare subsistence level on semiarid lands and produced little surplus. This was particularly true of nomadic and seminomadic peoples living in the grasslands of East Africa, in what is today Kenya and Tanzania. For many of these small groups, government remained quite simple and small. A local informant told Professor Gideon Were that:

> We used to be ruled by the Weng'oma (the one of the drum). His duties were to protect and to care for the country; to prevent wars; and to stop fighting; and to bring peace and harmony among the people. The weng'oma was neither a war leader nor a rainmaker nor a magician; he had his elders

who discharged the functions of foretelling the future, rainmaking, and officiating at sacrifices.[1]

Professor Were, in further studies, indicates that since the sixteenth century the neighboring pastoral Abashieni peoples of western Kenya have been ruled by the *Omwami Omukhongo,* or "great ruler." He was elected by the elders on the basis of his ability to settle quarrels. The elders, in turn, were elected by the whole community, consisting of clans and subclans. In some societies, clan organization tended to work against the evolution of any form of executive authority. The Luo people of western Kenya were divided by the late nineteenth century into clan groupings, some of which numbered over 60,000. Each grouping had its own chief, who ruled through a council of clan elders. But there was no tendency toward the concentration of power in the hands of one official.

Centralization of power in some societies was a response to the growing pressure of population and competition for land. By acquiring control over land distribution, an official could become extremely powerful, particularly if he claimed an ancestral affiliation with the spirits of the earth. Some societies made a deliberate effort to prevent control of land distribution from falling into the hands of a single official. Among the Sukuma of East Africa, land distribution and the assignment of labor were firmly in the hands of village age-grade organizations which jealously guarded their privilege. They ensured that chiefs would be weak.

LAW AND JUSTICE

Customary laws in precolonial Africa were not written or codified but were passed down through generations as proverbs, maxims, or adages. They had a spiritual logic rooted in a social milieu undergoing constant change. Many laws were linked to religious customs and rituals. In small-scale stateless societies, religious practices often acted as informal legal procedures.

Almost universally, religious systems helped to affirm a society's values, and, in so doing, they discouraged criminality or deviant behavior. Unwritten laws appeared to be immutable because of their links to religion and ritual. Yet, in truth, the lack of written codification made many laws remarkably flexible and responsive to social change. While judges looked to long-established rules of behavior and hallowed precedents for guidance, their final decisions reflected contemporary values and social relationships. However, courts existed mainly for the purpose of conciliation and were not viewed as agents of social reformation.

Customary laws were laid down, reiterated, and sometimes reinterpreted

[1] Gideon S. Were, *Western Kenya: Historical Texts* (Nairobi: East African Literature Bureau, 1967), p. 93.

by a wide variety of decision-making bodies. They may have included secret societies, informal open meetings of kinsmen, assemblies of elders, or perhaps formal councils of chiefs. In centralized kingdoms we might find a king and his nonfree advisors sitting in judgment. In most societies there were no officers of the law, only representatives of interested parties.

The severity of punishment often was decided by one's status in society. For example, under Nguni law in southern Africa, the accused individual paid a higher penalty if the offense were against a chiefly family. A condemned man in Asante, in some instances, could save his life through payment of a heavy fine in gold dust. However, even an Asante chief could not escape capital punishment if he had killed someone equal to or above him in rank. High status, in fact, could be a liability.

A serious crime in one society might be a minor offense in another or no offense at all. Africans understood this and tended to be tolerant of differences in law among different clans or ethnic and cultural groups. Nevertheless, in precolonial Africa certain transgressions received general condemnation. Witchcraft, sorcery, murder, and treason were defined universally as serious crimes. One could receive the death penalty in Dahomey for comitting arson, rape, chronic theft, or adultery with a member of the royal family. In the Mossi states, in what is today Upper Volta, theft, adultery, indebtedness, and trespassing were minor offenses whereas arson, witchcraft, kidnapping, and rape brought capital punishment. The more common and relatively less severe crimes were marital altercations, land disputes, petty jealousy between women, and disrespect for elders. Breaches of custom or ritual could be minor or serious, depending on the infraction. In all cases, an understanding of the social relationship between disputants was essential to deciding the proper procedure for resolving the case. African judges viewed some crimes as offenses against family or clan, others against the state. Acts considered more serious were usually those against the ancestors or God—both creators of law and the final judges of men. Yet divinely revealed laws depended on secular considerations and social precedents for their interpretations and implementations.

Justice in precolonial Africa could sometimes be arbitrary if the accused were found guilty after consulting oracles or spiritual mediums. Usually, considerable effort and care would be taken to obtain evidence. Individuals in Igboland handled their own cases by calling and cross-examining their own witnesses. Sometimes, one even could win a court case by citing a more pertinent proverb than the plaintiff could.

Every judge had the responsibility for maintaining or restoring the social equilibrium within a community. Consequently, the social implications of a specific dispute were important, and the aim of the judge was more to restore order and good relations than to punish the offender. Yet minimizing or localizing the social effects of an offense was not always easy. African societies had a strong sense of collective or shared responsibility, of which the individual was perceived as an integral part. Asante clansmen expressed this as: "I am because we are; and since we are, therefore I am." This summarizes the African conception of one's responsibility to his fellow man. An offender's guilt had to be shared by his entire family. If the offender were found to be mentally ill, his family would be allowed to practice communal psychotherapy on him in hopes of curing his deviant behavior. African judges usually drew a distinction between mental illness and criminality. Local diviners and religious leaders would be asked to help the offender's family in rehabilitation through ritual sacrifice and by interpreting the spiritual or magical causes of his deviant behavior. According to Dr. T.A. Lambo of Nigeria, "A supernatural belief system . . . is not a sphere of arbitrary dreams but a sphere of laws that dictate the rules of kinship, the order of the universe, the route to happiness."[2] Responsibility for an offender's actions had to be shared by his entire family.

Compensation became an effective means of restoring tranquility, but more serious conflicts usually warranted harsher punishment. Before the nineteenth century, few Africans had any concept of incarceration. Among the nomadic Masai of Kenya, punishment was judged in terms of loss of livestock. To a Masai, losing cattle as a form of punishment was far more painful because one's wealth and status were measured in cattle.

With the escalation in warfare throughout much of Africa in the late nineteenth century, imprisonment became more common. By 1880 nearly every town in Yorubaland had a prison. In Buganda, the accused was detained by shackling an arm or leg in stocks secured with a heavy log or a stake. Death appeared to have been more common in centralized states. Capital punishment sometimes was decapitation, as in nineteenth-century Asante.

Maiming was another severe form of punishment. In Bunyoro, for example, adultery could bring a fine of two household women plus the loss of a limb, eye, or ear. In Asante, public ridicule was occasionally viewed as a punishment tantamount to death. In Igboland, banishment from one's community was also a much dreaded form of castigation.

Justice in precolonial Africa was not administered solely on the basis of customary law. New procedures complemented and challenged traditional legal conceptions in areas of Muslim trade and leadership. Islam led to the separation of judicial and executive systems. It embodied a legal system based on the *Shari'a*—the sacred law of all Muslims. From early times, two important codes of law prevailed: The *Shafi'i* in East Africa and Egypt, and the *Maliki* in West Africa. Islamic law was usually dispensed by clerics (ministers of the Qur'an) or by judges, called *Qadi* or *Alkali*. Over the centuries, a compromise developed between customary law and Islamic law. This is not surprising, for the two had much in common. Both accepted the concept of collective responsibility. They also had the twin objectives of compensation and reconciliation

[2] Thomas A. Lambo, "Psychotherapy in Africa," *Human Nature,* March, 1978, pp. 32-33.

in settling disputes. There was a mutual recognition that fines could be levied according to age, sex, and status. In addition, the Shari'a left much room for the imposition of customary law. Homicide and cases of physical injury were handled as torts, whereas only theft, illicit sexual relations, and drunkenness lay clearly within its definition as crimes.

To serious students of Muslim law, the Shari'a remained the sacred law of Islam—governing all aspects of life. For them, insufficient emphasis fell on the legal and religious aspects of Islam. They saw African ruling elites returning to traditional religions and legal customs for answers to their judicial problems. This concern sparked the jihadic movements and a consequential Muslim revival in the Western and Central Sudan of West Africa.

Islamic law spread rapidly during the nineteenth century. It grew most dramatically in the newly created theocratic states of the Futas Jallon and Toro, in the Tukolor empire of al-Haj Umar, and in the Sokoto Caliphate. Under al-Kanami, Islamic law continued to flourish in the Bornu empire in what is today northeastern Nigeria.

Some nineteenth century African nation-builders were well versed in Maliki law and emphasized the legalistic aspects of Islam. Under them, qadis became more influential. In the emirates of the Sokoto Caliphate, they were made financially independent of the government by receiving their own revenue-producing estates. The chief Alkali in each emirate held a life appointment, and emirs could not remove them without permission from the Sarkin Musulmi in Sokoto. This made the central judiciary in emirates fairly independent of the executive branch of government. By the same token, the chief judge was expected to operate entirely within the judicial realm and not to make political decisions. Only in extreme cases could appeals be made by the chief Alkali's court to the emir and ultimately to the Sarkin Musulmi.

Even though Islam underwent a renaissance in the nineteenth century, traditional legal concepts were not destroyed completely. Muslim and non-Muslim courts often existed side by side and respected each other's areas of competence and jurisdiction.

MILITARISM AND WARFARE

Militarism and warfare had become common in Africa and paramount in the conduct of inter-African affairs by the late nineteenth century. Often, military strength was viewed as necessary for diplomatic negotiations. War had become a major industry in many African economies, and the estimation of a person's worth in those areas was based in part on his ability to wage war. Blacksmithing and shield making rose to occupational prominence.

Some rulers were imperialistic and conquered for the sake of personal aggrandizement. Others inherited confederacies and empires created by their predecessors but not constitutionally or institutionally consolidated. They therefore needed a strong military presence to keep the newly conquered areas from seceding. Not a few rulers built strong armies to defend themselves against European encroachments and to forestall their territorial ambitions.

Massive importation of European arms into Africa after the Crimean and Franco-Prussian Wars contributed to this destabilizing situation. Ironically the conquest of Africa by Europeans was immediately preceded by the conquest of much of Africa by Africans: the Christian king, Menelik II (c. 1889–1913) defeated the Muslims in the Ogaden and elsewhere, annexed their lands, and ruled them as colonies: Mzilikazi's indunas conquered and colonized Mashonaland; Shaka's regiments burst into the lands of the northern Nguni and Sotho with destructive force; the Nguni destroyed thousands of peaceful communities from the Zambesi River to the shores of Lake Tanganyika and created a number of mini-conquest states; and in West Africa's Sudan, Samory Touré created a military state in the upper Niger region between 1879 and 1895 by conquering the Senufo and others. Likewise, after 1854, the Muslim Tukolor under Umar and later his son, Ahmadu, plundered the states of Kaarta, Segu, and Massina in their quest for a theocratic empire. In western Nigeria, the Yoruba states battled each other for supremacy. These are only a few examples of the general breakdown of security, law, and order, as well as of local independence.

African peasant and servile populations had the most to lose by this constant warfare, because it was they who were drafted into service, they whose farms were left desolate, and they whose families had to take refuge in stockaded villages. In some regions, outlying farms no longer were adequately tended and gradually became unproductive. Local and long-distance trade continued, but often on a smaller scale, because merchants feared to travel unarmed or alone.

Obviously, many parts of Africa escaped the ravages of war, and life continued as peacefully as in the past. But without question, the incidence of physical violence generally increased as the nineteenth century progressed. Because of this, Africans acquired the unfair reputation overseas of being bloodthirsty warriors. If viewed in its proper historical perspective, during the period prior to the late nineteenth century, much of Africa would appear far more peaceful and stable than Europe. Nevertheless, European powers could now rationalize their imperialist programs and set them in a crusading jargon by arguing that Western, Christian intervention would save Africa from itself, from anarchy and barbarism. The apologists of empire neglected to mention that Africa's problems were partly a product of the penetration of Western, Christian, and capitalist values, which contributed to the tensions and contradictions within and between the various states.

By the eve of the European scramble for Africa, the military had gained ascendancy over civilian leaders in many indigenous governments. The great leaders of Africa were no longer men of peace and statesmanship, but of war. In the 1870s, King Kabalega of Bunyoro and others like him, created large standing armies, depleted state treasuries on increasingly sophisticated weaponry, and transferred military responsibilities from the chiefs to new groupings of professional soldiers. Yet the chiefs still were expected to contribute a growing number of fighting men, arms and war matériel. In some emirates of the Sokoto Caliphate, the general populace had grown so weary of war that it had become difficult to conscript able-bodied men. To meet war requirements it was often necessary to sweep down upon unsuspecting non-Muslims and non-Fulani in their fields. These unfortunate victims would either be impressed into the army or sold into bondage in order to finance purchases of more matériel. As more Africans were sold into slavery, especially in the interiors of what are now Tanzania, Malawi, and Mozambique, slavery became more pervasive.

Some African armies were quite large. In Ethiopia, by 1896 Menelik had built up an army of more than 100,000 men and had, over the years, secured modern guns and cannon from the Italians and other Europeans. At the Battle of Adowa in that year, he defeated the Italians with what was considered the best equipped African army on the continent.

Ethiopia was the only precolonial African state to resist successfully the European imperialists. Many African rulers had demonstrated courageous military resistance to the Europeans. Their defeat lay partly in the superiority of European tactics, strategy, training, and weapons. But there were other, more subtle reasons. Some African rulers had so alienated, divided, and demoralized the lesser chiefs and the civilian populations that Europeans encountered little difficulty in recruiting them as mercenaries. The British West African Frontier Force, which conquered the sprawling Sokoto Caliphate, consisted mostly of former slaves, Hausa discontents, and the Tiv, who had been constantly raided by Fulani cavalry. The French, in their conquest of Dahomey, first secured the support of the coastal people who had long been Dahomean vassals. In Senegal, the French expanded their indigenous army, the *tirailleurs,* and utilized them in the conquest of the western Sudan. In the Congo, the Belgians organized a Force Publique consisting of unemployed locals.

African rulers also failed to establish alliances among themselves in the face of European solidarity. Many leaders suffered from a political myopia that made it impossible for them to stand together. In the West African savanna, Samory Touré failed to cooperate with Ahmadu Seku and his Tukolor to turn back French expansionism; Ahmadu refused to assist his relatives in the Sokoto Caliphate in resisting the British. In the Niger Delta, the Itsekiri failed to join the Edo of Benin in repulsing British intrusions, because they hoped that a conquered Benin would open the hinterland more fully to Itsekiri trade. To the west, the Fon of Dahomey declined to aid their old Yoruba overlords or to work together in an effort to play the French off against the British. Moreover, the Fante along the Gold Coast seemed almost pleased to see the British crush their ancient tormentors, the Asante. In Central Africa, King Lobengula of Matabeleland sent an emissary to the neighboring Lozi king, Lewanika, inviting him to become his blood brother and to resist jointly the whites. On the advice of a British missionary, he declined the offer.

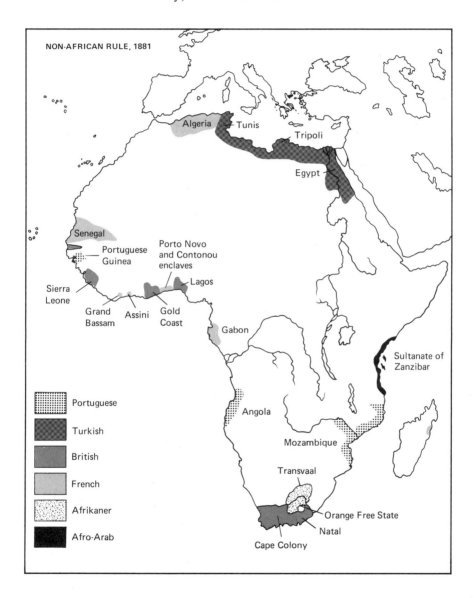

NON-AFRICAN RULE, 1881

Algeria
Tunis
Tripoli
Egypt
Senegal
Portuguese Guinea
Porto Novo and Contonou enclaves
Lagos
Sierra Leone
Grand Bassam
Assini
Gold Coast
Gabon
Sultanate of Zanzibar
Angola
Mozambique
Transvaal
Orange Free State
Natal
Cape Colony

Portuguese
Turkish
British
French
Afrikaner
Afro-Arab

THE EUROPEAN CHALLENGE

African rulers failed to recognize European imperialism as a common danger. They lacked knowledge of the historical forces that impelled Europeans to act as they did. They were unable to grasp the significance to the outside world of events like the discovery in South Africa of gold and diamonds, or the potential of palm oil exploitation in the Benin kingdom, or the strategic importance of the Nile Valley to the Suez Canal, or of the Zululand coast to international shipping. Nor did they fully comprehend European languages. They relied on poorly trained local people or supposed European missionary or trader friends as interpreters. Moreover, they held an entirely different conception of territorial sovereignty and land ownership.

Recently, historians have argued that many African states on the eve of the European conquest were in the process of rapid social changes and political modernization. By the late nineteenth century, slaves in the West African savanna were moving into such specialized occupations as weaving, masonry, and carpentry. In centralized states throughout Africa, slaves were increasingly assuming positions of influence in the expanding bureaucracies. More rulers had begun to recognize clearly the potential value of slaves as political agents of their own power. All this is true, but this was only a minority of the total servile population. If some slaves were growing in political and economic stature, their rising expectations were stifled by continuing social and judicial discrimination. Every free person in most societies was entitled to the protection of his or her kin group and could appeal to the chief against injustice or maltreatment. The nonfree could not appeal, and hence had little security. Nor could they hope to participate in the social and religious activities of the free population. As interstate conflicts persisted, they were viewed by the freemen as easy recruits.

Political scientists argue that in the nineteenth century, African political entities were becoming steadily larger as small, ethnically based states were amalgamated into empires or confederations with plural populations. Surely, this was the case with the newly created empires of the Tukolor, Mandinka, Fulani, Ethiopians, Ndebele, Bechuana, and a number of others. Some leaders, such as Khama III of the Bechuana, Samory Touré of the Mandinka, and Menelik of Ethiopia, consciously attempted to modernize their nations along modified Western lines. Yet even there, the African polities and economies were not modernizing fast enough to meet the European challenge, not fast enough to satisfy European demands for raw materials and foreign trade. Europeans were prepared to export capital to the less developed world, and to finance mining operations and infrastructure, but not on the terms or at the seemingly slow pace set by the traditional African governments. The weaknesses, internal divisions, and economic instability of the interior governments in some cases contributed to deeper capitalist penetration, which ultimately led to imperial conquest.

In the colonial era, the choice of indigenous collaborators influenced the character and organization of European rule. The degree of functional specialization in the bureaucracies of a given African government often would determine the extent to which a given society would be subject to alien control.

chapter 2

Economic Horizons

TRADE, MARKETS, AND TRADERS

The last quarter of the nineteenth century found most sub-Saharan Africans still living at a subsistence level. Most of life's necessities were produced and consumed by the producers and their immediate and extended families. If a surplus existed, producers bartered it for such necessities as iron for making spears, hoes, and machetes, or salt for preserving meat or for cooking.

European "legitimate commerce" had generated little substantive change in the economic structures of most interior African societies. More than nine-tenths of Africa's produce remained outside the commercial and monetary systems of the coastal towns. Trade with Europeans, though historically significant, in reality had only a minor impact on the everyday economic lives of the masses. Imported European goods, mainly alcoholic beverages, cloth, beads, and utensils, were nonproductive and had little practical value in raising the yields of peasants or pastoralists.

Most Africans were engaged in either agriculture or raising stock. But they still devoted much time to gathering wild foods such as nuts, fruits, seeds, and honey, to fishing, and to hunting wild game. Great herds and flocks of wild animals continued to roam across much of Africa, following long-established seasonal migratory patterns. These natural resources were an excellent dietary supplement, especially in periods of prolonged drought.

Africans remained proudly self-sufficient in meeting their basic food needs and did not rely on overseas imports. Yields per acre were remarkably high, considering the generally poor condition of African soils, the low state of agricultural technology, and the dearth of fertilizers. Food production usually kept pace with population growth. Starvation was not uncommon, but it rarely occurred on a large scale. Cultivators were very conscious of weather conditions and went to extraordinary lengths to store food for years of light rainfall. Every family compound contained a granary and storage areas.

By any standard, agriculture in Africa was extremely arduous and time-consuming. Farmers had to cope with soils devoid of humus and vulnerable to leaching during periods of high rainfall. Yet agriculture was the mainstay of Africa and its greatest natural resource.

Only a minority of Africans were dependent on markets as the basis of their existence. Beyond West Africa, very few people lived within the context of the market place or were significantly affected by the market principle of supply

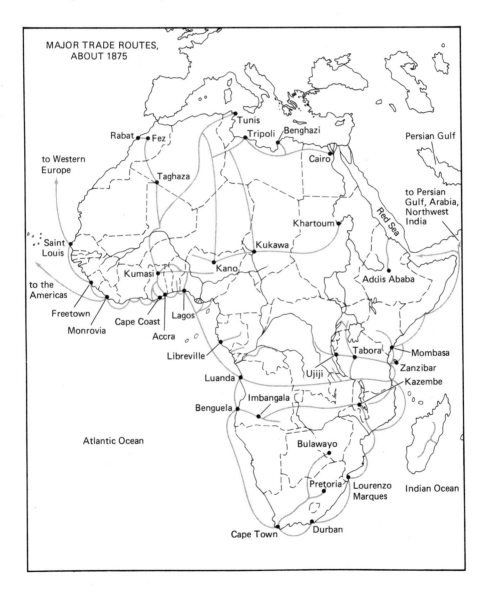

MAJOR TRADE ROUTES, ABOUT 1875

and demand. Large markets with well organized craft guilds flourished in towns of West Africa and the East African Swahili coast. In the interior of East and Central Africa, most people operated almost entirely in relatively closed barter systems until after the mid-nineteenth century. Nearly everywhere communities contained specialists in such trades as ceramics and basket weaving, wood carving, cloth weaving, and metal working.

Sub-Saharan Africa for centuries had been covered by local and regional trade networks, some extending over a thousand miles. International trade linkages also existed, though mainly in West Africa, the Congo, and along the East African coast. By 1875, the coastal areas of South, East, and West Africa, along with the Saharan-Sudanic periphery, were well integrated into the capitalist world economy. Each major coastal and sudanic town usually boasted its own interior trade network. The coastal Africans affected by these networks became increasingly dependent on overseas trade for a wider range of goods they had formerly produced themselves or did not have. European manufactured and Indian imported cloth was lighter in weight than local textiles and less expensive. Poorly ventilated and less comfortable European leather shoes were favored over local sandals, for prestige value.

Precolonial African trade was characterized by the exclusive ascendancy of one ethnic group or clan over long-distance trade. This was often achieved at the expense of their neighbors who found themselves exploited for their natural and human resources. In some instances, trade was tantamount to raid as weaker neighbors lost their cattle, crops, and family members.

It had always been in the interest of African rulers to control the centers of long-distance trade for reasons of power and prestige. Rulers, once exposed to external trade, attempted to monopolize it. "Free trade" was a totally alien concept, for the interests of free intercourse ran counter to those of the ruler. In the more politically centralized kingdoms, state enterprises were established by the monarchs and given special protection from competition from the private sector. In the Asante confederacy, for example, the initial kola crop was handled exclusively by officials of the Asantehene. As in the kingdom of Dahomey, royal traders worked for the king on commission while engaging in their own private trade on the side. In the Benin empire, Europeans could trade only with the Oba's agents for the lucrative palm kernels. In order to trade, special permission from the Oba was needed along with payment of a right-to-trade fee. European traders could not move about freely through Benin's internal markets but were restricted to Gwato, the empire's international seaport.

Throughout Africa, it was common for a ruler to accept a *dash,* usually in the form of gifts, before trade could commence. Traders expected a few small gifts in return. Reciprocal gift-giving was a visible expression of mutual trust and was not considered bribery.

The accumulation of luxury goods for hoarding or for distribution to clients continued to be emphasized over capital investment in economic development and infrastructure. Rarely did market trade produce sustained economic growth. Foreign trade continued to be more of a curiosity than a necessity, unless it dealt in firearms.

By 1875, a growing number of African states were deeply engrossed in the firearms trade with Europeans. The conclusion of the Franco-Prussian War in Europe provided an enormous surplus of sophisticated and inexpensive rifles. Many of these found their way into Africa. African rulers tried to monopolize the distribution of firearms and powder in order to defend their kingdoms against better armed rivals. The escalating trade in arms contributed to economic instability, insecurity, and lawlessness and encouraged some states involved in the traffic to intensify their raids against neighbors. For example, the introduction of Manchester repeaters, Mausers, Remingtons, and Schneider rifles in western Nigeria helped to prolong the destructive Yoruba civil wars. Everywhere in Africa, farmers became less willing to cultivate land too distant from the secure confines of walled villages. Consequently, large areas fell out of production. In the Asante Confederacy, firearms traffic fomented secessionist movements, which in turn weakened central authority and disrupted trade to European, African, and mixed-race traders on the coast.

The Brussels Act, which came into force in 1892, bound European signatory powers to restrict arms traffic in much of tropical Africa. The act further prohibited the sale of modern rapid-firing rifles into territories already under European control. Africans were restricted to the purchase of antique flintlocks which immediately placed them at a disadvantage to the modern weapons of the European imperialists. The smuggling of sophisticated arms nevertheless continued, especially in South Africa where weapons of all kinds were easily obtained by both whites and blacks.

By the last quarter of the nineteenth century, economic expertise, as much as birth or lineage, had become a major requisite for leadership over wide areas of Africa. Opportunities afforded by the deeper penetration of the capitalist world economy led to the emergence of powerful self-made entrepreneurs who often were not of royal birth. They built and defended their commercial empires through a combination of politics and warfare. In East Africa, Arab and Swahili traders became beneficiaries of a tradition of long-distance trade initiated by interior Africans, especially the Yao, a century or so earlier. The Yao people had established regular contact between the East African interior and the Sultan of Zanzibar's southern ports.

Many of the new aggressive traders attacked defenseless communities, took their able-bodied men as captives, and shipped them as slaves to the coast. They also organized ivory-hunting parties and decimated the great elephant herds. The ivory was carried to the coast by their human capitives. Many of the African, Swahili, and Arab traders were a socially disruptive force, operating to the detriment of peaceful populations between Zanzibar and the Congo basin, more than a thousand miles distant. Others organized disparate refugee groups into totally new tribal units, ready to serve the interests of trade and warfare. These people only a generation earlier had fled from Zulu and Boer imperialism in South Africa and sought sanctuary in the relatively lightly populated grasslands of East Africa.

One of East Africa's leading traders was Tippu Tip, an Afro-Arab who by 1872 had created a huge trading state based on the export of slaves and ivory. Tippu Tip's Swahili state, centered in the ivory-rich eastern Congo (now Zaire), stretched from Lake Tanganyika as far north as the Ituri forest and down the Congo basin.

Tippu Tip's contemporary, a Nyamwezi chief named Mirambo, established a vast commercial/territorial empire among his people in central Tanzania. In the 1870s and 1880s Mirambo exerted a powerful influence along the vital routes between Lake Tanganyika and the East African coastal ports. Mirambo was one of the few East Africans to challenge successfully Swahili and Arab competitors. Between 1870 and 1876, after a series of wars, he gained ascendancy over the Arabs in Tabora; by 1880 his influence extended along much of Lake Tanganyika's eastern shore. The economic spheres of Tippu Tip and Mirambo converged at the southern end of the lake, where the two formed an uneasy though productive alliance.

The Nyamwezi were one of the most active ethnic groups in the interior trade. One Nyamwezi trader, Msiri, arrived in Katanga in 1856 and within the next two decades had gained economic and political control over all the old Kazembe lands west of the Luapula River. Msiri monopolized the region's ivory, copper, and slave trade, and established a caravan network that linked Luanda on the Atlantic coast of Angola with Zanzibar on the Indian Ocean.

The Arabs and Indians of Zanzibar must share the greatest responsibility for the explosive growth in East Africa's trade. Arab traders of Middle-East Omani origin settled along the East African coast before the tenth century A.D. They married local Bantu, out of which evolved the Swahili people and civilization. Eventually, their city-states became politically independent of Oman. Arab control over the coast and offshore islands was reasserted after 1833 when the Arab Sultan Sayyid Said transferred his capital from Muscat in Oman to Zanzibar and laid historic claims to the vast coastal area. By 1850 Sayyid and his Arab friends had developed a labor-intensive clove and coconut plantation complex, worked by African slaves captured on the mainland. The islands of Zanzibar and Pemba soon became among the world's largest exporters of cloves. Concurrently, world prices for ivory soared, and East and Central Africa provided the largest source of elephants.

Sayyid Said attracted Indians to Zanzibar to finance the Arab ivory and slave caravans. By the late 1830s Arab traders had reached Ujiji on Lake Tanganyika and within another decade, they had crossed the lake into eastern Congo (Zaire). The Arab penetration of East Africa's hinterlands was not for empire-building or colonizing. They sought trade, not territorial conquest or the propagation of

Former Arab residence in Zanzibar city, probably constructed in the early nineteenth century, when Sayyid Said, Zanzibar's sultan, attracted Arabs from Oman in the Persian Gulf to establish plantations and operate slave caravans into the mainland's interior.

Islam. Some Arabs forged commercial alliances with Africans, others became fierce rivals. In both cases, the peasants were exploited and lived with the fear of possible raids.

Although slave trading networks still flourished in Central Africa in the 1870s and 1880s, Portuguese middlemen preferred to remain on the coast. Portugal's actual economic penetration was limited to a few decaying seaports such as

Fort Jesus, in the ancient Swahili city of Mombasa. Built by the Portuguese in 1593 in a futile effort to control the trans-Indian Ocean Arab-Swahili trade.

Luanda and Benguela in Angola, the island of Mozambique in the Indian Ocean, and the virtually independent plantations (*prazos*) up the Zambezi River.

The successful abolition of the slave trade in West African waters by 1840 led to the growth of economic substitutes: a timber trade emerged in coastal Sierra Leone; peanut oil exports grew in the Gambia and Senegal; and palm oil, used as a lubricant for machinery, became "king" in Dahomey and the Niger Delta. The profits of Niger Delta palm oil spawned a class of new commercial men. Similar to their East African counterparts, they tended to be of humble origins. One of the most prominent was Jaja, a fomer Igbo slave who consolidated numerous African trading houses and competed successfully with European, Creole, and other African commercial groups.

The Niger Delta's and Oil River's "houses" were in fact a combination of trading corporations and units of government. They were ruled initially by royal families and worked by their slaves, who took a share of the profits. From their origins in the seventeenth and eighteenth centuries, they competed with each other. House slaves who operated the oil-bearing canoes, began to gain wealth and power as the slave trade declined and oil prices boomed on world markets. Jaja became so powerful in the oil trade that in 1872 the British consul in the Niger Delta recognized his base at Opobo as an independent city-state. Jaja, like Mirambo in East Africa, symbolized the ascendancy of new men who had risen to positions of economic wealth and power through profits from palm oil or ivory. They often achieved this preeminence at the expense of the traditional authorities.

There was far more to West African trade than coastal produce. The last quarter of the nineteenth century also witnessed the continued growth of the great inland leather-working, cloth manufacturing, and embroidery industries. The markets of the cities of Kano, Kuka, Kumasi, Salaga, and many others remained filled with local craftsmen and their fine products. Most interior ethnic groups preferred their own designs, colors, and clothing styles over imports. European textiles were making deep inroads but did not seriously threaten local industries except in the coastal towns. There, Africans and Creoles adopted Western styles and readily bought up cheap, machine-manufactured European and Indian textiles. In East Africa, people hitherto had either gone naked or dressed in animal skins and woven-grass or bark-cloth skirts. Now Arab and Swahili traders began to introduce cotton cloth and coastal Muslim Swahili fashions.

Throughout Africa, local mining and smelting industries were faltering in the face of European imports of cheaper mass-produced iron products such as utensils, hoes, machetes, and firearms, which replaced spears. Nevertheless, the local gold and kola nut trade in West Africa's forests remained strong. Gold, mined by thousands of slaves and under Asante control, flowed south to the coast, along with dried fish for local consumption. Kola nuts, a tasty stimulant, were shipped in growing quantity out of the forests of Yorubaland to the Sokoto Caliphate and beyond the Sahara. Meanwhile, European demand grew for such tropical products as vegetable oils, timber, and gum used for manufacturing paper and confectionery, as a dye fixative, and for fabric sizing. The economy of South Africa presented a somewhat mixed picture by the last quarter of the nineteenth century. Major exports consisted of mohair, wool, wines, and ostrich feathers. Whites in Natal colony had begun to cultivate sugar and to import contract workers from India. Some wheat and oranges were grown, but mostly for home consumption. For white Afrikaners, the economy rested primarily on extensive ranching and for Africans, on subsistence agriculture. Very little African produce appeared in the markets. Other than a few thousand English-speaking whites, few people were engaged in commerce or manufacturing. By any measure, South Africa was an economic backwater before the late 1860s. Indeed, the commerce of all southern Africa south of the Zambezi River did not equal in value that of West Africa from Sierra Leone to the Cameroons.

All this changed with the discovery of diamonds in 1867 and gold in 1886. These vast finds heralded a mineral revolution, and the lure of those minerals triggered a flood of foreign immigrants, overseas capital, and capital goods. Between 1870 and 1897, trade rose by 800 percent. In 1898, the region was responsible for nearly 75 percent of the total external commerce of sub-Saharan Africa, far exceeding that of West Africa. Gold bullion, the mineral upon which the international economy's monetary system rested, accounted for more than 45 percent of southern Africa's exports. Gold projected the economy of southern Africa into a position of international prominence, and overnight the region became a magnet for the big British and continental European investors, merchants, and skilled workers.

The new wealth in gold and diamonds greatly reduced public debt, increased state revenues, and triggered the rapid expansion of public works and railways. An autonomous capitalism, capable of financing its own expansion, emerged in South Africa's colonies and republics. New economic forces were unleashed, working toward the integration of the hitherto, economically nonviable, interior Afrikaner republics of the Orange Free State and the Transvaal with coastal ports of Natal and Cape colonies. A wider, more unified market economy developed. Agricultural communities everywhere were drawn into the exchange economy. The range of agricultural products widened as the wage-earning population grew, and as transportation improved and became faster and less expensive. Farmers found profitable new markets in South Africa and abroad for their produce.

MEDIUMS OF EXCHANGE

In much of tropical Africa, the barter system of trade impeded the establishment of a monetary economy. Even in societies utilizing a form of currency, financial transactions were cumbersome because of the nature of the money. Traditional forms of currency included standardized lengths of cloth, cowrie shells, some metals such as iron bars (*manillas*) or copper wire and bracklets, standardized bundles of crops, particularly corn, and in a few economies, silver dollars. One or more currencies may have been in use in a given market place. The bulkiness and weight of these currencies made them difficult to carry and may help to explain why so many interior Africans preferred to barter. By 1875 African cowrie and metal currencies had undergone a serious depreciation. Cowries and copper and brass manillas were being imported in increasing quantity by European traders. Their overabundance and consequential loss in value made traders of all races lose confidence in them. Imported silver dollars soon became more popular in the coastal towns of West Africa and in the large Sudanic markets of the Sokoto Caliphate. Likewise, Indian rupees were used more widely in the Swahili coastal markets of East Africa.

As the value of cowries plunged, these shells became increasingly cumbersome to carry and time-consuming to count. By the 1890s cowries were so depreciated that it was hardly worthwhile to carry them at all. At that time, a standard "bag" of twenty-thousand cowries weighed fifty pounds and in Dahomey, could buy only two-thirds of an ounce of gold.

TRANSPORTATION AND MIGRATION

Poor transportation severely limited trade and economic development. Wheeled vehicles were unknown and pack animals were impossible to use in many areas because of the tsetse flies. Donkeys and camels were found only in dry, open savannas, mainly in the West African Sudan. Zebras and gazelles could not be domesticated. Camels continued to be essential carriers of goods across the Sahara to North Africa. Their strength and endurance may explain the late nineteenth-century boom in trans-Saharan trade. Among the white Boers of South Africa, produce was transported by ox wagon.

In most of tropical Africa, goods had to be moved on human heads and shoulders. This was a painfully slow and inefficient mode of transport and one which placed Africa in an increasingly less competitive position vis-à-vis other regions of the world. Canoes, made from hollowed or burned-out tree trunks, were used along Africa's rivers, estuaries, and lagoons. These vessels carried palm oil through the Niger Delta to markets in the various coastal city-states. On interior bodies of water such as Lakes Chad, Tanganyika, Victoria, and Malawi, African fishermen used boats made of woven or lashed reeds and other grasses. In the Indian Ocean, Arab designed sailing vessels, called *dhows,* were propelled by seasonal monsoon winds between East African coastal city-states and the markets of the Arabian peninsula, Persian Gulf, and western India. These vehicles also were unable to transport large amounts.

River transportation in Africa was impeded by a frustrating combination of cataracts, few natural harbors, and seasonal fluctuations in river-water level and flow. Most ocean-going vessels had to anchor offshore or in lagoons and wait

Woman with calabash bowls on her head. Before the twentieth century, head porterage was the major means of transporting goods. Northern Nigeria.

long periods for goods to reach them by hand-paddled canoes. Before the twentieth century, few large, modern, international, deep-water ports existed other than those at Dakar, Senegal, Freetown, Sierra Leone, Cape Town, South Africa, and at Zanzibar off the East African mainland. Arteries stretching inland from coastal ports were little more than footpaths maintained in varying degrees of repair, depending on the whim of chieftaincies through which they meandered.

These limitations did not prevent trade, nor did they block the migration of people driven from one area to another by famine, disease, overgrazing, soil exhaustion, or from a need for more land or greater security from slave raids. Local migration was not unusual for farmers, who generally practiced shifting cultivation. Under shifting cultivation, parcels of land were cultivated for a few years until the soil was exhausted and crop yields fell. The farmer then moved on to another area while the first parcel laid fallow and regained its fertility. Artificial fertilizers were nonexistent in the humid rain forests, and in the open grasslands cow manure was more frequently used for fuel than for fertilizer.

The shifting of agricultural settlements was practiced extensively in many parts of Africa in the precolonial era. Long-distance migration across ecological zones was more common among nomadic pastoralists and was seasonal. West African pastoralists, raising cattle, sheep, and goats, were an important provider of meat for the large commercial markets of the Sudanic belt. They drove their herds seasonally from the northern grasslands on the Saharan fringe to the pastures and markets of the Sudan and southwards to the forest edge. Pastoralists in East Africa tended not to sell their cattle for market slaughter but kept them for milk and for prestige and bride price. For the pastoral Tutsi, Masai, and others, cows had a certain spiritual and social value and were not to be judged by the commercial ethic of the marketplace.

LAND AND LABOR

Labor was the key to production in precolonial Africa. Indeed, for centuries Africa's most valuable resource had been manpower. Population densities were generally low and therefore labor needs became acute, especially in the centralized states.

Africans considered land a spiritual commodity, owned not by the living members of a community but by their founding ancestors. Responsibility for determining land use and allocation rested with the descendants of those first settlers, be they elders, priests, chiefs, or king. It was they who acted as trustees for the entire community—dead, living, unborn. Most land was held communally, for the concept of private, freehold ownership of property was totally alien.

The clearing, cultivation, and harvesting of land were usually performed by the extended family, working as a labor unit. In more highly stratified societies, their work may have been supplemented by groups of young men organized in a particular age category or with nonfree servants. Sex differentiation in labor also existed in some areas. Among the Yoruba of western Nigeria, men did all farming; women marketed their produce. Only a few hundred miles away, in the Muslim Sokoto Caliphate, markets usually were run only by men. In the Benin empire, only men could cultivate yams, the staple food. Secondary crops, such as peanuts, corn, melons, and beans were the responsibility of women.

Land occupation was considered a privilege not a right. If a ruler believed a family was abusing the land, or not taking full advantage of its productive potential, he could transfer the parcel to more deserving members of the community. Some authorities bestowed land upon individuals in recognition of their service to the state or in return for their loyalty. To deprive a person or family of land was tantamount to expulsion from the community.

In the late nineteenth century, many traditional authorities abused their control over land by alienating the most mineral-rich or fertile areas to European concessionary companies in return for firearms, money, or exotic luxury goods. These trustees for their ancestors naively believed that at will they could demand the return of the land. They failed to understand the European conception of private ownership of property, based on individual freehold tenure. To the European speculator, land was a purely economic commodity, an exclusive instrument for private, not communal, profit.

In white-controlled South Africa, the lack of land became an increasingly serious problem for blacks after the early nineteenth century. After 1836, as Boers pushed inland from the Cape Colony, Africans became squatters on the lands of their ancestors. By the 1880s, a growing number of Bantu in the Cape Colony held land under freehold conditions. But in the Afrikaner-dominated Orange Free State and Transvaal, individual African freehold tenure was forbidden. Instead, mining companies moved into the Transvaal after 1886, acquired large tracts of land for future exploitation, and temporarily settled African peasants on them. The peasants had to pay rent and faced eviction at any time.

The system of maintaining blacks not needed in the white economy on "native reserves" was established in the Natal Colony in the mid-nineteenth century. It was developed fully after 1897 when Zululand was conquered, annexed, and bifurcated into a native reserve and an area for white freehold tenure.

In precolonial Africa, labor could not easily be obtained in societies lacking coins or paper currency. Often, the agricultural goods or livestock a ruler received as taxes or gifts were invested in the control of labor. A ruler would distribute the produce of his subjects with the understanding it would be repaid in labor. In some African states, the labor that a peasant was expected to give his chief was figured as a fixed number of days in a year. If the peasant were prosperous, the labor obligation would be performed by one or more of his slaves.

Rulers reserved the right to call upon their male subjects to clear and maintain footpaths, and to build and repair the palaces, markets, and other public places. By 1875, with the escalation in internal slave-raiding, this was done mostly by nonfree people. Indeed, slave raids became common means of obtaining laborers. Internal slave-raiding was particularly widespread in the hinterlands of what are today Nigeria, Angola, Mozambique, Tanzania, Uganda, and the Sudan, though for centuries, slaves had been used by free Africans in barter transactions, much like iron hoes and salt.

The North Atlantic slave trade diminished greatly after 1840. However, we have seen that in the South Atlantic, in the Indian Ocean, and down the Nile Valley it continued to flourish for another three decades. Portuguese, Arab, and half-caste traders annually exported thousands of slaves to Brazil from the region which today is eastern Zaire, northern Zambia, Malawi, and Mozambique. Black slaves were still in demand by Arabs in the Middle East and on plantations along the East African coast. The African institution of slavery, once remarkably benign, became more prevalent and far less humane in the late nineteenth century as internal slave-raiding grew and captives multiplied.

In 1876 the Sultan of Zanzibar was forced by the British consul to outlaw the export of slaves from East Africa. Afterward, the Indian Ocean traffic slowed considerably. The internal slave trade died less quickly, especially among the Ganda around Lake Victoria and the Yao in the Lake Malawi and southern Lake Tanganyika regions. Even the Nyamwezi and Gogo people in central Tanzania accumulated large numbers of captives and put them to work on farms and in carrying ivory to the coast for shipment to India and Europe. In South Africa by 1875 a labor pattern had just begun to develop in which African men were taken off their farms and away from their families to work for several months in the mines of the Transvaal and Orange Free State. By 1899 this oscillating migration brought some 100,000 blacks to the gold mines alone. Workers were recruited from all over southern Africa and at the turn of the century, nearly sixty percent of the African gold miners came from Mozambique.

TAXATION AND REVENUE

Taxation and revenue, so crucial to sustained economic development, were already a part of the African scene in the politically centralized states. The territorially expansive Sokoto Caliphate of northern Nigeria boasted of an extensive system of occupational taxation, under the jurisdiction of each emir in its emirates. Taxes also were levied on cattle and were paid in the form of a percentage of the herd. Hut or compound taxes were paid in bundles of corn. By 1890 ten percent of all bundles harvested were given to the government. In addition, customs duties as a portion of items carried, were levied upon

One of the great gates of the walled Hausa city of Katsina, northern Nigeria.

goods passing through the gates of the caliphate's major walled cities. These duties were apportioned among the emir, the *Magajin Gari* (mayor), and the provincial chief who happened to be in charge of a given gate. Gifts from subordinate emirates to the central government were also a major form of revenue. Nonpayment was tantamount to treasonable defiance. Revenue was supplemented by presents given to the caliph and to emirs by newly appointed officials. Another source of revenue was booty, often in the form of captives, of which at least twenty percent had to be sent to the caliph. Non-Muslims paid a special tax in order to "buy" protection from enslavement and as a price for government nonintervention in their cultural and religious beliefs.

The king of Dahomey also benefited from a multitude of revenue sources, including a capitation tax, death duties, a palm oil tax, market fees, and tolls collected along the major trade routes. In Asante, a poll tax was levied directly by the central government. By 1896 it was extremely burdensome and generally resented by the people. Generally, the level of taxation in Africa rose dramatically in the late nineteenth century, as rulers spent increasing amounts of their wealth on maintaining internal security against attacks from both neighbors and Europeans. Revenue was expended on more than the military. Royal households and palace functionaries also had to be supported and in the Muslim states, alms given to scholars and the poor.

THE ECONOMICS OF INFORMAL EMPIRE

The British government always had insisted that its African colonies be self-supporting and not a drain on the public treasury. Every colonial enclave was responsible for meeting the cost of its own administration, and customs therefore had to be imposed in order to raise the necessary revenue. The home government argued that any expansion must be commercial, undertaken by private entrepreneurs at their own risk and expense.

Because each colonial enclave existed to promote so-called "legitimate trade," its consuls or governors inevitably bcame embroiled in the affairs of interior African states, to ensure that trade flowed freely and steadily. If African rulers impeded trade, the colonial enclave would risk a drop in its own revenue, and the colonial authorities often would dispatch a military expedition to force the recalcitrant regime into collaboration. African rulers were intimidated into abolishing commercial monopolies, lowering their own tariffs, and opening the trade routes and markets to so-called "free trade." Unfortunately, such raids often produced the opposite effect. The African rulers lost face with their people, central authority weakened, peripheral provinces seceded, civil war followed, and trade was disrupted further. Indeed, British interference in Asante and Yorubaland did much to prolong internal strife among warring factions within the various states. But it was not British policy to conquer permanently, occupy, or govern hinterland African states. Few people in Great Britain were prepared to support territorial expansion for its own sake. A formal empire, most believed, would entail enormous costs which taxpayers would refuse to pay out of public funds.

Before the last quarter of the nineteenth century, other European powers shared Britain's reluctance to create and financially support territorial empires in sub-Saharan Africa. However, from about 1875 onward, competition did intensify between an expanding number of British, French, German, and African private firms. Larger-hulled, steam-powered ships were used more widely. Shipping volume increased, freight rates fell, and traveling time was reduced. Together with the telegraph, these ships brought Africa closer to European markets and opened new opportunities for those interested in overseas trade. Consequently, competition heightened as more European merchants entered the picture. In 1876 King Leopold of Belgium founded the International African Association to explore the possibilities of commercially developing the Congo basin. Two years later the Livingstonia Central African Trading Company was established to erect depots in the area between Lakes Malawi and Tanganyika. Scarcely a year had passed when the English merchant George Goldie formed the United African Company. Its aim was to monopolize trade along the lower Niger in order to reduce the prices paid to Africans for their produce. Within a few months, a multitude of small English and French firms established themselves in the same area. In the early 1880s Carl Peters founded the Society for German Colonization with the intention of creating a colony and commercial operations in the hinterland of what is now Tanzania. William Mackinnon, who for two decades had been operating a steamship service in the Indian Ocean, formed the British East Africa Association in 1887 to trade in the mainland dominions of the Sultan of Zanzibar. Most noteworthy is the dramatic growth in the number of non-British firms operating in Africa.

Since 1815 the African overseas trade had been dominated by Great Britain. After the European market crash of 1873, there was a shift in the economic balance of power and Germany and France again openly challenged British hegemony. Capitalist classes in Europe by 1879 understood the need to secure and protect future opportunities for foreign commerce and investment in a world of growing nationalism. Germany, France, and the United States were now well into their own industrial revolutions and found themselves in a position to challenge Britain's domination of international trade and finance. Their burgeoning industries looked to new and cheaper supplies of raw materials, particularly metal ores.

Between 1879 and 1880 in France, old notions of infomal empire were discarded in favor of the government assuming the financial responsibility for expansion, and the establishment of formal political control as a prerequisite of economic exploitation. France now plunged into tropical Africa in the expectation of profit in the distant future. Henceforth, the French government demonstrated a willingness to lay both political and economic claims to African territory. They became convinced that British hegemony in Africa could not be overcome by purely private commercial means nor through the efforts and expense of their governors and their small enclaves.

Events in Egypt did much to win French public opinion over to the cause of militant imperialism. The Suez Canal in Egypt, built by private British and French capital, opened in 1869. Overnight, it brought East Africa, the Indian Ocean, and India closer to European markets. It also revitalized the Egyptian economy, enabling the *Khedive* (king) to undertake an ambitious program of modernization. Anticipating future wealth, the Khedive borrowed foreign capital for prestige projects, military, and other nonproductive purposes. He aimed too high and in 1876 the regime went bankrupt. Britain and France then imposed drastic financial controls and constitutional reforms on the Egyptian government in return for further loans. Such European intervention reduced the popularity of the Khedive in the eyes of his people and strengthened the nationalists. It provoked a nationalist uprising which destroyed European property and endangered the canal. The uprising also threatened to end dual Anglo-French control over the Egyptian treasury, which was intended to restore Egyptian solvency. Neither European power wished to assume full responsibility for a bankrupt regime, and preferred to maintain an Egyptian collaborator, like the Khedive, in power. But the political situation now bordered on anarchy. France was embroiled in its own domestic crises, and so in 1882 Britain reluctantly acted alone by invading and occupying the country.

Within months, the French parliament ratified a treaty with the Bateke of central Africa, largely because the Congo River was seen as a commercial highway to the heart of the continent. It was a propitious moment to seek ratification, for public opinion was outraged over the unilateral British invasion of Egypt. Since the days of Napoleon I, the two nations had been rivals there. Now British paramountcy had been established. The treaty with the Bateke people also confirmed France's intention of establishing a colonial possession in central Africa. Less than a year later, French protectorates also were formed in Cotonou and Porto Novo on the coast of West Africa.

In West Africa, French military personnel, not capitalists, initiated the late nineteenth-century territorial advance into the grasslands of the Senegalese interior. French industry, still small-scale and family-dominated, lacked the capital to undertake bold expansionary projects, and all but a handful of them were really concerned with sub-Saharan Africa. It was therefore the French military advance to the upper Niger in 1879, to support plans for railway construction, which launched that nation on a course of aggressive imperialism. Military engineers dreamed of railway networks extending from the eastern and western coasts and northward across the Sahara to Mediterranean ports. Such dreams seemed realistic after successful railway construction in Russia, the United States, and France.

Visions of Sudanese wealth merged with strong trade protectionist sentiments at home. France's small but rapidly growing industries looked to the state for protection from British competition. After the early 1880s, tariff walls were thrown up, and the state was recognized by many as the principal instrument of territorial expansion.

Rising European interests in African economic exploitation converged in late 1884 when German Chancellor Bismarck convened in Berlin an international conference on West Africa. Fourteen European nations and the United States were invited. Not a single African state was included. From the Berlin West African Conference came a declaration (the Berlin Act) of freedom of trade and navigation in the Congo basin and freedom of navigation on the Niger. But the limits of future territorial expansion behind existing European coastal enclaves were defined only vaguely. The conference's most definitive act was the legalization of Belgian King Leopold's sovereignty over his so-called Congo Independent State. The Europeans avoided the possibility of Great Power rivalry in the heart of Africa by allowing the monarch of small, neutral Belgium to be sovereign there. Tragically, decisions were reached at the Berlin Conference without the consultation or approval of the affected African states. Indeed, traditional rulers in central Africa had not been informed of these conferences and had never granted King Leopold sovereignty over their domains. Nor did they agree to a European free-for-all in matters of trade and navigation.

CHARTERED COMPANIES AND AFRICAN ENTERPRISE

The scramble for Africa was well underway before the Berlin Conference. Surprisingly, in view of his previous distrust in colonial ventures, Bismarck decided that Germany needed protectorates. In early 1884 he sanctioned the establishment of protectorates over areas in which German merchants had been threatened by foreign competition. Thus, even before the conference convened, Bismarck had extended formal protection to German firms operating in Togo, Cameroun, East Africa, and Angra Pequeña in South West Africa. A year earlier, Jules Ferry, the new French prime minister, annexed the Dahomean coast, driving a wedge between Britain's old coastal possessions of Lagos and the Gold Coast. The British, fearing the expansion of German and French activity in the lower Niger, declared a protectorate over the Oil Rivers.

Despite these measures, between 1885 and 1891 the Great Powers returned to the seventeenth-century principle of using chartered private companies as agents of territorial expansion and administration in the interests of their respective nations. The granting of royal charters by Britain, Portugal, and Germany reflected a public reluctance to finance territorial expansion and colonial administration at the taxpayers' expense. British statesmen saw it as the only means of forestalling the French advance in Africa short of committing its own armed forces and risking a direct confrontation with them.

In the early 1880s, the Compagnie Française de l'Afrique Equatoriale and the Compagnie du Sénégal were almost as strong as George Goldie's United African Company. But when they refused to join him, Goldie destroyed them by using his personal family fortune to undercut their prices. By 1886, he had destroyed all competing French and British firms along the lower Niger north of the Oil Rivers Protectorate. After such a stunning success Goldie secured a royal charter for his firm, renamed the Royal Niger Company. Like many other chartered companies, the Royal Niger Company was given wide power to trade and govern under concessions and treaties obtained from local rulers. Goldie's company soon exercised a virtual monopoly over trade and treaty-making in what would eventually become much of southern Nigeria. Although the Berlin Act and British law prohibited such monopolies, Goldie insisted that the crown, which granted the charter, was not bound by British law and that the Berlin Act merely required free navigation on the Niger River itself. Other than African traders and rulers, no one seemed concerned that the company was given such sweeping powers. Goldie, the private entrepreneur, was in effect given powers normally bestowed only on nation-states.

European governments rationalized to the public that the internal African slave trade could be abolished only by establishing other, competitive forms of trade. The charter companies gained respectability by pledging, ambiguously, that the "condition of the natives would be improved." Commercial aims were couched thus in humanitarian jargon.

A series of civil wars between 1880 and 1895 brought economic ruin and political anarchy to the Niger Delta city-states. Ja Ja of Opobo had refused to allow British traders free access to his domains or to deal directly with his sources of supply. In reply to this resistance, in 1887 the British deported him to the West Indies. Goldie shrewdly played upon traditional rivalries among the city-states and encountered little difficulty in finding African collaborators only too willing to see the demise of the city-states and an opportunity for themselves to trade directly with Europeans. Sadly, they failed to grasp Goldie's long-term goal of establishing his own company as sole middleman for the Delta palm oil trade. Through intimidation, war, and monopolistic practices, Goldie eliminated remaining European, Creole, Kalabari, and other small traders. The death knell sounded for the African middleman in 1895, when the Royal Niger Company in concert with the Royal Navy destroyed the last pocket of resistance, the trading state of Brass. According to one historian, "the real issue had never been monopoly and free trade, but rather whether the monopoly should be enjoyed by Delta merchants or by British firms."[1]

Eugène Etienne, France's ambitious Under-Secretary of State for the colonies, did much to galvanize French politicians behind publicly financed imperialist ventures. Anxious to strengthen the nascent colonial department, in 1892 he

---

[1] J.B. Webster and A.A. Boahen, *The Growth of African Civilization: The Revolutionary Years, West Africa Since 1800* (London: Longmans Group, Ltd., 1967), p. 205.

obtained from the National Assembly funds for a war against King Behanzin of Dahomey. After Colonel Dodds, a Senegalese mulatto in charge of the French expeditionary force, had conquered the kingdom, he pressed his African mercenaries towards the Niger, thus threatening the gains made by Goldie's company. French military advances also were made in the Ivory Coast, Guinea, and in Gabon.

In 1895 the arch-imperialist Joseph Chamberlain became British colonial secretary. Within a year he launched Great Britain on an aggressive expansionist course, arguing that as long as Britain espoused free trade, the government must protect resources in existing coastal enclaves. Chamberlain played up to the industrialists, who feared that the nation's natural resources eventually would be exhausted. The dynamic colonial secretary warned that new areas for future exploitation must be found and reserved for posterity, that if the hinterlands of the British enclaves of Freetown, the Gold Coast, Lagos, and the Oil Rivers were not secured soon, they would be swallowed up by protectionist France who would divert trade to its own seaports. In that event, the enclaves would no longer be self-supporting and would have to draw upon public funds for their survival or go bankrupt. Chamberlain's lobbying among the newspaper magnates and his eloquent speeches before Parliament won the day. Direct military intervention in Africa commenced in 1896 when government-financed expeditions conquered the Yoruba states of western Nigeria, occupied the Asante capital, deported the king, and gained control over the Sierra Leone hinterland in anticipation of French military advances. Similarly, when the Oba of the economically disintegrating Benin empire refused to permit free trade, his nation too was crushed. Because the Oba's frequent cessation of trade between the Benin oil producers and the Itsekiri middlemen had affected European traders on the coast, the issue of who would control trade, the Oba or the British consul, was resolved in 1897 by the British conquest of the empire.

Chamberlain had become impatient with the Royal Niger Company's slow rate of conquest in Nigeria. In the same year (1897), responsibility for the conquest of the remainder of the present Nigeria was transferred to a British-backed military force. This was done to forestall French expansion into the lower Niger and across the vast Sokoto Caliphate in the north. Inevitably, British and French forces confronted each other and tensions rose. The French backed down and signed the Niger Convention in June 1898. The scramble for West Africa was over. But Britain still feared French control of the Nile's headwaters and the possibility of a dam to divert its waters, thus economically crushing Egypt. The British argued that to protect the Suez, lifeline of the empire, they had to hold Egypt. Another Ango-French confrontation resulted, this time at Fashoda on the upper Nile. France was at a disadvantage. The British already had conquered the Sudan and had a large army in the field. France was weak on land and at home the government was tottering. In September 1898 another Anglo-French accord was signed, signaling the end of the scramble in East Africa.

The Fashoda incident culminated more than a decade of intense European activity. East Africa's indigenous traders at first welcomed European commercial penetration as a possible counterbalance against the growing Arab presence. Three private firms, the German East Africa Company, the German Witu Company, and the British East Africa Association all pushed rapidly inland from early 1884 through 1886, signing treaties with numerous African rulers. The Sultan of Zanzibar, by then a puppet of the British consul, lacked the necessary leadership to assert administrative and formal territorial sovereignty over the interior peoples. His influence hardly extended beyond the coastal Swahili towns. Inland, Arabs and Swahili traders operated independently. The Arabs, particularly, never numbered more than a few hundred at any one time, were generally disunited, and thinly spread.

Arab and European traders tolerated each other at first, but this changed after 1885 when it became apparent that the Europeans had political and territorial as well as commercial designs. The facts spoke for themselves. European commercial presence in the Lake Nyasa (Malawi) region was large enough to warrant a permanent British consul in 1883. In 1885 Bismarck authorized the establishment of a protectorate in the areas of East Africa under the German East Africa Company treaty. Two years later the company secured a charter from the government. In 1888 William Mackinnon's East Africa Association received a royal charter from the British Crown and was renamed the Imperial British East Africa Company. These companies became, in effect, agents for their respective metropolitan governments, with responsibility for opening up and developing the interior.

By 1885 the Arab, Swahili, and African traders were quickly losing their economic autonomy. The death that year of Mwinyi Kheri, the great Arab merchant and political force in Ujiji, seemed to signal the ending of an era. Kheri had cultivated strong relationships between Arabs and Africans in the Ujiji area and no one possessed the leadership to carry on after him. To make matters worse, the great trader Mirambo had died only months earlier. His half-brother lacked the military leadershp and political acumen to defend Mirambo's extensive trading network. The success of Kheri and Mirambo was based in large measure on the force of their own personalities rather than on an institutionalization of power. Mirambo's empire slowly crumbled, and in 1893 his successor was defeated by the Germans, who were a far more formidable enemy than the Tabora Arabs of Mirambo's day.

Arab hegemony already was doomed. Five years earlier the Germans gained control over the Tanganyikan coast by crushing a revolt led by the Arab trader Abushiri. Consequently, Arabs, Africans, and Swahili were deprived of their Indian Ocean outlets for trade, and their middleman position in the East African interior could no longer be sustained. The Arabs also were expelled from the powerful kingdom of Buganda in the same year by African converts to Christianity. The fate of Arab power in East Africa was sealed in 1890 when Great

Britain declared a protectorate in Zanzibar, and the Germans bought out most of the Sultan's coastal possessions. The remainder was ceded by the Sultan to the Portuguese in Mozambique and to the Italians in Somalia.

Arab and African economic power was destroyed also in Central Africa. In copper-rich Katanga, the great Nyamwezi trader, Msiri, was murdered in 1891 after refusing to recognize the sovereignty of King Leopold's Congo Independent State. King Leopold did hire Tippu Tip, who for years had been one of the most powerful and knowledgeable ivory and slave traders in the eastern Congo. However, once the Belgians were firmly established, Tip was no longer needed as a collaborator. A series of futile wars between King Leopold's mercenaries and the Arabs from 1892 to 1894 led to the expulsion of the Arabs from the area. Henceforth, the ivory trade gravitated towards the Atlantic ports rather than to the old Swahili coast of East Africa.

With Arab, African, and Swahili economic power crushed, the rival European powers had to face themselves. At first, indirect influence through chartered private companies seemed safer than direct involvement, for the latter risked military confrontation among themselves. But as in West Africa, the chartered companies were poorly conceived, mismanaged, and grossly under-capitalized. They lacked the ability to finance effective armies for conquest or to generate the capital necessary for effective administration or economic development. The costly Abushiri revolt of 1888 had to be put down by imperial forces and made Germany recognize the military ineffectiveness and administrative incompetence of the German East Africa Company. Two years later its charter was revoked, and administrative responsibility for its domains was assumed by the German government.

The British experience was somewhat similar. Britain regarded the Imperial British East Africa Company as an instrument for securing the Nile Valley. The kingdom of Buganda was seen as critically important because of its proximity to Lake Victoria, a major Nile headwater. Captain Lugard had successfully extended company control over Buganda between 1890 and 1892, but at a ruinous cost. The firm went bankrupt in 1891 and threatened to withdraw from Buganda altogether. Only a last-minute grant of money from local European missionaries and their supporters back home delayed the firm's departure and bought valuable time. By the end of 1892 the French were advancing towards the Upper Nile. Meanwhile, British legislators urgently debated the strategic importance of Uganda, a Nile source, to the defenses of Egypt and Suez. The Foreign Office saw Uganda as a gateway to the Nile Valley and argued that a withdrawal would leave the area open to French occupation. They won their case and in 1893 the government took over the company's interests in Buganda. A year later a British protectorate was declared in the present Uganda, which covers many former African states, including Buganda. In 1894 the remainder of the company's possessions (now Kenya) became the East Africa Protectorate.

Britain assumed responsibility for the latter, not because of its strategic or economic potential but as as a corridor from the Indian Ocean to Uganda.

Southern Africa after the 1880s became another focal point of rivalry as it experienced an unprecedented economic boom. In 1886 the Witwatersrand gold reef was found in the heart of the Afrikaner's Transvaal Republic. Miners flocked in by the thousands, and the white population doubled between 1880 and 1890. They generated a market for food and provided greater opportunities in agriculture and commerce. The hitherto poor and backward Transvaal now experienced dramatic growth. Railway construction had begun in the 1870s from Cape ports to the diamond fields and after 1892 to Witwatersrand and much of the republic. These lines opened up the South African hinterland to commercial agriculture.

Mining, manufacturing, and commerce more than ever became the preserve of the English-speaking whites; the economically depressed Boers and black Africans were drawn into English mines and factories. A young Englishman, Cecil John Rhodes, emigrated to South Africa and quickly united the claims of individuals and syndicates into the DeBeers Consolidated Mines Ltd. and the Consolidated Gold Fields Ltd. The DeBeers company soon monopolized both the production and the marketing of diamonds.

Rhodes became the prime minister of the Cape Colony and sought to implement his dream of a railroad and communications system extending from Cape Town to Cairo, Egypt. He also believed in an economically united South Africa under Anglo-Saxon capitalist control. But the interior Afrikaner republics of the Orange Free State and Transvaal jealously guarded their autonomy and saw Rhodes as a threat. In 1895 the Transvaal completed a railway to Delagoa Bay on the Indian Ocean in an effort to divert mineral exports from ports in the British controlled Cape and Natal Colonies. Rhodes feared the growing economic strength of the Transvaal and the possibility of its alliance with Germany, which had established a protectorate in nearby South West Africa. Nevertheless, a raid in 1895 into the Transvaal by Rhodes's mercenaries under the direction of his advisor, Dr. Jameson, was squelched by the Afrikaners after it failed to win the miners' support. The Jameson Raid was a disaster for Rhodes. It strengthened the hands of Paul Kruger, the Transvaal's president, and weakened the credibility of the imperial position throughout southern Africa and overseas.

Rhodes also had hoped to destroy the Transvaal by encirclement. Since 1886 land between the Limpopo and Zambezi Rivers had been eyed by speculators as another possible source of gold. Both Rhodes and the Transvaal's President Kruger sought control. The British government shared Rhodes's fears that the Transvaal might eventually become so rich that it would dominate all of southern Africa, including the Cape and Natal. It was therefore in both their interests to bring as much of southern Africa as possible into the British commercial system before the Transvaal became powerful enough to secure those areas for itself.

The British government was unwilling to pay for such expansion, so Rhodes formed and personally financed the British South African Company to acquire lands north of the Limpopo River. By October 1888 his agents had concluded a treaty with Lobengula, the ruler of the Matabele empire, which transferred "complete and exclusive mineral rights" in return for arms and ammunition. Rhodes ignored the Brussels Protocols prohibiting such sales.

The British rewarded Rhodes the following year with the grant of a royal charter. In effect, he obtained a free hand to contain Transvaal expansionism, conduct diplomatic relations with African rulers, and prevent the Portuguese from linking their Angola and Mozambique possessions into a transcontinental empire. Portugal chartered the Mozambique Company and the Niassa Company to advance its own imperialist interests. But Portugal, a poor nation, had few financiers and the two companies soon were neutralized when their shares fell into the hands of British and French capitalists.

In 1890 Rhodes marched a Pioneer Column of one hundred-eighty European traders and farmers and five hundred company police, and took physical possession of Mashonaland. It was a blatant violation of his treaty with Lobengula. But this intrepid imperialist needed white settlement to supply his miners and as a counterpoise to the Afrikaners and Portuguese.

While the Africans suffered from the trauma of alien occupation, their woes were compounded by a severe drought, poor harvests, a locust plague, and a devastating outbreak of rinderpest. The company also began to levy a hut tax and killed the Africans' diseased cattle in order to protect their own herds. After two futile wars of resistance, the so-called Matabele Wars of 1893 and 1896, the Ndebele and Shona sank into despondent passivity. Within a year, the company completed a railway line from South Africa to Bulawayo, Lobengula's old capital, and plugged what was to become Southern Rhodesia into the capitalist world economy.

By 1895 Great Britain was committed to a policy of maintaining imperial supremacy throughout southern Africa. The Jameson Raid on the Transvaal that year was a fiasco and ruined the political career of Cecil Rhodes, its perpetrator. It also brought Afrikaner sentiment throughout South Africa closer to the Transvaal. Joseph Chamberlain was now at the helm in the Colonial Office and pushed hard for public support of the Transvaal's destruction. Rhodes, in declining health and discredited, could no longer be relied upon to prevent the Transvaal from forging the various South African colonies into an Afrikaner-controlled nation, beyond British dominion. Chamberlain argued that only the military conquest of the Transvaal could save South Africa for the British Empire. From 1895 to 1899 the British failed to curb the Transvaal's growing economic power and autonomy through diplomacy and were unable to coerce it into a railway and customs union with the British colonies of the Cape and Natal. In frustration, Great Britain provoked the Transvaal and Orange Free State into a second Anglo-Boer War. It lasted from 1899 to 1902 and resulted

in the political absorption of the two Afrikaner states into a Union of South
Africa dominated by Great Britain and the English-speaking white capitalists of
South Africa.

AFRICA, EUROPE, AND THE WORLD ECONOMY:
THE ECONOMICS OF DISCORD

Before 1875 at least ninety-five percent of sub-Saharan Africa lay beyond the
direct control of the Western capitalist economy. By the beginning of the twentieth century, nearly the entire continent had fallen under European capitalist
hegemony. This dramatic transition was caused largely by shifts in the balance of
economic and political power among the major European nations. Before 1879
Africa was insulated from the rivalries of European powers. Metropolitan ministers, legislators, and merchants generally were not interested in expanding
their formal contacts with African empires, kingdoms, and city-states. To them,
Africa was an economic backwater and a white man's graveyard. For nearly a
century, New World slavery and the slave trade had seemed inhumane and un-
economical. Slaves from Africa were therefore no longer needed and European
capital went elsewhere in search of profits. The Danes, Dutch, Prussians, and
Swedes either abandoned their decaying forts and warehouses or sold them to
the British who only reluctantly accepted them.

After the mid-nineteenth century, legitimate trade began to grow in a few
geographical areas, encouraging the British and French to add a little more
territory to their small coastal enclaves. But they did this only to make them
more financially self-sufficient. European merchants were for the most part
content to trade with Africans and not to conquer them. Moreover, most European merchants in Africa resented government interference in trade.

King Leopold II of Belgium in 1876 was the first European ruler to embark
on a policy of territorial empire by seeking formal treaties with Africans in the
Congo region. At first, other European rulers seemed unperturbed. After all,
international law forbade the territorial violation of Belgium neutrality, and the
country itself was small and powerless. Even the French military advance into
the western Sudan in 1879–81 failed to cause serious alarm. Since the 1860
Cobden Treaty, trade between Britain and France was virtually free of tariff
restraints. In Africa as well as in Europe, the two nations had been remarkably
cooperative for decades.

This harmonious picture changed dramatically after 1879. France and Germany shifted to a high tariff policy in an effort to prevent cheap British imports
from weakening their own industries. It was a shift resulting from rising nationalist sentiments, spurred on by the unification of Germany and the humiliating
French defeat in the Franco-Prussian War of 1870. It was a consequence of the

pressures of industrialists seeking government protection from the competition of British products in world markets.

After about 1871 European industrial capitalism extended its scope and in so doing transformed itself. Small-scale entrepreneurs declined greatly in number and their richer, more powerful successors cultivated closer ties to government. They looked to government to reduce competition and to finance the transportation systems so necessary for economic development. One of the most common forms of government assistance to private enterprise was the protective tariff.

Britain had begun to lose its lead in commerce and by 1895, found it could no longer rely on free trade, private enterprise, or even its own colonial consuls and governors to safeguard its overseas economic interests from foreign encroachment. France and Germany had abandoned free trade and threatened to exclude Britain from European as well as from colonial markets and resource areas. France and Russia were gravitating diplomatically towards each other, thus endangering Germany with political encirclement. In 1884 Bismarck plunged into colonial adventures to draw France and Germany closer together over imperial disputes with Great Britain.

Matters were complicated further by rising Afrikaner nationalism in South Africa. After 1887 Britain was concerned that the gold-rich Transvaal Republic would draw itself and all of southern Africa out of the British imperial orbit. Such an eventuality would threaten the strategic sea route between Great Britain and its holdings in the East. To contain Transvaal expansionism, they conquered the Zulu nation along the coast, annexed Bechuanaland to secure the road to the north, allowed Rhodes to take Matabeleland, declared protectorates in Northern Rhodesia and Nyasaland, and tried unsuccessfully to buy Delagoa Bay from the Portuguese in Mozambique. Gold, the blood of the European monetary systems, was in growing demand as Western Europe industrialized. The Transvaal's gold resources seemed infinite, irresistible, and absolutely essential to the maintenance of British supremacy in the world economy.

The reasons for Africa's absorption into the world economy do not lie entirely in Western Europe. On the eve of European conquest, African rulers were weaker and less secure in their positions than they had been for several centuries. Their hold over indigenous political, economic, and social structures was slipping, and many of them had begun to resort to extraconstitutional means to remain in power. Some African states were relatively young and had not had time to develop a national consensus among their ethnically diverse populations. Many were beset by dynastic rivalries, militarism, and civil wars, all of which retarded real economic growth. The situation was exacerbated by European armaments. Indeed, by 1888 guns were filtering into East and Central Africa at the rate of eighty to one hundred-thousand annually. There may have been even more flowing into West Africa. Often, ambitious European consuls and arms traders took sides and further fractionalized the internal struggles.

They obtained concessions to land and minerals from pretenders to power who sought arms to overwhelm their rivals.

Much of this tragedy grew out of the nearly four hundred years of the overseas slave trade. It left a legacy of bitterness and suspicion, not only between Europeans and Africans but among various African ethnic and social groups. Rulers of the more powerful clans and tribes had attacked their weaker brothers and had sold them into bondage.

During the heyday of the slave trade, most of these captives were bought by Europeans and mixed-race traders on the coast for shipment overseas. The export sector of many economies became geared to slave raiding and trading. In some states, the practice of slave raiding became institutionalized and endemic, even after the decline of the overseas slave trade. Just before the European conquest, many of these captives still had not been assimilated into the culture of their captors, and the African rulers therefore could not count on them for support against foreign attack.

The Yoruba empire of Oyo and the kingdom of Dahomey expanded between the seventeenth and eighteenth centuries because of profits from the overseas slave trade. When the trade waned in the early nineteenth century, the economies of both states declined. Dahomey survived by developing a centrally planned economy, held together by a despotic totalitarian regime. The king built up a huge army and espionage network to control the masses and supported it through a plethora of taxes levied on the working population. In addition, the kingdom diverted slaves from export to plantation labor on state-owned palm-oil estates. In the neighboring Oyo empire, civil authority collapsed after 1817 and thousands of its Hausa and Fulani slaves revolted. Subordinate kingdoms seceded, massive pillaging followed, and waves of refugees sought the protection of self-appointed warlords. By the 1870s the military state of Ibadan was exploiting fellow Yoruba states as sources of wealth and cheap labor. They imposed unpopular and ruthless rulers who enjoyed intolerable privileges. Ibadan and other powerful Yoruba kingdoms took captives and sold them for arms and powder. The Yoruba civil wars brought great human suffering and economic chaos to a once prosperous empire.

Eastward, the economically decaying Benin empire had shrunk in size and found itself locked in bitter trade wars with once-subordinate states. Not far away, the Niger Delta city-states were destroying each other in competition for the palm-oil trade with the Europeans. The once-powerful Asante Confederacy also began to disintegrate and by the mid-nineteenth century was held together largely by military force. Many of the southern states had seceded by 1875, and the Muslim north followed after the deposition of Asantehene Mensa Bonsu in 1883. Later, slaves were put to work in the government gold mines in order to bolster the dwindling treasury.

In East Africa, the situation was no better. The peaceful indigenous populations were being harassed not only by Arabs and Swahili slavers but also by waves of armed Ngoni who had learned the art of war from the Zulu-Boer conflicts in South Africa. From the 1840s these foreigners fanned out over wide areas of Central and East Africa as far north as Lake Tanganyika. In Buganda the kabaka had to contend with competing Muslim, traditionalist, and Christian factions at his court. At one point in 1888 he killed innocent Catholic converts in an effort to achieve a semblance of authority. In Central Africa the peaceful Shona peoples, who had lived in the area for more than a thousand years, were invaded in 1837 by Ndebele warriors from South Africa. The Ndebele established the Matabele empire, after driving many Shona off their ancestral lands. King Lobengula, on the eve of Rhodes's conquest, had been raiding and extorting tribute from the defenseless Shona.

These are but a few illustrations of a general pattern of the economic and political discord prevailing over much of independent Africa on the eve of the European conquest. This situation weakened the ability of African rulers to unite against the alien imperialists and enabled the Europeans to couch their conquest in humanitarian jargon. The imperialists convinced the public that only they could restore peace and security and provide the conditions necessary for "legitimate trade" and for moral regeneration through Christian missionary enterprise. Many of the oppressed at first viewed the European imperialists as liberators. But as the subsequent colonial era wore on, the liberators came to be regarded by the people as their oppressors. Ironically, the traditional authorities, at least in British Africa, who at first resisted the conquest later viewed the colonialists as upholders of their positions attacked by the new generation of African nationalists.

POPULATION AND DISEASE

Diseases were a major deterrent to economic growth in precolonial Africa. Ironically, the increase in long-distance trade contributed substantially to the spread of infectious diseases. Such trade facilitated intercourse between groups and communities, and therefore accelerated disease transmission. Caravans served as deadly conveyors of alien and indigenous epidemic diseases.

Africa's generally low population density may have been a reflection of high disease mortality rates. From about 1650 to 1900 Europe's population grew by over 600 percent while Africa's expanded by only 20 percent or less. Surely, this may be explained in part by losses from the slave trade, for it is estimated that from twelve to fifty million people perished in the process. Within Africa itself, internal slave-raiding in the nineteenth century caused demographic disruption and devastation which in some areas created periodic food shortages and famine. People tended to cluster more closely for security. The concentration of population in river valleys contributed to soaring rates of chronic bilharzia (schistosoma), a disease which affects the bladder and large intestine causing physical lethargy and ultimately death.

West and Equatorial Africa (the Niger Delta, the coastal lagoons, and humid rain forests) were hosts to mosquitoes carrying malaria and yellow fever. Malaria was especially common and inflicted severe and debilitating fevers upon humans. People living in malarial zones either died of the disease during childhood or developed partial immunities. Yellow fever invariably resulted in death.

Even more widespread in the nineteenth century was trypanosomiasis, or sleeping sickness, which was carried by the tsetse fly and affected both men and cattle. Typhoid, and a variety of debilitating dysenteries, were common in areas of contaminated water. Typhus also remained a formidable disease and measles and smallpox ravaged the newborn. Infant mortality rates in the nineteenth century were the highest in the world. Though the birth rate was estimated to exceed an astounding four percent per annum, fewer than ten percent of those infants could expect to reach the age of five.

Africa was almost entirely free of cholera until the 1820s when it was brought to the East African coast by Arab traders from Muscat. It then followed the slave traders inland and at times devastated entire communities. Isolated cholera outbreaks also occurred in Egypt, the Sudan, and along the West African coast. The increased incidence of disease not only suppressed an otherwise explosive population growth but also contributed to social upheaval, dislocation, and tension, as people blamed their misfortune on foreigners or on evil elements within their own communities.

In 1896 a cattle virus, called rinderpest, spread into East, West, and southern Africa from the Nile Valley and Ethiopia. The death of millions of head of cattle led to severe malnutrition among pastoralists who in their weakened condition fell victim to other diseases.

chapter 3

Patterns of Culture

THE CENTRALITY OF RELIGION AND ANCESTOR WORSHIP

Religion in precolonial Africa was characterized by a wide diversity of belief systems and ritual forms. Each of the hundreds of different cultures maintained its own religious patterns yet many had striking similarities in outlook, strengthening the thesis that African religions were not immutable. They innovated and borrowed from each other, tailoring "foreign" concepts to their own needs. It was not unusual for several isolated cultural groups, separated from one another by hundreds or thousands of miles, to have similar religious stories. The names of the characters and the setting may have differed, but not the basic theme or moral. Religious beliefs and practices shaped, and were shaped by, the livelihood of the society, be it pastoral, agricultural, aquatic, or hunting and gathering, and by the scale and degree of social and political organization.

Religious belief for most precolonial Africans was the center of life. Everything revolved around it, was inextricably linked to it, and was subordinate to it. Religious practice thus took precedence over politics and social and economic concerns. Central to religion was the concept of "power", or "vital force" as most Bantu called it. Through prayers, invocations, sacrifices, witchcraft, and sorcery, Africans sought to activate, increase, or diminish that vital force which lay within themselves and within all animate and inanimate objects. Everything had a certain energy locked within it but releasing it was a major problem. Magical objects were placed at the entrances to family compounds and at community gates to ward off evil spirits and disease. Sacrifices in the form of offerings of livestock, beverages, and in a few cases, of humans, were intended to keep man in harmony with the spiritual forces, especially his ancestors, and to guard against misfortunes. In a prescientific world, religion seemed the only way to understand and control events, to relieve doubt, anxiety, and guilt. African religions also tried to explain how and why the world was created and developed. Nearly all the hundreds of distinct religious systems reflected philosphical concerns in that they considered questions such as the meaning and significance of life, death, and life beyond death.

Nearly all African civilizations believed in a Supreme God. In nearly every case, God's residence was in the heavens above. There were many names for God: "Leza" among the Tonga of Central Africa, "Mawu" among the Ewe of West Africa, and "Nyame" among the Akan of today's Ghana.

God was seen as the creator of both world and man. He established an order and gave it a life force found everywhere in nature that enabled man to exist in the world. God was the creative force; He had made the sun, moon, sky, air, water, and all living creatures including man, animals, and plants. God rewarded goodness but ruthlessly punished evil. God knew all, saw all, and was both omnipresent and omnipotent. He was responsible for sorrow and joy, sickness and well-being, fertility and impotence.

God was never worshipped, except by the Akan people and a few other groups. The Asante, a branch of the Akan, believed that everyone had direct access to God and they expressed this in the maxim: "No man's path crosses another's." In other words, everyone has his own, direct route to God.

Africans believed that the powers in the world were not all equal but were arranged in a sacred order, with God at the pinnacle. The Akan hierarchy moved from the Supreme God, to the spirits of the dead, to the spiritual powers over trees, mountains, and rivers. Everything had a vital force, but in varying degrees.

In many African societies there were tales of God living on earth but subsequently moving to heaven because of some human fault in his people. According to an Asante tale, Onyankopon lived on earth long ago. But he became unhappy with man and moved up into the sky beyond their reach. An old woman thought of a way to reach him and to bring him back. She told her children to go out and gather all the rocks they could find. Then she told them to pile them one on top of the other until they could reach Onyankopon. Her children complied, until they reached the point at which they needed only one more to get to Onyankopon. Since they could not find another rock anywhere, the old woman told them to take one out from the bottom and put it on top to make them reach. So her children removed a rock from the bottom and all the others rolled and fell to the ground, causing the death of many people.[1]

In Susan Feldman's anthology *African Myths and Tales,* there is a similar tale from the Barotse peoples living on the upper Zambesi River in south-central Africa. The creator, Nyambi, once lived on earth. One of his creations, named Kamonu, tried to imitate everything Nyambi did. Finally, Kamonu became violent and killed living creatures. Nyambi sent him away, but he returned and continued to commit violent acts. Nyambi tried various means

[1] Geoffrey Parrinder, *African Mythology* (London: Hamlyn Publishing Group, Ltd., 1967), pp. 34–35.

to flee Kamonu and each time Kamonu found him. Nyambi finally sought counsel from a diviner who told him that his life depended on a spider. A spider then spun a thread from the earth to the sky and Nyambi climbed it. After Nyambi disappeared into the sky, Kamonu gathered some men and ordered the construction of a tower that would reach Nyambi's heavenly abode. They cut down trees and put log on log, higher and higher towards the sky. But the weight was too great and the tower collapsed. So Kamonu never found his way to Nyambi's home.[2]

These tales established the imperfect nature of man vis-à-vis God, and they explained the need for man to search constantly to discover God's will and to reconcile himself to God. The Yoruba of western Nigeria attempted to do this through a complicated system of divination. They had seventeen hundred different divinities or *orisa,* which were lesser deities under the Supreme Being. *Ogun,* one of the leading divinities, was the owner of all iron and it was he, as a hunter and warrior, who paved the way for the other deities to come to earth. Divinities were intermediaries between man and God. Organizations of priests or diviners were responsible for the divining process. In a prescientific world, divinities like Sango, god of thunder, could explain the forces of nature. It was important for the individual to know what each spiritual power was doing. Peter Morton-Williams has noted that the Yoruba would consult two divine mediators, called Ifa and Esu. Esu was the divine trickster who might intervene in one's life to magnify his misdeeds and shortcomings to the extent that the chief, the ancestors, and others may become angered. Ifa would tell how to conform to society, to convention, and to the will of the orisa. It was therefore quite important to discern the intentions and wishes of the spirits. Seldom were state decisions made in the Oyo empire without prior consultation with the cult in charge of the appropriate orisa.

To the Yoruba, the cosmos consisted of sky-heaven, earth, and world. Olorun was the god of heaven. Those who resided in sky-heaven were the spiritual doubles of those who dwelled on earth. Olorun's counterpart was Onile, the goddess of the earth. She would receive the souls of the dead, in other words, the ancestors. The orisa mediated the relations between sky-heaven and the world of the living. Life in this third cosmic realm, world, was good only if the deities and spirits of the other two realms were in harmony with the world. While the orisa priests were concerned with maintaining this harmony, the ancestors occupied themselves with controlling behavior among kinfolk. The ancestors were interested in upholding the morals of the living community. The Tutsi and Hutu of Ruanda believed that the *bazimu,* or spirits of the dead, sometimes returned to the world of the living. The ancestors would protect their living descendants, if they led a good life, if they followed tradition and prec-

---

[2] Susan Feldman, ed., *African Myths and Tales* (New York: Dell Publishing Co., 1963), pp. 36-37.

Tano shrine house, built during the precolonial era by the Asante near the city of Kumasi in Ghana.

edent, and if they made offerings to them. So in order to appease the ancestors, the living regularly held observances in their memory.

Ancestor worship was common in precolonial Africa and served as a stabilizing social force. Some argue today that it discouraged innovation and change and that it was a conservative force. Though this may be true, ancestor worship was crucial to African civilizations. It was the core of religious behavior. Some say it was its "spiritual essence." In Yorubaland, ancestor worship assumed a universal form in the *egungun,* or masqueraders. According to G.J. Ojo, "these . . . were supposed to be ancestors from heaven who had returned to hear and put right the complaints of the people left behind, to bless them with human and crop fertility and also with general prosperity."[3] Egungun masqueraders were found in almost every Yoruba community and were both respected and feared as the spirits of the ancestors. They had the vital role of regulating community behavior in accordance with the norms of society. The egungun ceremony achieved the purpose of honoring the ancestors and in so doing ensured that the people who are still living would be protected.

Ancestor worship was very much a part of African artistic traditions because of the many masked dances accompanying such ceremonies or festivals. In the Benin empire since at least the sixteenth century, ceremonies have been held annually in honor of the deity Ekpo, who taught people how to prevent certain

[3]G.J. Ojo, *Yoruba Culture* (Ifé: University of London Press, Ltd., 1966), p. 140.

deadly epidemics. The aim of the ekpo cult or society, according to Osarenren Omoregie, is to combat disease and to keep towns clean or in a state of ritual purity. He adds that the Bini people believed "that serious illness was caused by supernatural forces acting against man, either in retribution or out of sheer malevolence."[4] When the elders felt their village was in danger, they would call upon the ekpo society to make sacrifices, perform purification rites, and stage masked dances.

Prayer was also a part of the traditional African religious systems. However, few African societies built houses or temples for the worship of the Supreme Being. In some nineteenth-century Asante villages there were temples for the worship of Nyame, or God. But in most African civilizations, the people preferred to build shrines for the worship of lesser deities, such as gods of rivers, hills, or rocks. This is not to say that Africans did not pray. The Yoruba and others prayed frequently, at any place at any time of the day.

It would be wrong to believe that Africans were "pagans" before their conversion to Christianity or "kaffirs" before their conversion to Islam. African religions were polytheistic but with a belief in a Supreme Being. They were convinced that there were close links betwen the world of the living and the world of the spirits. The Asante, like most Africans, kept their ancestors constantly in mind. KA. Busia has stated:

> . . . prayer expresses the sense of dependence on the ancestors. They are believed to be constantly watching over the living relatives. They punish those who break the customs, or fail to fulfil their obligations to their kinsfolk.[5]

None of the classical African religions became universalistic, though a few were embraced by more than one ethnic group. Priestly orders were intensely secretive and did not see themselves as missionaries bent on prosyletizing people outside their own localities. The religions also were intimately tied to ancestor veneration which had little importance other than for the descendants of specific familes and clans. Many of these religious systems were as complex as Christianity and Islam.

Islam was the largest of the precolonial African religions and easily cut across ethnic, lineage, political, and social lines. It had existed for many centuries in North Africa, the West African savanna, and along the East African coast, intermittently growing and declining with the rise and fall of various economic and political entities. In the late nineteenth century, there were still a number of ancient centers of Islamic learning, and Africans continued to make pilgrimages to Mecca. Islam always had given Africa an important cultural link with the

---

[4] Osarenren Omoregie, "Ekpo Ritual in Avbiama", *African Arts* (Summer 1969), p. 9.

[5] K.A. Busia, *Africa in Search of Democracy* (London: Routledge & Kegan Paul, Ltd.), p. 29.

outside world, particularly with the Middle East. The Qadiriyya brotherhood maintained lodges in many towns and villages of the West African grasslands.

The nineteenth century, however, was the era of militant Islam, a time when its adherents rejected compromise or syncretism with traditional African religions. Islamic clerics and their students came out of their mosques and Qur'anic schools, declared jihads, and became revolutionaries. After the early eighteenth century, these religious rebellions led to the establishment of theocratic states and empires in the West African Sudan, from the Futa Jalon to northern Nigeria. We spoke of this in its political context in earlier chapters. Here, it is important to remember that these *jihadi,* or revolutionaries, called for a restoration of the classical purity of the Islamic faith and the purging of the religious system of corrupt, syncretistic forms. Under some of them, the more militant Tijaniyya brotherhood spread quickly, often at the expense of the Qadiriyya. The Tijaniyya order preached a more egalitarian Islam and drew its popularity from ritual simplicity. A missionary order, it was founded by Ahmad al-Tijani of Fez in the late eighteenth century. In contrast, the Qadiriyya order was the oldest in Islam, founded in Iraq in the twelfth century and introduced to West Africa via Timbuktu four centuries later. The Qadiriyya was more purist, rigid, and socially intolerant.

Islam was imposed by force, and many people, notably the Mossi of Upper Volta and the Asante, stoutly and successfully resisted. Others were defeated and their religious symbols, masks and sculpture, were destroyed. Islam did grow somewhat in the 1840s in East Africa, under the Zanzibar rule of Sultan Sayyid Said. Arab and Swahili caravan drivers and traders penetrated into the mainland interior as far as the eastern Congo. But unlike the West African Muslim jihadi, their main concern was trade and the establishment of economic spheres of influence. In the last quarter of the nineteenth century, the European Imperialists destroyed the West African theocratic states and empires and broke the economic back of the East African Muslims. Militant, political Islam declined, yet ironically, the colonial era facilitated the diffusion of Islamic religious ideas.

Before the last quarter of the nineteenth century, Christianity was confined largely to the European enclaves along the West African coast, South Africa, and the ancient Coptic Christian kingdom of Ethiopia. After the 1820s there were various missionary groups in West Africa: principally the powerful Anglican Church Missionary Society (CMS), the Wesleyan Methodist Missionary Society, the Foreign Mission Committee of the United Presbyterian Church of Scotland, the Southern Baptist Convention of the United States, and the Catholic Society of African Missions of France. As adherents of the antislavery movement, they championed not only Christianity but also European "legitimate" commerce and civilization. The missionaries also were anxious to create a Christianized and Westernized African middle class that might implement the social reforms the missionaries favored and that would provide agents for proselytizing Africans in a seemingly "disease-ridden" interior. In the Cape Colony of South Africa, after the early 1800s the English-speaking Congregational London Missionary Society led the struggle against racial discrimination and defended the civil liberties of the Khoi and coloreds against the Afrikaans-speaking, white population. In this endeavor, they came up against strong resistance from the conservative Dutch Reformed Church.

After the 1840s missionaries began to push into the interior: the Rhenish Missionary Society into South West Africa, the Basel and Bremen missionaries from Germany and Switzerland into the Gold Coast hinterland, the CMS into Yorubaland in western Nigeria, the Holy Ghost Fathers, Lutherans, CMS, and others into the East African interior. In West Africa, Sierra Leone's Fourah Bay College educated freed slaves as clergymen. One student, Samuel Ajayi Crowther, became Anglican Bishop for all West Africa in 1864 and served in that capacity for nearly three decades.

Geographical explorations and discoveries in the interior and great medical strides in the control of such tropical diseases as malaria, made European penetration of the interior less dangerous and more attractive. Missionaries received even greater inspiration from the ideas and activities of the Scottish missionary, Dr. David Livingstone. Livingstone's best selling books set into motion an era of almost frenetic missionary expansion. His own work was based in southern Africa, between the Limpopo River and the southern shores of Lake Tanganyika. Livingstone believed that missionaries must establish "centers of Christianity and civilization for the promotion of religion, agriculture and commerce."[6] In his prolific writings and public addresses in Great Britain he called upon missionaries to develop local industry and to displace the slave trade with legitimate trade. He and such famous explorers as Henry Morton Stanley spoke widely of the cruelty of the interior slave-trading and raiding, and were convinced that only European enterprise could provide an economically viable alternative.

The global attention given to Livingstone's death in 1873 and his burial in Great Britain's Westminster Abbey, greatly aroused public sentiment and interest in expanding missionary programs in Africa. The last quarter of the nineteenth century thus witnessed a dramatic growth in missionary endeavor. African clergy like Bishop Crowther were overwhelmed, and their authority was eclipsed as European missionaries flooded into the continent. In 1876 Scottish missionaries of the Church of Scotland Mission set up stations around Lake Malawi. A year later the London Missionary Society established their own mission posts around Lake Tanganyika. The CMS established settlements for freed slaves along the East African coast. The Universities Mission to Central Africa (UMCA) also became more active, using Zanzibar as its base. In 1876 the CMS moved into the kingdom of Buganda, becoming more deeply embroiled in the political and social life of the people. The new Protestant thrust inspired a competitive

[6]Tim Jeal, *Livingstone* (New York: Dell Publishing Co., Inc.), p. 416.

response from the Catholics. France's Father Lavigerie established the White Fathers, and in 1879 this order arrived at Ujiji on Lake Tanganyika. By the 1880s they were active in Buganda, competing with both Arabs and the CMS for the peoples' hearts and minds, and also had established posts as far south as the present Zambia. At the same time, the Jesuits moved into Matabeleland, an area where they had not been since the seventeenth century, in the days of the old Mwenemutapa empire.

Everywhere, the missionaries followed the precolonial trade routes and discovered that the interior was far more accessible than Europeans had originally thought. In many cases, the missionaries gained the friendship and trust of local chiefs. These enthusiastic Europeans, most of them in their twenties, studied African civilizations, and published grammars and dictionaries of local languages.

By the 1880s, the European powers had become interested in territorial acquisitions, and the missionaries, who knew more about Africa than anyone else, wittingly and unwittingly were transformed into agents of militant imperialism. Roland Oliver stated, "They wished to ensure that the intervention would be carried out by their own countrymen or by the power most likely to offer the best opportunity for the work of their denominations."[7] At home, missionaries helped shape public opinion behind the "Imperial Factor" in order to "save" Africa from the domination of Arab slavers or other European powers. In Africa, they introduced agents of European governments to African chiefs, acted as diplomatic interpreters, and facilitated the signing of treaties of "protection." In Matabeleland, the Reverend Helm, who purported to be a friend of King Lobengula, was in fact secretly employed by Rhodes. Missionaries in Matabeleland were convinced that the Ndebele system of government had to be destroyed before Christian conversion could succeed, and in 1890 they warmly greeted the arrival of Rhodes's British South Africa Company forces.

In much of tropical Africa, the missionaries, not the European traders and enclave administrators, were the torch-bearers of Western influence until at least the early 1890s. They favored imperialist intervention and colonialism, because it would offer them protection and security and would stimulate capitalist enterprise, which in turn would provide new economic opportunities for the Africans, especially those who had suffered from slaving activities. From about 1875, missionary propaganda gave imperialism an undeserved moral justification.

The Christian missionaries, with their denominational varieties and rivalries, undermined traditional social, religious, and political institutions and obscured true European intentions. This made African leaders even more vulnerable to imperial conquest. In many ways, the missionaries paved the way for European colonialism.

---

[7]Roland Oliver and Gervase Mathew, eds., *History of East Africa,* I (Oxford: Clarendon, 1963), p. 69.

EDUCATION

Africa was mostly preliterate before the colonial era. Only in the Muslim areas, in the Coptic Christian Church in Ethiopia, in European coastal enclaves, and among Europeans in South Africa were there bodies of literate people. Elsewhere, literacy was absent and there were few written languages other than a handful embodied in missionary-produced vernacular Bibles, grammars, and dictionaries. In Liberia, however, Momolu Daolu of the Vai people developed a new system of writing in the early nineteenth century. The Vai script was cumbersome and could not compete with English. Nevertheless, it is a testament to the ability of Africans to devise their own system of writing when a need for it arose. By 1875, a majority of adult Vai males could read and write in this script.

Liberians of American descent also were fairly literate, using English in their schools and at Liberia College which was founded in the 1860s. In South Africa, a local variant of Dutch, with a vocabulary incorporating Malay, Khoi, French, and Portuguese words evolved into a new language called Afrikaans. By the late 1870s Afrikaans had become a literary as well as an oral medium of expression.

In traditional African education, children were educated in the home by parents, grandparents, and clan elders. Until age five or six they were confined largely to the family compound. Afterwards, boys joined adults to learn the art of observation in the forest, fields, and in the market place. Weather indications were taught through rhymes and sayings. Boys also were taught to identify and to trap or eliminate crop pests, rodents, and dangerous animals. The art of hunting and bird, plant and aquatic identification, of clearing land, sowing, and harvesting also was emphasized. Crafts were learned by direct observation and imitation. A knowledge of ethics and moral values was imparted by family or clan elders through the recitation of legends, proverbs, maxims, and didactic songs and poetry, all with philosophical meaning. The following are a few examples:

"One falsehood spoils a thousand truths" Asante
"Do not call the forest that shelters you a jungle" Asante
"A man with excessive ambition will not sleep peacefully" Lunda
"Knowledge is better than material riches" Kanuri
"Two fish disputed about a morsel of food when a third swam over and
    carried it away" Songhay
"He who learns, teaches" Galla
"Mutual gifts cement friendship" Baule
"Virtue is better than wealth" Kikuyu[8]

[8]Charlotte and Wolf Leslau, eds., *African Proverbs* (Mount Vernon: Peter Pauper Press, 1962), pp. 42-66.

The importance placed on education is revealed in a Hausa proverb "Want of learning is like the yoke on a slave." Education also taught toleration, as shown in another Hausa proverb, "The camel brags about the Asben trail but will never go to Asante." Camels are excellent in desertlike conditions but cannot withstand tropical rain forests. In other words, different people have different aptitudes.

Role-playing and dramatizations were used to instruct youth in proper etiquette. If a child were of royal birth, he or she would be sent to the palace compound to learn from the palace retainers and the ruler about the mystique of divine-right power. They would study gestures and symbols of diplomacy, clothing for appropriate ceremonies, history, and gestures. Daughters of commoners remained near the family compound and learned household tasks, especially the preparation and cooking of food. They also learned to identify medicinal herbs used to treat ailments and developed skills in handicrafts such as basketmaking and ceramics.

Historical knowledge of the general community was passed down in some societies through groups of professional raconteurs, poets, and jesters, called *griots* by the Manding (Mande) ethnic group. Their intellectual energies focused on memorizing and reciting important events concerning the ruling family and the polity it governed. They transmitted to the younger generations the genealogies, social, legal, and political traditions, and the important accomplishments of ancestral leaders. As historians of traditional Africa, griots were the major repositories of oral literature and were its leading educators. They developed exceptional skills in memorization and were in effect the archives of the communities and families they served. In humid tropical climates, paper, subject to mildew and termites, disintegrated quickly. Thus, information was best stored within the mind. The griot, then, was the most revered educator of all and gave his listeners a crucial sense of continuity, collective consciousness, and will.

At puberty, children underwent a period of intensive education before becoming responsible members of adult society. Initiation rites, or "rites of passage" prepared youth to cope with sex, marriage, family management, and social and legal customs. Only after their elevation to adulthood could they gain admission to the prestigious secret societies. The latter were not only agents of social control. They provided a number of community services including the education of youth, the appeasement of benign and malign spirits, the enforcement of taboos, and the punishment of offenders. In conclusion, the major aims of traditional education were to maintain the status quo, to inculcate in people a respect for and understanding of authority, to provide continuity, to impart practical skills, and to promote a spirit of mutuality. Students were not encouraged to cultivate abstract, critical reasoning, particularly if it challenged the words and deeds of the ancestors. Education was conservative and moralistic, stressing respect for older people and discipline.

Education acquired an additional dimension in the Muslim areas. The Qur'anic schools in the Sokoto Caliphate of northern Nigeria were open to all, regardless of rank in society. Only a tiny fraction of the population actually attended and most were males. Normally, students studied in local Qur'anic schools, often attached to mosques, for one to five years. They memorized portions of the Qur'an and learned to read and write the Hausa language in Arabic script. Advanced scholars wrote in classical Arabic and studied commentaries of the Qur'an. Teachers, called scribes, clerics, or *mallams,* depended on their students' families for gifts, usually crops, livestock, or clothes, and on the compulsory ten-percent Islamic tax, called *zakat.*

In the Sokoto Caliphate, the intellectual community was divided into two categories: the urban mallams who had permanent schools and personal libraries and who doubled as mosque officials and government advisors, and the itinerant rural mallams who spent a limited time in each community. Rural mallams in the West African savanna were more than mere teachers. They also served as physicians, family counselors, and officiators at weddings and funerals. One usually became a mallam by memorizing significant portions of the Qur'an and by demonstrating some comprehension of Islam's social, legal, and ritual regulations. A sure route to advancement was to study under some prominent mallam or cleric and to perform a *haj* or pilgrimmage to Mecca, Islam's Holy Land. The leading teachers of Muslim Africa often were called *al-hajis.*

Islamic education spread rapidly in the savanna of West Africa and along the East African coast in the nineteenth century. By 1875, there were more than ninety-five Qur'anic schools in West Africa with enrollments exceeding a hundred students. Most of them were in the Sultanate of Bornu, the Sokoto Caliphate, and in the theocratic state of Massina. Many scholars traveled widely, sometimes beyond their own states and occasionally to North Africa. Some became important political leaders and founders of theocratic states, like Usuman dan Fodio, Seku Ahmadu, al-haj 'Umar, and al-Kanami, to mention only a few from the early nineteenth century.

There were very few institutions of higher education in sub-Saharan Africa before the twentieth century. Nearly all of them were missionary-operated, with a classical and theological curriculum designed to turn out clergymen. South Africa led the way but their institutions almost exclusively catered to English-speaking whites. In 1873 the University of the Cape of Good Hope was founded as an examining and controlling body that awarded degrees but left instruction to eight existing colleges. The most famous institution was Victoria College in the Cape Colony (1887) which later became the University of Stellenbosch. In Sierra Leone, Fourah Bay College, founded by the Church Missionary Society in 1827 for freed slaves, became affiliated with Durham University in England after 1876. Most of the Western-educated elites of British West Africa in the nineteenth century were graduates of Fourah Bay College. Liberia College, founded in 1862, was mainly a national university and emphasized political science and diplomacy with an accent on Greek and Latin.

Most Africans qualifying for a higher education, and there were only a few handfuls, went to institutions in Western Europe, mainly in Great Britain and France. After the late 1880s a few black South Africans attended universities in the United States.

SOCIAL ORGANIZATION

Stratification, according to Margaret Peil, may be defined as "institutionalized inequality of access to advantageous positions."[9] In viewing precolonial Africa in the late nineteenth century, many examples and degrees of stratification can be found, particularly in the savanna and forest zones of West Africa, along the East African Swahili coast, in Ethiopia, in the interlacustrine areas of East Africa, and in South Africa. In less accessible and ethnically homogeneous rural areas, role differentiation was limited to age, sex, and physical and mental capacity. In nearly every society, older people commanded higher esteem. Peil distinguishes between status, referring to prestige, honor, and social privilege, and class, implying economic and cultural interest. Status differentiation was found almost everywhere but class distinctions were limited to societies involved in accumulating material wealth.

Precolonial African societies exhibited a wide spectrum of social organization from hereditary aristrocracy, free peasants, castes, and involuntary servitude, to highly egalitarian communities receptive to achieved mobility. Many communities expressed a tripartite division in society consisting of aristocrats, commoners, and the nonfree. The aristocrats often came from different ethnic stocks and had entered the indigenous society as invading conquerors. Societies without institutionalized political leaders usually conferred superior status upon such ritual leaders as rainmakers, diviners, prophets, and priestesses. Low levels of technology inhibited the growth of significant economic inequality, particularly in societies not engaged in long-distance trade or possessing markets. Most people lived at much the same economic level and enjoyed similar lifestyles and living standards. The major differentiating principle in precolonial societies was power, both physical and mental. Class consciousness was rarely manifested because of the low level of occupational specialization and the strongly entrenched ethnic and clan feelings that often transcended class interests.

By the second half of the nineteenth century, involuntary domestic servitude and chattel slavery had become important elements in the social organization of many societies. Slavery lacked the racist overtones and much of the ideology of innate inferiority so common to South Africa and the Americas. Ethnic discrimination, on the other hand, was often inextricably linked to

---

[9]Margaret Peil, *Consensus and Conflict in African Societies* (London: Longman Group, Ltd., 1977), p. 79.

the institution, for only infrequently would Africans enslave people of their own ethnic origin.

Master-servant relationships in black Africa go back long before the heyday of the Atlantic slave trade and the plantation system of New World slavery. Nonfree groups of peoples were usually found in socially stratified societies under powerful and highly centralized political control. It is difficult to label all nonfree people as "slaves," in the Western sense, because many of these groups had considerable mobility and were not deprived of their self-esteem, dignity, or humanity.

There are at least five categories of nonfree peoples: laborers (fieldhands, men working on public projects, gardeners), eunuchs (performing household chores but some also holding administrative positions), concubines (women for harems), administrators (forming the rank and file of government bureaucracies as tax collectors and overseers of local government) and soldiers (usually infantrymen and bowmen). Nonfree persons were the backbone of many African societies; they were important to agriculture and to the military sector, to defend the country. Free peasants as well as nonfree peasants were dependent on their masters for food, clothing, and shelter, particularly in times of famines. The master in turn was morally obligated to meet the servant's needs, otherwise risking social ostracism and loss of standing among his peers. Some would say that the wealth or poverty of a master was written on the faces of his servants.

Masters were dependent on their servants for harvesting crops, a portion of which would have to be remitted to state officials as tax payment. Also, they depended upon their servants to maintain compound walls and to keep paths clear.

The chores of free and nonfree peasants differed very little. Free people enjoyed a higher social status and could inherit personal property and real estate. The nonfree in many societies were without kin to support and defend them in time of need. Without a lineage of their own, they were more completely dependent on their masters than a free client might be. For convenience and clarity, let us say that "lineage" consists of all the descendants of a common ancestor in the same line. A clan is composed of a number of lineages whose members claim descent from a common ancestor. Lineage affiliation to this day is vital to the social cohesion of African communities. Nonfree groups usually were not connected to a lineage or clan and were not buried in the community cemeteries. Among the Asante, certain community secrets were kept from nonfree people, placing them at a disadvantage.

In some societies, nonfree people did not have equality before the law, but this varied widely. In the Asante Confederacy, a nonfree person could give evidence in court against his master and could change masters. Once freed, it was a legal offense for anyone to speak publicly of his servile origins.

It was very difficult in some cultures for a group or individual to secure freedom. In the kingdom of Ruanda in East Africa, the pastoral Tutsi peoples had complete control over the distribution of cattle. Cattle was not only a status symbol but was vital to the nation's economic wealth. The Hutu people, who differed in physical appearance from the Tutsi, were denied equal access to cattle. Consequently, they were forced to do all the manual labor and to till the fields. The Tutsi, though numerically fewer acted as protectors of the Hutu, offering them shelter against raids by neighbors. In return, the Hutu were forced to supply their Tutsi overlords with agricultural produce—goods which afforded the Tutsi a very high standard of living. The Tutsi disdained working the soil and left such dirty work to the Hutu. Indeed, the Tutsi had a greater share of the so-called good things of life and got it with little physical effort.

Nonfree peoples, usually of a different ethnic origin, in some states were physically segregated from the free. Until recently in Botswana, bushmen, or San, were serfs of their Bantu masters. They had to live in settlements on the outskirts of their masters' villages and commute in for the day. Politically, they had no power within the framework of the village government. In the Sokoto Caliphate in the nineteenth century, nonfree peoples were segregated into special villages, called *rumada.* Later, when the Igbo, a free people, moved into the area, they were unable to settle in the existing cities but instead had to reside on the periphery in what were called *sabon garis,* or "strangers' towns."

Life without freedom was not always a happy one, but in many parts of Africa there were opportunities for freedom. Nonfree people in Benin were allowed to farm and trade for themselves and could become independent enough to secure their emancipation by paying off their master or by buying a replacement. Jaja, in the Niger Delta, was born a slave but through his own hard work manning canoes laden with palm oil, he bought his freedom and went on to establish his own state, complete with palm-oil plantations and a seaport. As one authority on the Niger Delta peoples wrote, "Slaves and freemen together belonged to closely knit trading corporations in which slaves had opportunities to acquire wealth, demonstrate their energy and intelligence and thus to improve their status."[10]

A distinction can be made between slave and servant in precolonial Africa. Both were valued for the economic and commercial utility of their labor. They were also a public expression of their master's personal power and wealth. In effect they were his personal property, and he could will them to others upon his death. Yet there were basic differences. Servants, though not free, enjoyed a closer relationship with their masters. They had been born in their master's compound and raised there. They were rarely sold, except for serious offences or in times of dire financial need. Often they had either their own garden plots or were entitled to a percentage of the fruits of their labor. Children of servants played with their free counterparts. When a child matured, the master would

[10] A.J.H. Latham, *Old Calabar 1600-1891* (Oxford: Clarendon Press, Ltd., 1973), p. 97.

pay for the wedding and possibly pay the bride price as well. Some servants held important government offices and thus had power over free men.

Who then were the slaves? They were individuals or groups who had been captured in raids or wars and who lived apart from their master's compound. These people were seldom well known by their master and were considered economic or commercial instruments and little else. They might be bought or sold at whim or used as tribute or in payment of taxes. They might be put to death as part of the sacrificial rites on the death of a monarch. These were people whose life was little better than that of their brothers on plantations in the Americas. But slavery of this nature was not common in Africa, though it was widespread. The institution of slavery, as opposed to servitude, grew tremendously as a result of the Atlantic slave trade. In some kingdoms, slaves were a great proportion of the total population. In the emirates of Katsina and Kano in the Sokoto Caliphate by the 1850s, they were estimated to be more than fifty percent of the population. In 1860 the emir of neighboring Zaria left an estate of nine thousand slaves. About one-third of the Wolof, Serer, and Fon populations included slaves of all categories, and C. Meillassoux estimated that between thirty and sixty percent of the people in the entire western Sudan were in servile positions.

There were a few isolated cases of plantation slavery, akin to that found in the southern United States. On Zanzibar island, nineteenth-century clove plantations were worked by African slaves under Arab masters. The king of Dahomey in West Africa established slave-worked palm-oil plantations in the mid-nineteenth century. At the same time, not a few Fulani chiefs forced slaves to work on plantations in northern Nigeria. While coastal West Africa responded to the growth of "legitimate" trade in the early nineteenth century, the Sokoto Caliphate expanded dramatically their plantation sector. Slave-worked plantations sprang up near all the major towns. By the 1880s in the outlying provinces, plantations vied with slave-raiding and tribute collection as the basis of the economy. In the Asante Confederacy, slaves were employed in the mines. Between 1790 and the 1820s, the kind of Asante employed from eight to ten thousand slaves in a single gold-mining region in his domain.

The Atlantic slave-trade system accelerated the internal system, corrupting local "legitimate" trade and in effect creating a demand for more slaves in the local economies, for use as well as for sale. While a certain element of continuity existed in master-servant relationships, the Atlantic slave trade altered the degree of intimacy and coercion in those relationships. It became more difficult and less likely for the acquired "outsider" to become incorporated into the institutions of the host society. As European demands for slaves increased, the acquired person had a smaller chance of remaining in Africa and gradually gaining for himself or his descendants the status of "insider" within the master's kin group.

Ironically, New World slavery grew even more with the decline of the Atlantic slave trade. European traders, searching for "legitimate" goods to trade (in place of slaves) unwittingly encouraged the use of slaves to produce cash crops and other products demanded by Europe and the Americas. There was a continuing domestic demand for people to serve as units of labor and to expand the social and political scale of local societies. In the late nineteenth century a growing number of slaves were found as trading agents, court officials, and soldiers. African chiefs assigned others to work on farms and in mines in an effort to make the necessary readjustment from economies structured around the export of slaves to economies once again based on the exploitation of natural resources. Those captives not put to work in these capacities were integrated gradually into free society. Indeed, there are indications that most slaves, after the first generation of enslavement, moved steadily towards incorporation into the institutions of the host society. Most eventually acquired kinship connections. This was important, because as I. Kopytoff suggested, "kinship relations and the kin group were dominant elements in most African social systems."[11]

In the Niger Delta, around Old Calabar, tension began to develop between the urban dwellers and the expanding number of agricultural slaves. A.J.H. Latham states, "Slaves were expected to support and identify with the interests of their masters, for whom they had to work, and if necessary, fight. This gave them opportunity to achieve both wealth and influence despite their lack of kinship."[12] In the Niger Delta, slaves and ex-slaves revolted because free society would not allow them to hold political positions commensurate with their economic strength. By 1850, they were becoming reluctant to recognize any direct master at all. The agricultural slaves late in that year bound themselves with a blood oath to resist the arbitrary treatment of the freemen, and so they formed the Order of Blood Men. In some areas these slaves, once they had achieved this unit, did not overthrow the freemen but chose instead to support their masters in political power plays. In other words, they transformed themselves into a powerful political lobby.

It should be understood that servitude was accepted almost everywhere in precolonial Africa as perfectly natural. In a precapitalistic society, it was an effective means of mobilizing labor to meet the political, economic, and military requirements of a given state and labor was one of Africa's greatest resources.

To summarize, nonfree persons could be bought, sold, or inherited by a private individual, were denied choice of occupation, employer, or lifestyle, and were unable to dispose of property, marry freely, control their offspring's life, or gain equal access to the law. In essence, African slavery revolves around the rights that an individual or group exercises over another, in other words, the

---

[11] Suzanne Miers and Igor Kopytoff, eds., *Slavery in Africa* (Madison: University of Wisconsin Press, 1977), p. 22.

[12] A.J.H. Latham, *Old Calabar 1600-1891* (Oxford: Clarendon Press, Ltd., 1973), p. 97.

"rights-in-persons." Transactions in rights-in-persons were an integral part of traditional African social organization, free and nonfree. Important to any discussion of master-servant relationships is an understanding of the legal position of the individual within a kin group. In determining the status of a "slave" or free person, one must assess the degree of coercion or compulsion in the transferral of a person from one group to another. One must also consider that individual's subsequent relationship to the acquisitor's kin group.

URBANIZATION

It is widely believed that before the colonial era, black Africans had little understanding of the dynamics of urban design and architecture. African dwellings were described as "shelters" or "huts" and their communities as "bush villages." It was assumed that what little urban life did exist, resulted largely from European inspiration. Until recently, urbanologists concentrated on the colonial period thereby strengthening these myths. It cannot be denied that most sub-Saharan Africans lived and indeed continue to live in small villages and hamlets. Yet magnificent towns and cities flourished as well, and only a minority of Africans in the late nineteenth century were completely unaffected by them.

For the convenience of definition, precolonial African cities and towns were collective bodies of inhabitants under the jurisdiction of an elite with political, economic, or religious authority. Sheer numbers do not determine a town, or for that matter, a city. Rather, a town or city must be seen as a center, not only of population but of religion, the arts, government, the military, industry, and commerce. Towns and cities also act as cultural transmitters; the mark of a truly great cosmopolis is its ability to disseminate its institutions. Medieval Timbuktu and Jenné were important cities of the western Sudan. Their educational and religious institutions (based on Islam) and their architectural forms became prototypes for a multitude of West African savanna communities. The cosmopolitan Swahili city-states of the East African coast did not become powerful transmitters of culture until the nineteenth century. For centuries they had attracted peoples from Arabia, Persia, northwest India, Indonesia (via Madagascar), and the East African interior.

Traditional African towns and cities were more than mere transmitters: they also received and synthesized. Perhaps the sudanic and Swahili cities came closest to becoming "ecumenopolises," or urban synthesizers of diverse cultures. In their central market places it was not unusual to find many ethnic groups, speaking different languages and having different lifestyles.

Unlike Western European counterparts, African cities and towns were basically agrarian. Seventy percent or more of their male residents commuted regularly to outlying farms. In a sense, some cities, particularly those of the

West African forests, could be described as village-cities. Their social and political organization almost mirrored that of the outlying rural communities.

Some urbanologists insist that an urban agglomeration is not a "town" unless a significant proportion of its inhabitants devote most of their energies to nonagricultural pursuits, namely, to handicrafts or trade. In other words, to qualify as a town, a population center must provide specialized services. Although this qualification may be debated, many towns and cities conformed to this pattern. It is equally important that we define cities and towns by the functions they perform, their capacity for assimilation, and their ability to transmit a new cultural synthesis. It would be an exaggeration to assert that cities and towns shaped the destinies of all African peoples. Some societies, like the nomadic Masai of Kenya or the Dogon of Mali, were affected only remotely by life in urban centers lying beyond their cultural and occupational frontiers. In other areas, particularly along the West and East African coasts in the West African savanna, cities and towns played a crucial role.

If sizeable towns did exist in precolonial Africa, what led to their emergence and growth? It was not unusual for some towns to evolve from spiritual centers. Two cities of the Sokoto Caliphate, Daura and Kano, originated before the eleventh century as headquarters of the important local deities and priestly orders connected to them. In some instances, towns emerged from the residences of kings, chiefs, or important traders. For centuries, successive kings of Buganda staked out their own capitals on one of the many flat-topped hills near modern Kampala. The capital, inevitably relocated by each new ruler, did not contain a central market place. Rather, people flocked there solely because of its status as the kingdom's administrative and judicial nerve center.

Many towns in the nineteenth century East African interior were produced by the energies of dynamic trader-chiefs. These communities, as meeting places for converging itinerant traders, were fragile and fell as rapidly as they had risen. Lacking an institutional base, their fate was often directly related to the destiny of the leadership supporting them.

Other towns, serving simultaneously as political, economic, or religious centers, lasted longer. Kumasi, the capital of the Asante Confederacy, started out as a market place in about 1633. By 1699 Osei Tutu had transformed it into a politico-religious center as well. It became the repository of the Golden Stool, the *sum sum* or soul of the nation. Kumasi, therefore, was able to sustain external African threats to its integrity. It was not conquered and occupied until the late 1890s, and then only by the British with their vastly superior firepower.

Many African towns contained large markets, even though they remained agrarian in nature. With the possible exception of the East African coastal towns, it was common for more than seventy percent of the residential population of any urban center to commute daily to suburban farms. Nevertheless, well-organized craft guilds did exist. Some towns even gained wide repute for their artisans' work. The northern Nigerian city of Kano, for example, enjoyed centuries of fame for its expert leather workers and cloth dyers, and Bida City was known for its copper and brassware. In contrast, Benin and Ifé for centuries had dazzled their visitors with naturalistic, brass commemorative heads and wall plaques made from minerals obtained thousands of miles away in desert mines along the paths to the Nile.

Ironically, war and slave raiding accelerated the tendency towards urbanization in some societies. By the eighteenth century, a series of defensive settlements had arisen from the Gambia to Liberia. Many new towns in Sierra Leone were laid out defensively, surrounded by wooden stockades and stake-filled ditches. By the mid-eighteenth century, some of these war-towns had populations approaching a thousand. Satellite villages, usually lying within a five-mile range, supported the townsfolk with food. Another chain of war-towns appeared between 1825 and 1830 to defend against Fulbe and Mane raids.

As the Asante grew territorially from the mid-eighteenth century, new towns were created by transferring prisoners-of-war to the Confederacy's metropolitan core. These towns, like those which arose in the same period in Dahomey, served as "colonies" or centers of cultural assimilation. The vanquished learned Asante, or, in the case of Dahomey, the vanquished had to assimilate the dominant Fon culture. It was an ingenious and surprisingly successful attempt to forge disparate peoples into homogeneous nations.

In western Nigeria, the Yoruba had already acquired a propensity for living in large, nucleated settlements. This might be explained by the functioning of their centralized, authoritarian institutions. Indeed, permanent nucleated settlements have existed in Yorubaland since at least the sixteenth century, following the establishment of the old Oyo empire. The Fulani invasion of the early nineteenth century, followed by internecine civil wars, accelerated urban development. Warrior camps mushroomed everywhere, many of them evolving into large though amorphous and poorly planned cities of refuge. New cities, like Ibadan, emerged because of their ability to protect refugees from devastating civil wars. Ibadan began in 1829 as an insignificant Egba farming village on the edge of the grassland. Within three decades, it had grown into the most powerful city in Yorubaland, with a population exceeding 70,000.

War, slave raiding, and massive, abrupt migrations had similar repercussions in parts of East Africa's interior. Here, too, they were a powerful stimulant for the development of town life. For centuries, East African homesites were scattered throughout cultivated fields and gardens. Compact, nucleated settlements were almost nonexistent. Indeed, the prevailing system of land tenure encouraged isolated dwellings on individual *shambas* (farms). With no foreign threats, there was little need to cluster for survival. However, after 1840 some groups in central Tanzania constructed stone fortress-towns to shield themselves, their farms, and livestock against Ngoni invaders and avaricious Arab/Swahili slavers.

It should be clear that the nineteenth century was a period of town building in sub-Saharan Africa. Historians formerly attributed the commencement of rapid urbanization to the colonial era. Yet recent evidence indicates that many of the "colonial cities" sprang from the need for self-defense and survival against alien forces in the precolonial period.

Many precolonial cities grew by accident, beyond the control of the human will. Others were defensive responses to external or internal threats. Some cities did reflect an act of will, a bold attempt to build a new society. Muhammad Bello in 1808, after forging the disparate Hausa city-states into a unified Fulani caliphate, created a new capital city on the Sokoto River. Overnight, Sokoto city became the administrative center of the caliphate bearing its name. On the East African coast, many decaying Swahili cities were revived by Sultan Sayyid Said. Zanzibar Town and Mombasa in particular, enjoyed rapid new growth in the mid-nineteenth century. Under Said's successor, Majid, a bold though not too successful effort was made to establish new cities. In 1862 the foundations of Dar es Salaam were laid, but this seaport did not become an important shipping and administrative center until the twentieth century, under German and later British direction.

Very little urban development occurred in areas without centralized institutions of authority and not exposed to external threats or massive infusions of new, culturally dissimilar ethnic groups. In comparison to other parts of the world, Africa, on the eve of the colonial era, was probably the least urbanized region (outside of Australia), in terms of proportion of population living in towns or cities. The Igbo of eastern Nigeria are an example of a densely populated people without an urban ethic. Igbo families chose not to construct cities. Disdaining the institution of centralized, divine kingship, they had no leaders to whom tribute was paid. Thus, there was no centralized, bureaucratic authority to command mass labor for the construction of public edifices. Instead, the Igbo lived in loose clusters of homesteads, irregularly scattered along paths that radiated from central meeting places. The Igbo lived in what modern planners would call "cluster communities."

The human and structural contours of African communities were governed by a variety of factors, including geography, kinship organization, and occupational orientation. The basic unit of African society, the extended family, was reflected in the overall pattern of town and city living. Private dwellings were often situated according to relationships created by clan affiliations. The very design of buildings reflected not only family and tribal structure but religious, political, and economic institutions. In situating community structures, elites paid greater attention to social relationships than to geometric design.

The cohension of lineage in urban areas obviated instability, criminality, and violence. True, ghettos did exist in large towns, kings sometimes monopolized homesite allocations and separated themselves from the exploited masses, and patterns of segregation—social, ethnic, and religious—were not uncommon. Yet urban dwelling did not become oppressive, nor did it weaken kinship bonds or lineage structures. Indeed, urban social cohesion prevailed in black Africa until the colonial era.

THE POWER OF ART

Today, people flock to museums and art markets to view African art and sometimes to buy it. African art enchants, excites, and haunts the imagination of modern man. A few years ago, a sixteenth-century Nigerian bronze figure of a flute player commanded $442,000 at an art auction.

What else do most viewers and buyers know about African art than meets the naked eye? Museum brochures tell very little, yet much traditional African art was made to be practical, and not meant to be viewed in a detached manner. Indeed, most African art was essential to life. Masks in particular were used by secret societies which held ceremonies aimed at aiding and controlling the fertility, health, and productivity of the community. Such ceremonies also attempted to protect the community from sorcerers, witches, or evil spirits. An individual wearing a mask in a dance would become possessed by the mask's spirit.

African sculpture, most of which was wood, served as dwelling places of benevolent spirits. Traditional African sculpture expressed religious belief and therefore gave form to the deepest cultural values. As one expert said "spirits were personalized forces which Africans feared and could not fully understand in a prescientific age."[13] African art answered philosophical questions, brought psychic comfort, solved problems of personal and corporate identity, and united communities and cultures.

Art objects were used for many purposes: in puberty ceremonies, rites of circumcision, at death, in the worship of ancestors, and in the rendering of judgments. In the last, the mask represented judicial authority. African sculpture thus had a function crucial to the order and survival of the community. Carvers had to bear enormous responsibility for their work, knowing full well the tremendous power their objects might wield. It is no wonder that artisans were held in both fear and awe and commanded great respect, even though they suffered from low social standing. Carvers were rarely invited to participate in the ceremonies in which their arts were used or even to view their work in action.

Some Western art critics complain that African art lacks expression. In many cases this is true. But it must be remembered that African artists usually did not seek to achieve visual reality in their works. Much of their art represented invisible, spiritual forces, or symbolized fertility. It should also be emphasized

[13]K.A. Busia, *Africa in Search of Democracy* (London: Routledge & Kegan Paul, Ltd., 1967), p. 42.

Ancestral twin dolls (ibeji) in the style of the city of Oyo, western Nigeria. (Photo, Lascell studios)

that Africans did not worship their artifacts per se. Rather, they worshipped the spiritual being that the art object symbolized. Actually, African art ranged from almost completely abstract stylization to a relative naturalism.

Not all African art fulfilled spiritual needs. Some art objects were secular in intent and served a political, economic, or social function. Nevertheless, most art was for life's sake—not for art's sake. Rarely were works of art produced purely for aesthetic purposes. Most art tended to reinforce the beliefs and value patterns of society.

Art was power. To the Bantu-speakers, all beings in the universe possess a vital force of their own: human, animal, vegetable. As Father Placide Tempels said, "Each being has been endowed by God with a certain force, capable of strengthening the vital energy of the strongest being of all creation: man."[14] To Africans, everything possessed energy and power. Thus, when an object was carved, a ritual was performed in order not to disturb that power.

Who created the art of Africa? In many cultures, art was produced by professional families or castes. In highly centralized polities, such as kingdoms, these castes remained detached within large palace compounds, and the secrets of their craft were kept from would-be competitors. In Senufo country, sculptors were in guilds, ethnically and culturally distinct from the farmers who acquired their art. Not everyone in precolonial Africa could simply take up a craft or art

[14] Placide Tempels, *Bantu Philosophy* (Paris: Presence Africaine, 1969), p. 148.

even if he was so creatively inclined. Normally, one was born into a family of artists or artisans.

The major stylistic regions of the continent and the areas where most African wood sculpture was done, extended from the western Guinea coast, through the Nigerian forests, across Cameroun, and into the Zaire/Angola area. One finds a tremendous diversity of shapes, sizes, and uses. The plastic, representational arts, particularly sculpture, were found mainly among sedentary agriculturalists in the forest or on its periphery, and rarely among nomadic pastoral societies. Pastoralists were better known for their body decoration, jewelry, small milking stools, basketry, and in some areas, weaving. With the exception of the Makonde along the Tanzania/Mozambique border, almost no southern or eastern African peoples expressed themselves through sculpture.

The lack of wood cannot wholly explain this paucity of sculpture in eastern and southern Africa. Strong artistic traditions were found most commonly in societies with some political and social centralization, in highly structured sedentary cultures led by chiefs or kings whose wealth could support artists and artisans, and who needed their work to glorify their own authority. Art, particularly mask-carving, also flourished in cultures with well organized and powerful secret societies. Such secret men's and women's organizations used masks in their ceremonies.

MUSICAL TRADITIONS

Traditional music, like art, was largely functional. It connected cultural values with political, social, and religious life. It reflected the deepest thoughts of the individual and the collective community. On occasion, musical instruments performed extramusical functions. They could be symbols of authority and rank. In the Katsina emirate of the Sokoto Caliphate, the so-called Bachelor Drum was beaten three times on the turbaning of senior chiefs and twelve times on the installation of a new emir. Iron bells or gongs in the Kongo kingdom were used as signaling devices in battle. To the neighboring Kuba, they were an emblem of kingship. The Igbo and Ijaw town-criers used them to summon the people. In Bambara country, the mythical symbols of the ancestral pantheon were the *tabale* drum and the harp; in parts of Ghana, Uganda, and the Transvaal of South Africa, the heavy drums were associated with the courts of important chiefs and had a certain sacred quality. The hour-glass talking drums of the Yoruba had the range of an octave. Yoruba's musical composers discovered at some point that all sentences in their Oyo dialect stayed within the range of an octave in a typical conversation. The talking drum thus was designed to imitate verbal communication. For the Asante and the Yoruba, talking-drumming was an important means of communication. It can be compared to the modern telegraph and was used to send messages long-distance as well as to add a deeper dimension to musical scores.

Some musical instruments were restricted for use by men or women only. Sometimes a given clan or village was responsible for making music on certain instruments. There were families and villages of drummers, flautists, or xylophonists.

Music-making in some societies was a prestigious profession; in others, particularly in the Wolof and Hausa communities, it had a low social rank. Everywhere musicians and singers performed activities with high social importance. Griots, or praise-singers, of the western Sudanic royal courts sang topical songs relating historical events. Songs were the prime carriers of history and legend among preliterate peoples throughout Africa.

Musical instruments can be placed into four categories: idiophones (bells, rattles), membranophones (drums), chordophones (lutes, harps), and aerophones (flutes, trumpets, horns). Some instruments were more predominant in one region than in another—for example, xylophones, flutes, and trumpets in the West African savanna, drums in the West African forests, gongs in Central Africa, and zithers and harps in the interlacustrine regions of East Africa. By the last quarter of the nineteenth century, percussion instruments were widespread.

In most societies, music and song were part of almost every form of human activity: work, war, weddings, sowing, harvesting, and hunting, drinking, lamenting the dead and praising important people. Thus, music, like art, was inseparable from the entire social and political structure of the people.

DANCE AND DRAMA

Dance, inextricably a part of music, has been, along with music, one of Africa's major cultural contributions to the world. Many dances served a ritual purpose. In western Yoruba country, at the annual Yam festival, the stilt dance had to be performed before farmers could take in their crops. To this day, the ten-foot stilts are the preserve of certain dancing families. In the old Dahomean kingdom and elsewhere team-dancing took place at the installation of important chiefs.

Drama was also a well developed and highly sophisticated artistic form. In Africa, musicians, their instruments, singers, dancers with their masks, and dramatists often interacted with their audiences to create a dynamic theatrical unity. The great value of dance was in its ability to synergize all the various cultural elements.

Song and dance, like other arts, were effective tools of social and political comment. Every Yoruba community in western Nigeria possessed its own

Oriki music, which blended song, dance, and poetry. Oriki music described, praised, or condemned certain village characteristics, including historical evolution, contemporary leadership, and its relations with neighboring communities. In times of trouble, Oriki music invoked ancestral heroes and spiritual forces for guidance, assistance, or comfort. More important, Oriki songs enabled performers to voice legitimately their opposition to royal authority, corruption, or oppressive conditions. New songs and dramatic sequences were developed therefore to reflect changing conditions. In a sense, Oriki music served the same purpose as our editorial column or literary essay in modern newspapers and journals.

Ekon dramatic associations in the Calabar area of eastern Nigeria served a similar purpose. Their members, drawn from various patrilineages, studied the habits of local communities for six years. They composed songs and dances satirizing individuals, institutions, and customs. In the seventh year, the association went on tour with their entertaining, though often scathing, repertoire.

By the mid-eighteenth century, Yoruba entertainers had organized traveling-theater companies that staged dramas and dances, and performed acrobatics. Unlike most groups of artisans, these companies consisted of full-time professionals. They deserved great credit in the nineteenth century for maintaining the integrity of Yoruba culture at a time when civil war and Fulani invasions convulsed the crumbling Oyo empire.

PRECOLONIAL LITERATURE

Because Africa was overwhelmingly nonliterate before the colonial era, most poetic and prose traditions, and they were extremely rich and varied, were transmitted orally. Some prose traditions consisted of legends, folk-tales, proverbs, and riddles; others of fine oratory and serious conversation. Poetic traditions were found in poems of praise, invocation, incantation, relaxation, satire, lamentation, and dance. Among the Asante a vast body of proverbs included such wisdom as: "one falsehood spoils a thousand truths", "the ruin of a nation begins in the homes of its people", "no one tests the depth of a river with both feet", "one head, or man, does not constitute a council", and "the hearth is only absent where human beings cease to live". In the corpus of Yoruba proverbs we discover "the thread follows the needle", "peace is the father of friendship", and "the young cannot teach tradition to the old". A Yoruba riddle conveys: "two small birds fly over a thousand trees", which means that a person's two sharp discerning eyes will carry him far in life. Among the Wolof of Senegal one could hear the proverb "Don't try to make someone hate the person he loves, for he will still go on loving but will hate you." Their neighbors, the Serer, often recited: "to know nothing is bad, to learn nothing is worse". This seems to echo the Masai phrase "virtue is better than wealth" and the Fulani words, "knowledge is better than riches".

The value, ethical, and belief systems of Africans were also beautifully revealed in personal names. We can discern much of the structure of African culture through an examination of personal names, which were sometimes of deep psychological import. Among the Yoruba, Olaiya meant "the glorious influence of mothers"; Babalola, "father is the source of honor". The name Obileye carried the meaning "parents have dignity and respect" and Ayodele "joy reaches our abode". In Asante, children's names reflected the day on which they were born or the order of their birth. Thus, a child born on Saturday was named Kwame and the first born was named Baako.

African writing was confined largely to the scribes and mallams in the Muslim areas and to a few handfuls of Western educated intellectuals in South Africa and in the coastal European enclaves. Writing in the South African Xhosa language, T. Soga (1831-71) and W.W. Gqoba (1840-88) produced a small quantity of short stories, essays, and proverbs. The Sotho scholars, E.L. Segoete (b. 1858) and Z.D. Mangoaela produced collections of folk traditions. In the Gold Coast, the Reverend C.C. Reindorf in the 1890s wrote *The History of the Gold Coast and Asante,* one of the first systematic histories of black Africa ever written by an African in a European language. Earlier, the Yoruba Bishop Samuel Crowther, wrote *Journal of an Expedition up the Niger and Tshadda Rivers* (1855), a work containing much anthropological information on the peoples living along those rivers. In 1887, Edward W. Blyden, a Liberian citizen of West Indian birth, completed *Christianity, Islam and the Negro Race.*

The writings of these literary men had little effect on the minds of the masses of Africans. Before the twentieth century, most African literature depended on oral transmission for its survival, and the proverbs, tales, songs reflected most completely the deep thoughts of Africans. Oral literature embraced the entire traditional philosophy of the communities it served. There were no recognized authors or dates of origin, no copyrights other than some traditions which belonged to certain important families. African literature represented the accumulated wisdom of societies whose roots often lay centuries in the past. Its repositories were not libraries but the fertile brains of its transmitters.

part **II**

THE COLONIAL ERA

4

Patterns of Authority

THEORY AND PRACTICE OF COLONIAL AUTHORITY

The British and French had established municipal governments in their small coastal enclaves decades before the late nineteenth-century interior conquest. Between 1862 and 1888 legislative and executive councils were formed in the British possessions of Bathurst (Gambia), Freetown (Sierra Leone), Cape Coast and Accra (Gold Coast), and Lagos (Nigeria). The legislative councils were composed mainly of the principal colonial officials and a minority of nominated nonofficials, consisting of Europeans, mixed-bloods, and Africans representing special interests, primarily commercial. These councilors advised the governor on administrative matters. The nonofficials, so few in number, were rarely able to initiate or veto bills.

The political pattern in French West Africa was somewhat similar, although the populace was granted full rights of French citizenship and ultimately acquired institutions of local government identical to those in metropolitan France. In 1848 the Senegalese towns of Saint Louis and Gorée received elected municipal councils, with the additional right of all men, regardless of color, to elect representatives to the National Assembly in Paris. This right was suspended during the Second French Empire but restored in 1872 under the Third French Republic. This special status was extended to the nearby towns of Dakar and Rufisque by 1887. Until 1914, the elected deputies were French or Afro-French. In Portuguese Africa, the constitution of 1838 declared the free population, numbering only a few hundred, to be Portuguese citizens. However, they had no representative municipal councils. Indeed, Angola since 1592 and Mozambique since 1752 had been under the almost dictatorial rule of governor-generals, with little participation by the local populations.

In the nineteenth century, Westernized Africans and Afro-Europeans played increasingly important roles in colonial administrations of the French and British enclaves. For example, James Bannerman, an Afro-European merchant, acted as governor of the Gold Coast from 1850 to 1851. G.K. Blankson, another prominent merchant, in 1861 became the first full-blooded African member of the legislative council. In the British colony of Lagos in 1875, the heads of police, harbors, telegraph, and customs were Africans.

By the late 1880s, Charles Darwin's theories of struggle for survival among plant and animal species were distorted by other "experts" to "prove" that a struggle for survival also exists among a single species, Homo sapiens. Social Darwinists, as they came to be called, argued that Western Man and his institutions had evolved into a position of superiority vis-a-vis the seemingly inferior non-European counterparts. The latter were therefore destined to become extinct.

Before the rise of Social Darwinism and pseudo-scientific racism in the late nineteenth century, British and French liberal thought held that all men are basically equal in intelligence and potential and that through Western education and exposure, Africans could be raised to the level of civilization of even the most sophisticated European. A few Portuguese thinkers held similar views. The French concept of "Mission Civilisatrice" or "Civilizing Mission" went hand-in-hand with assimilationist ideas. French imperialism implied the right of Frenchmen to dominate and instruct the conquered savages, and to encourage them to absorb French institutions and values based on universal, natural, and immutable laws. The British equivalent of this was the "White Man's Burden."

Conversionist ideas were strongest among the French, and had originated in the revolutionary period, in the era of the Declaration of the Rights of Man. Liberty, equality, and fraternity, should be for all men, at all times, and in all places. This eighteenth-century Cartesian universalism quickly evolved into notions of assimilation. Government founded upon reason could apply to all people, they argued. That what is good and important to a Frenchman is appropriate to everyone, because French language, mores, and laws are rooted in human reason. These concepts deviated somewhat from the British empirical view which theoretically held that societies must develop their own institutions and that it should not be British policy to transform the indigenous populations into black Victorians. In reality, Western-educated Africans and Afro-Europeans were encouraged to adopt many of the values and lifestyles of their European counterparts. Moreover, they were given Christian names and expected to speak English.

French universalism began to be placed on a legal footing in 1792 when black slavery was abolished and all men in the French colonies became French citizens. Three years later, the French constitution stated that "the colonies are an integral part of the Republic and are subject to the same constitutional law."[1]

---

[1] Michael Crowder, *West Africa under Colonial Rule* (Evanston: Northwestern University Press, 1968), pp. 165–167.

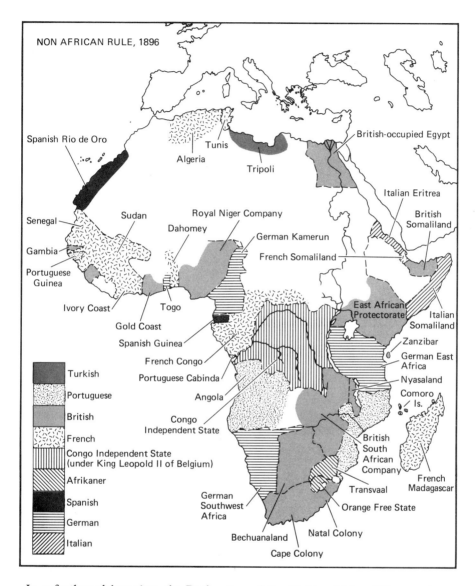

NON AFRICAN RULE, 1896

Spanish Rio de Oro

Tunis

Algeria

Tripoli

British-occupied Egypt

Italian Eritrea

Senegal

Sudan

Royal Niger Company

Dahomey

German Kamerun

French Somaliland

British Somaliland

Gambia

Portuguese Guinea

Ivory Coast

Togo

Gold Coast

Spanish Guinea

French Congo

Portuguese Cabinda

Angola

Congo Independent State

East African Protectorate

Italian Somaliland

Zanzibar

German East Africa

Nyasaland

Comoro Is.

British South African Company

French Madagascar

Transvaal

German Southwest Africa

Orange Free State

Bechuanaland

Natal Colony

Cape Colony

Turkish

Portuguese

British

French

Congo Independent State (under King Leopold II of Belgium)

Afrikaner

Spanish

German

Italian

In a further elaboration, the Declaration of the Rights of Man, "Men are born and live free and equal in rights."[2]

These universalistic, assimilationist ideas were suppressed by Napoleon I, reinstituted in the Revolution of 1848, abolished again by Napoleon III who believed that colonies must be governed by distinct legislation, and then resur-

[2] Ibid.

rected again by the new republican regime in 1872. Most Frenchmen believed that colonial policy must be uniform and be applied uniformly throughout the overseas possessions. The tariff law of 1892 economically assimilated the colonies into metropolitan France. In other words, France and its possessions were to be viewed as a single economic entity.

After the military conquest of Africa in the 1880s and 1890s, the European powers found themselves with an area more than ten times the size of their own nations, with millions of people and literally hundreds of different ethnic groups and systems of government. This awesome situation forced the Europeans to rethink their relationships with the Africans.

In West Africa, the British in the nineteenth century first had federated the Gambia, Sierra Leone, and the Gold Coast and later the Gold Coast and Lagos. Now, after the acquisition of vast interior territories behind their coastal colonies, they abandoned the federal concept and governed each separately. The French, on the other hand, established a Ministry for Colonies in 1894 and between 1896 and 1904, shaped their West African territories (excluding the four communes) into the Federation of French West Africa and the Federation of French Equatorial Africa. Although both powers continued to give their old coastal possessions special, favored status, after the conquest of the interior, the British changed their collaborators from the Western educated elites of the coastal enclaves to the traditional African rulers. In the expanding civil service, the former gradually were replaced by British expatriates. In the French areas, the reverse was true. The traditional rulers were stripped of all real power and the Westernized, assimilated Africans assumed greater influence. More of this will be said later.

Initially, private companies were given responsibility for colonial administration in some of the newly conquered areas. Much of Nigeria was governed by the Royal Niger Company, Uganda by the Imperial British East African Company, Tanganyika by the Imperial German East Africa Company, and Southern Rhodesia by the British South Africa Company. Private companies lacked the financial resources to assume such responsibilities while also making a profit for their stockholders back home. The private companies thus were phased out, the last one being the British South Africa Company which turned over administrative responsibility for Southern Rhodesia to the British crown in 1923.

A debate among French colonial theorists over policy questions began in 1881. Assimilationist notions came under attack by the Social Darwinists, who held that men are different and unequal, and that races and tribes do evolve in their own particular national and cultural environments and have their own unique characteristics. Some critics argued that the imposition of assimilation on non-Gallic peoples might lead to rebellions, as they did in Indochina. Others emphasized the desirability of variation in colonial practice and suggested that the colonized retain their own customs, institutions, and laws. These theorists were convinced that the masses of Africans could not assimilate

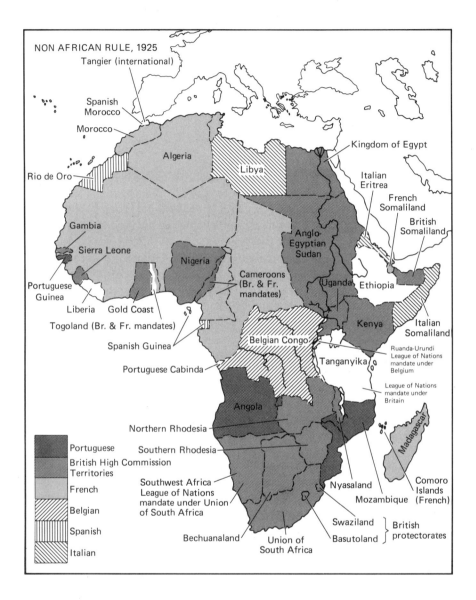

NON AFRICAN RULE, 1925

Tangier (international)

Spanish Morocco

Morocco

Algeria

Libya

Kingdom of Egypt

Rio de Oro

Italian Eritrea

French Somaliland

British Somaliland

Gambia

Sierra Leone

Nigeria

Anglo-Egyptian Sudan

Cameroons (Br. & Fr. mandates)

Uganda

Ethiopia

Portuguese Guinea

Liberia   Gold Coast

Togoland (Br. & Fr. mandates)

Spanish Guinea

Portuguese Cabinda

Kenya

Italian Somaliland

Belgian Congo

Ruanda-Urundi League of Nations mandate under Belgium

Tanganyika

League of Nations mandate under Britain

Angola

Northern Rhodesia

Southern Rhodesia

Madagascar

Portuguese

British High Commission Territories

French

Belgian

Spanish

Italian

Southwest Africa League of Nations mandate under Union of South Africa

Nyasaland

Mozambique

Comoro Islands (French)

Swaziland

Basutoland

British protectorates

Bechuanaland   Union of South Africa

French civilization, because of their inherent racial inferiority and that they must evolve along their own lines. By 1920, these theories had evolved into a coherent colonial policy, called "association," in which the colonized would develop within their own milieu in association with the French. In other words, the economic and political improvement of a region would be undertaken by Africans and Frenchmen within the context of the former's indigenous institutions. The great virtue of association policy was proclaimed to lie in its practicality, flexibility, and economy. By 1895 the Portuguese, too, had begun to question the thought of equality for the Africans. They argued that there should be two administrative codes, one for the Africans and another for the Europeans. We will return to this problem later in the chapter.

BRITISH RULE: INDIRECT AND DIRECT

While the French were debating the issue of association at the turn of the century, the British were putting it into practice, first in northern Nigeria, under the term "indirect rule." The example of Northern Nigeria before World War I became the prototype of indirect rule which later was widely copied throughout Britain's tropical African possessions, especially among the Asante of the Gold Coast, the Ganda of Uganda, the Barotse of Northern Rhodesia (now Zambia), and in Tanganyika. It would therefore be worthwhile to examine it in detail.

After 1895 the British public were won over to the idea of late Victorian, militant, territorial imperialism: that government, not private enterprise alone, had to undertake the conquest and colonial administration of tropical territories. Government had to provide the infrastructure and climate in which private enterprise could flourish.

In Africa, the major architect of indirect rule was Frederick Lugard, who was responsible for conquering much of Nigeria and Uganda. Its introduction can be traced to January 1900 when the British flag was raised over the town of Lokoja in Nigeria. Between 1900 and 1903 the British West African Frontier Force under Lugard conquered the Sokoto Caliphate and its immediate neighbors. But once conquered, there came the problem of governance. In 1903 Lugard's staff numbered less than seventy in all Nigeria. The British treasury in London was reluctant to spend public funds on a vast European bureaucracy. Lugard therefore had no choice but to devise the inexpensive system of indirect rule whereby the miniscule British staff would simply oversee and advise. Neither the British taxpayer nor the treasury would have tolerated the financial burden of direct and total British rule.

How did this system work? The Sokoto Caliphate was not dismembered, but control no longer emanated from the Sarkin Musulmi in Sokoto city. The old caliphate and surrounding areas were formed into a new entity, called the Protectorate of Northern Nigeria, and placed under a British High Commissioner. Under the protectorate were provinces, which often followed the old administrative boundaries of the emirates, and were administered by British residents. The provinces were further subdivided into divisions under a British Divisional Officer. Divisions sometimes corresponded to the boundaries of smaller emirates or parts thereof. For example, the old emirate of Katsina became a division of Kano province. At that level there were a British administration and a Native Administration existing side by side. The former was headed by a British official and the latter by the emir, his staff, and principal chiefs. Below the division and emirate were districts headed by district chiefs under the supervision of a British District Officer. The district tended to be the key administrative unit. The District Officer was in charge of all aspects of local administration, from judicial appeals to tax collection, public works, and education.

At the emirate level, the old African political structure was largely preserved, with its emir, chiefs, *alkali* (judges) and their traditional bureaucracies. Over these, British, Anglo-Saxon-inspired political and legal institutions were imposed. Lugard anticipated that these institutions would be grafted onto the African ones. The emir's authority had to be upheld and no one was to be Christianized or Westernized in belief or lifestyle for fear of upsetting the status quo and weakening the prestige of the hereditary rulers vis-à-vis the masses. Too, Christianity might have conflicted with the predominantly Muslim population and triggered schisms and conflict among the populations.

The British saw themselves on a great mission to restore and regenerate the Fulani aristocracy. A puritanical element was present, just as it was during the great Fulani jihad only a century earlier. The Fulani were not to be made into black Englishmen but rather would be encouraged to remain proud of their Islamic African heritage. Lugard wanted them to retain their own traditions and institutions but to adopt Western morality and Western codes of ethics. The British officer in Northern Nigeria easily identified with the Fulani aristocrat. Both were from the landed gentrv, both had received a classical education, both were accustomed to wielding authority in a male-oriented hierarchical system in which class confidence and the rituals of rule were highly regarded, and both placed more emphasis on character and style than on expertise and intellectualism. Together, they admired good horsemanship, family background, and a paternalistic attitude towards the poor.

Under indirect rule, the royal families became more entrenched, received clearer title to lands and position, but obtained little real power. This was the price for survival. Outwardly they appeared to be the effective rulers. In reality, power resided first with the British officer in charge and second with the emir. The British officer transmitted orders from the protectorate through the emir. Never was he to go to the people directly. The emir, his chiefs, and their staffs were to serve as his intermediaries.

Was indirect rule a fact or an illusion? In a sense it was both. The traditional administrative institutions were left fairly intact. British officers tended to rule not through the traditional hereditary chiefs but through men who had received their appointments from the British and not from the traditional electors.

Under Sokoto rule in the nineteenth century, a system of indirect rule had been in effect, operating entirely through the legitimate traditional rulers of component emirates. In Katsina they were the hereditary emir, his kingmakers, and the lesser nobility. Under Sokoto rule, the emir was prevented from becoming an absolute ruler. Sokoto was able to maintain a delicate balance of authority among emir, kingmakers, and titled nobility. Under British over-rule in the twentieth century, the traditional sources of power gradually were bypassed and new ones, suitable to the Europeans, were introduced. This re-structuring of authority permitted the British to control the emirate more directly and effectively, as compared with Sokoto rule, and allowed the emir and his British counterpart to assume powers far greater than anyone had had in the precolonial period. This exaggeration of the authority of ruler and over-ruler enhanced the powers of the central administrative structures to the detri-ment of local government. In consequence, it weakened the fabric of local traditional authority and made it more vulnerable to the infiltration after 1920 of European technical officers.

When Sokoto rule is compared with that of the British, there is little question that the latter was more far-reaching and direct. The differences were more of degree than of kind. One can reasonably compare the old offices of Sarkin Musulmi, Galadima Sokoto, and Dan Maliki, with those of British governor, provincial or divisional officer, and district officer. Yet the degree of inter-ference of the British, in comparison to Sokoto, was far greater. Under British overrule, African potentates in Northern Nigeria lost control over their armies, foreign affairs, and legislation. Although both Sokoto and later the British demanded a share of the revenue, the former had no control over budget esti-mates or audits. In addition, Sokoto's right to appoint or depose Katsina officials was limited to a few large fiefholders. By contrast, the British controlled all appointments and set the legal criteria for depositions. Sokoto's major concern in Katsina and the other emirates of the caliphate was to ensure that Sarkin Musulmi would receive a fair share of the annual revenue and could count on military support in time of trouble. The British were overseers of every aspect of the administration. They could sit in on native courts and adjudicate cases at will, they could personally assess taxes and by controlling educational cur-ricula, they could instill in the African mind the desirability of maintaining the status quo and respect for authority.

Ideally, both Sokoto and the British sought to govern Katsina and the other emirates through the emir who was to be responsible to the hereditary tradi-tional chiefs. However, theories and ideas did not always coincide with political realities and power politics. At the inception of British rule in Katsina in 1903, the uncooperative hereditary emir was sacked and replaced by a man who under the old order had had no clear hereditary claim to that office. The palace slaves, knowing the British were going to resettle the nobility on their fiefs and restore their function as tax collectors, were equally uncooperative. They were reduced to administrative impotence. In time, the British permitted their appointed emir to resort to an old tactic—that of circumventing the hereditary chiefs by creating his own parallel civil service.

The increasing bureaucratization of the "Native Administration," as the

African counterpart to the British administration was called, resulted in a shift away from indirect rule and towards that of greater European control.

Tied to the Hausa and English public-school criteria of what constitutes an educated man, their educational system failed to provide new "bottles" for the fermenting wine of progress. The reason for this is clear. A basic tenet of indirect rule was "to avoid as far as possible everything that has a denationalizing tendency, and to inculcate respect for authority, self-respect. . . ."[3] Nonaristocratic children were discouraged from attending the government-supported schools for fear they would gain an educational advantage over their "natural" hereditary rulers. Under such a system, the student would undoubtedly lose his "respect for authority" and if exposed to too much Western education, would become denationalized and lose his "self-respect." This was painfully apparent to the British in Southern Nigeria where mission schools were educating large numbers of nonaristocratic youths who, as a result, chafed under traditional authority.

Avoiding everything that had a denationalizing tendency meant avoiding Western technology. The British were prepared to endow Katsina and the other emirates of Northern Nigeria with a fairly modern and efficient administrative superstructure, but they dared not modernize the African governmental cadres in order to operate it, for fear this might disrupt the social and political status quo. They were willing to be revolutionary in introducing sweeping judicial and fiscal changes. But when it came to the question of education, the slogan of "evolution" prevailed. This indeed was a major contradiction in indirect rule and one which provided the germs for its failure to function in accordance with stated policy.

In order to avoid disrupting the political and social status quo, the British increasingly relied on Westernized, Southern Nigerians to act as subordinate clerks in their own offices. Ironically, this had the long-term effect of making the indigenous native authorities dependent upon technically more advanced ethnic groups for the development of their administration.

As the revenue of Katsina and other emirates began to grow in the 1920s and 1930s, greater demands were placed upon the native authorities. Deep concrete wells had to be sunk, and infirmaries, schools, government buildings, bridges, and roads had to be constructed. Few Africans were prepared to manage these complicated projects, so the British technical officers from government departments were seconded to the Native Administration departments as "advisors." However, more than advice was needed to effect these programs. The British technical officers had to become directors and set up priorities, plan and budget projects, and implement them. Their responsibility, as they saw it, was

[3] A.H.M. Kirk-Greene, ed., *The Principles of Native Administration in Nigeria: Selected Documents, 1900–1947* (London: Oxford University Press, 1965), pp. 98–99.

not to the emir, or even to the British district officer, but rather to their government department at the protectorate level. This created serious conflicts of jurisdiction and robbed both the local and central native authorities of their responsibility in the technical fields. True, although local Africans were appointed to head the native authorities departments, this was only to maintain the pretense of indirect rule. In effect, they had little power or responsibility. The inevitable consequence of this was an increasing degree of direct British intervention and a movement away from rule through the traditional authorities.

As early as the 1930s, articulate Europeans as well as Africans spoke out against indirect rule. The British stoutly defended the system, even though some colonial governors sought reform. By 1945 it had become all too clear that there were many contradictions in the system.

In the early years of the twentieth century, indirect rule had worked so well in Northern Nigeria that the method was extended to other areas. In some cases, where no kings or chiefs were visible, as among the stateless Igbo, the British created "warrant chiefs." Indirect rule had grown into a mystique. British officers felt that Lugard's principles as embodied in his *Political Memoranda* (1906), had to be applied rigidly and that it was the only way to administer effectively.

A great misconception of indirect rule was the assumption that the process of modernization would be towards democratization, that is, towards a modern democratic government along Western lines. The democratic system emphasizes achieved position. The British, however, were upholding a system based on lineage and heredity, not at all compatible with popular voting and government by the people.

The problem was that at the national, all-Nigeria level the notion of representative government was encouraged. Legislative councils in the Gold Coast, Sierra Leone, and Nigeria were moving towards elected majorities. But when it came to local government, British rule tended to perpetuate an autocratic, authoritarian system. At the national level, power was delegated more and more to talented, Westernized Africans. At the local level, it remained in the hands of paternalistic British district officers working with the traditional authorities. In the 1950s, the British tried to reform local government in some areas by introducing locally elected councils. In Southern Nigeria, these councils gradually overshadowed the chiefs.

The native authority system failed to incorporate young, Western-educated, nonaristocratic people into it. This spelled its ultimate downfall because the youth became disaffected, especially those in the South where Christian missionary education was permitted and where nonaristocrats swarmed into the schools in pursuit of a modern education. By the 1930s a gulf had formed between the nationalistic, nonroyal youths in the South, demanding control not only of local government but of the central government as well, and the traditional authorities who, along with the British, feared an upset of the status quo. This disparity fanned the flames of nationalism in the postwar era.

Northern and Southern Nigeria merged in 1914. While conservative traditional tendencies were encouraged and perpetuated in the North, the South rapidly was modernized and democratized. Yet when Nigeria was granted independence in 1960, it was given a constitution designed to perpetuate northern domination. This ultimately led to a civil war in 1966, between the forces of the status quo led by the Fulani of the North and the forces of modernization led by the achievement-oriented and modernizing Igbos and other southerners.

In the Gold Coast (today Ghana), the coastal area was declared a crown colony in 1874, and in 1901 Asante and the Northern Territories were made a protectorate. The Asante Confederacy was abolished, but local traditional institutions were upheld and the Asantehene was allowed to return from exile. It was not until 1946 that the colony and the old Asante political units were placed under common instruments, namely, the reconstituted legislative and executive councils.

Over the decades, indirect rule had shifted the focus of authority and responsibility from the Asantehene and chiefs to the British. Indirect rule outwardly strengthened the chiefs and enabled them to step beyond traditional limits. This ultimately weakened the effectiveness of the traditional political substructures. Although the Asante Confederacy as a political entity lost its significance in the Gold Coast, Asante subnationalism persisted and made it difficult for the central government of Ghana to achieve a national, Ghanaian consciousness in the decade following independence in 1957.

The British system of indirect rule operated in a similar fashion and had similar effects on Uganda in East Africa. The major chiefs in the old Buganda kingdom became a permanent aristocracy after the British gave them in 1900 private ownership of lands that previously had been held by the clan heads in trust for the peasants. Henceforth, *saza* (county) chiefs were paid by the colonial government, and the tenants on their land paid them rent. By giving these powerful chiefs freehold title to land, they ensured their interest in the status quo and gained loyal collaborators.

The British were so impressed by Buganda's traditional system of governance, with its kabaka and hierarchy of chiefs, that they used the Buganda officials as subimperialists in other parts of the Uganda protectorate. Buganda, after first helping the British to conquer their neighbor, Bunyoro, later became agents of British colonialism. Buganda agents were planted nearly everywhere as government officials. In that capacity, they provoked almost universal resistance, hatred, and envy.

Nevertheless, the British placed Buganda and its kabaka in a most-favored position vis-à-vis the other ethnic groups and political entities in the protectorate. The Buganda agents introduced their precolonial model of government to other societies though it worked successfully only in political contexts similar to their own.

When Uganda gained its independence in 1962, the British imposed a constitution which continued to place Buganda in a special, semiautonomous relationship, and which allowed the kabaka of Buganda to become Uganda's president. Almost immediately, tension developed between the central government and the Buganda government. In 1966, Milton Obote, the nation's prime minister invaded Buganda's royal palace and forced the kabaka into exile. This act only heightened divisions within the country and set into motion forces which led to a military coup in 1971 and the suspension of the constitution.

Northern Rhodesia (today Zambia) found itself in an analogous position. With the establishment of British South Africa Company rule in the early 1890s, all the traditional chiefs, except in the Barotse kingdom, lost their preeminent position. In 1924 the company transferred its administrative responsibilities to the British, and Northern Rhodesia became a protectorate. Lugardian concepts of indirect rule were introduced six years later and Barotseland, where traditional authority structures were strong, was granted a special position. Local authorities were reorganized in the 1940s, and chiefs were forced to share power with a council. In 1948 the colonial government established tribal councils consisting of chiefs, traditional councilors, and Western-educated Africans. The major urban areas, with ethnically mixed populations, could not be ruled by a native authority system. It was in the towns that African nationalism emerged in the 1940s and 1950s. There, the colonial government established African representative councils, which became instruments of nationalism. Northern Rhodesia became the independent nation of Zambia in 1964. Barotseland, clinging to its separate identity, made the task of nation-building in the 1960s a difficult one.

British colonial policy assumed a different character in colonies with a large European settlement. Local whites tended to be highly politicized and extracted significant concessions from the home government. Settlers began arriving in East Africa in 1896, a year after the declaration of the East African Protectorate. The Foreign Office, under whose jurisdiction the protectorate fell, encouraged European immigration in the hopes that their economic activity would support the railway from Mombasa to Uganda, which in turn might make the protectorate economically self-sustaining. That encouragement ended in 1905 when jurisdiction of the protectorate passed to the Colonial Office, which was less sympathetic to the colonists and their demands.

Three years earlier, the government had identified indigenous authority figures with whom the British district officers could deal. There were no large, highly centralized African governments, and consequently clan heads were converted into chiefs and given responsibility for tax collection and the recruitment of laborers for public works and European farms. White settlers were delighted with the British pledge that the rich highlands in the foothills of Mount Kenya and Mount Kilimanjaro would be reserved for them and that Indians and others would not be allowed to farm there.

As the white settlers secured longer rights of tenure to the lands taken from the Africans, more were attracted to the area. A legislative council was established in 1907, and it immediately became a forum for settler demands and an instrument for their political ambitions. A system of native reserves was instituted as a corollary to the segregationist "white highlands" policy. All Africans not part of the white economy were to be concentrated in such reserves.

In 1920 the East African Protectorate became a crown colony, henceforth called "Kenya Colony and Protectorate." White hopes for self-government and dominion status were crushed in 1923 when the Devonshire Agreement made it clear that Kenya forever would be primarily an African country, not a white nation in black Africa. To mollify the settlers, the agreement also provided a "dual policy," one for the settlers and the other for the Africans and Indians. Colonial policy aimed at confining African politics within a tribal context. In 1924 native councils were set up, presided over by British administrative officers, and designed to restore a measure of authority to the elders.

While Europeans and Indians struggled among themselves and collectively against the Colonial Office for political power, many Africans were becoming urbanized, Westernized, and politicized by the missionaries. A nationalist movement gradually formed in the 1920s and 1930s and accelerated in the postwar period.

Land grievances always had been the central issue. Almost from the beginning, the native reserves were overpopulated and agriculturally eroded. African grievances culminated in 1952 with the violent Mau Mau movement. It now became clear to the British government in London that the white settlers alone were incapable of solving Kenya's internal problems and accommodating African aspirations. A series of political reforms followed, broadening the franchise for Africans and in 1960, establishing a common electoral role and an African majority in the legislative council. The era of settler political domination drew quickly to a close, and in 1963 Kenya won independence under African majority rule.

In Southern Rhodesia, the European settler population was far larger and exerted greater influence over colonial policy. The first wave of settlers came in 1890 under the aegis of the British South Africa Company. The first and second Matabele Wars (1893 and 1896) resulted in the destruction of the Ndebele-controlled Matabele empire and its tributary state of Mashonaland. The Ndebele military leaders negotiated a peace with Cecil Rhodes which left their power at the local level fairly intact. The Shona resisted to the bitter end and their political institutions, already weakened by the Ndebele, largely collapsed.

The British South Africa Company established a form of direct rule over the conquered and demoralized indigenous populations. Chiefs were looked upon as local constables without recognized judicial powers and responsible to a native affairs department. Meanwhile, the company's constitution provided for a legislative council, which in 1907 gained an elected majority. Africans were virtually excluded from voting by property qualifications.

In 1922 the British government chose to terminate the company's administrative responsibilities and gave the local electorate, almost all of whom were of British origin, two alternatives: amalgamation with South Africa or internal self-government as a crown colony. They opted for the latter out of fear of Afrikaner domination. Thus in 1923, the white settlers gained control over the army and civil service and strengthened their hand in the new legislature.

Southern Rhodesia's land policies almost mirrored those in Kenya and South Africa. The Land Apportionment Acts of 1902, 1920, and 1930 reserved most of the cool, fertile uplands for European settlement and relegated most Africans not under contract as laborers to native reserves.

African nationalism, first confined largely to Ndebele dreams of a restored monarchy, gradually included Shonas and became more urban and far-reaching in the 1930s. The Southern Rhodesian African National Congress was founded in 1934, faltered, was revived in 1945, faltered, was revived again in 1957, and banned two years later. As in Kenya, colonial authorities hoped to blunt African nationalism by appealing to ethnic feelings and bolstering the traditional local authorities. In the early 1930s the old company method of direct rule was abandoned for indirect rule, which gave greater responsibility to the chiefs. Native councils were formed in 1937 but remained weak and ineffectual until further reforms two decades later. But as elsewhere in the British possessions, the native councils failed to accommodate the nonroyal, urbanized, and Western-educated youth.

The spectrum of Southern Rhodesian politics was vastly broadened between 1953 and 1963 in the British-imposed scheme to unite Northern Rhodesia and Nyasaland with white-dominated Southern Rhodesia into a multiracial Federation of the Rhodesias and Nyasaland. Africans from the three territories were elected to twelve special seats in a federal parliament of fifty-nine seats. Unfortunately, the overwhelming political sophistication and power of the white Southern Rhodesians intimidated and frustrated African nationalists. European settlers in Northern and Southern Rhodesia wanted, through federation, to eliminate Colonial Office control in Northern Rhodesia, which they considered an obstacle to European supremacy and to the perpetuation of social segregation in the South. The British government anticipated that the Federation would turn into an equal association between Europeans and Africans, even though the latter represented more than ninety percent of the Federation's population. African opposition to the scheme grew over the years, as it became obvious that they would not even achieve a simple majority in the federal parliament. After strong appeals to the British government in London, the Federation was dismantled in 1963 and within a year, Northern Rhodesia and Nyasaland became the independent states of Zambia and Malawi, under African majority rule. Whites in Southern Rhodesia, fearing a British attempt to broaden the African franchise, unilaterally declared their independence from the British crown in 1965. Southern Rhodesia became the Republic of Rhodesia, under firm settler control.

In South Africa, peoples of European descent exerted even greater control over internal affairs. In 1910 the Cape Colony, the Transvaal, Natal, and the Orange Free State together formed the Union of South Africa. Great Britain ignored the pleas for one-man-one-vote and a multiracial national parliament for fear they would impede attempts at reconciliation between the British and the Afrikaners whom they had just defeated in the Second Anglo-Boer War. Great Britain favored a union, or unitary form of government in hopes it would consolidate and strengthen the British position in South Africa and ensure its loyalty in the event of a war with Germany. The union provided for a bicameral legislature, to which only "Europeans" could be elected. Basutoland, Bechuanaland, and Swaziland remained administratively separate entities, under a British high commissioner directly responsible to the government in London.

The price of Anglo-Afrikaner unity and conciliation was the institutionalization of white supremacy. The new constitution could be altered fairly easily to suit the needs of the white community, the major exception being a clause that upheld the voting rights of coloreds in the Cape province. The coloreds, or people of mixed racial ancestry, had enjoyed that right since the Cape constitution of 1853.

Since the electorate was overwhelmingly white, South African politics tended to be concerned primarily with issues affecting their own interests. From 1910 to 1924 parliamentary activity centered on the question of cooperation between the Afrikaners and those of British descent. The Afrikaners, most of whom were economically depressed and undereducated, struggled to gain cultural and economic equality. They fought for bilingualism in government and soon secured a predominant position in the civil service. From 1924 to 1933 Afrikaners dominated the political scene, and the period was characterized by economic nationalism and efforts to draw South Africa further away from its linkage with Great Britain. The British Statute of Westminster enabled South Africa in 1934 to become juridically and legislatively independent and to pursue its own foreign policy. However, it remained tied to Great Britain through the crown. Even before this great turning point, South Africa had begun to put racial segregation on a broad legal footing. The Immorality Act (1927) prohibited racially different couples from living together. The Native Administration Act (1927) empowered the governor to transfer Africans to any geographical location in the country. Africans thus lost their right to freedom of movement. The government's "civilized labor policy," while aimed at assisting the absorption of poor whites (mainly Afrikaners) into industrial occupations, was in effect a policy protecting the white workers against nonwhite competition. This was a severe blow to the hopes of blacks for achieving a measure of equal economic opportunity. Their political position also was weakened in 1936 when Africans in the Cape province, the only province in which they could vote, were removed from the common electoral rolls and were forced to elect three whites to represent them in parliament. This marked the nadir in the decline of the liberal multiracial tradition in the Cape, which had had its origins in 1806 with the Anglican group called the London Missionary Society.

English-speaking peoples and moderate Afrikaners drew together during the Great Depression and the war years. But Afrikaner politics moved steadily to the right in the postwar period. In 1948 the Afrikaner Nationalist Party came to power in an electoral victory and has held it ever since. Nationalists argued that without a privileged position a "pure" and separate white race could not survive; without a "pure" and separate white race, a privileged position could not be perpetuated. Afrikaners stated further that the white population could remain pure only if it retained its color-consciousness.

Between 1948 and 1961 South Africa moved further away from Great Britain and more deeply entrenched its policy of separate racial and ethnic development, or *apartheid*. The Tomlinson Report (1950) represented the Afrikaner ideal of a racially segregated utopia. The report recommended consolidation of the 264 scattered African areas and native reserves into eleven Bantustans, or Bantu states. It warned that economic integration in South Africa could lead to political and social assimilation and to "biogenetic" amalgamation and an end to Afrikaner civilization. What it failed to appreciate was that the process of economic integration along racial lines had been going on since the mid-seventeenth century and that the nation's economy had become dependent on an integrated work force. Nevertheless, the report called for the territorial separation of every racial group.

The nationalist-dominated legislature had already begun to pass a series of apartheid laws. The Prohibition of Mixed Marriages Act (1949) made marriage between races illegal. The Population Registration Act (1950) provided for classification of the population into whites, coloreds, Asians, and Bantu. The Group Areas Act, passed in the same year, led to the division of South Africa into separate areas for different races. A series of racial legislation affecting public amenities resulted in legally segregated public accommodations. Other legislation applied to labor and denied Africans the right to be defined as "employees," to join racially mixed unions, and to strike. Still other laws placed public education at all levels on a racially separate basis.

The nonwhite populations could do little to prevent such racially inspired, discriminatory laws. The entrenched clause guaranteeing voting rights of coloreds in Cape Province was removed from the constitution in 1956. In 1959, the Promotion of Bantu Self-Government Act provided for the removal of the Africans' white representatives from parliament and the consolidation of the native reserves into eight national territories, or Bantustans, each consisting of a major tribe or ethnic group. The intention of this legislation was to give each Bantustan independence and to encourage it to maintain its own separate identity. It also was aimed at channeling black nationalism into ethnic nationalism in order to weaken the growing cries for African participation at the very center of government.

White fears were not totally unfounded. African nationalism was spreading across the continent in the various European colonies. Political activity among the other races in South Africa began in the 1880s in the Cape Colony. The principal organizations were the African National Congress (1912), the South African Indian Congress (1920), and the colored-dominated African Political Organization. All these bodies were initially small, moderate, Western-oriented elite groups without mass support. The African National Congress gradually became an urban movement, organized along modern political party lines. Between 1949 and 1952 the A.N.C. moved towards greater multiracial cooperation with other antisegregationist groups and waged campaigns of passive resistance to unjust laws. By 1956 they had launched a series of bus-boycotts and pass-burnings. A system of passbooks had been in effect for years as a way of controlling the movement of people. Nonviolent resistance did not prove to be an effective tactic for political change, and in 1959 the more radical youth broke with the A.N.C. and formed the more militant Pan-Africanist Congress, or P.A.C. A demonstration at Sharpeville in March 1960 resulted in South African police shooting nearly seventy participants. Within months, the A.N.C. and P.A.C. were banned by the government, and the African nationalist movement was driven underground and into exile.

FRENCH ASSIMILATION AND ASSOCIATION

We now must return to our examination of the colonial policies of France. The French imposed their rule on West and Equatorial Africa largely by force of arms rather than by treaty. The French military officers who directed the conquest initially stayed on to devise new means of administration. It already has been seen that an assimilationist policy was viewed as expensive, impractical, and excessively idealistic. The resources of French-controlled tropical Africa were clearly not sufficient, even to begin assimilating Africans into the same economic and social standards as those in France. France itself refused to pay the cost of implementing such a policy from its metropolitan budget. Consequently, the assimilationist approach was set aside in all possessions save the old Four Communes of Senegal. In the newly conquered areas, Africans were not considered French citizens but *sujets* (subjects).

The new policy of "association" was given official sanction in 1905, though was not fully implemented until after the First World War. It was now argued that only a small cadre of the most intelligent Africans be assimilated. The notion was that this new "Frenchified" elite would act as a bridge between the French administration and the unassimilated masses. This did not work very well, because the process of assimilation was too successful. The elite returned to Africa and wanted nothing to do with the rural masses. They recoiled from the prospect of becoming "bush administrators" and preferred to remain in such cosmopolitan urban centers as Dakar, Abidjan, and Brazzaville. Ironically, the Frenchmen themselves became a far better bridge to the masses than the *évolués,* or assimilated Africans.

Despite the program of Association, the colonies continued to be ruled by the Decree of 1854, and policy directives usually emanated from Paris. The two great federations were highly centralized, and all major services and administration fell under the control of a governor-general in each. Each federation was subdivided into colonies, and further into *cercles* (circles) under a French commandant de cercle. This system placed the chief in an entirely subordinate role to the commandant de cercle. The chief did not head a unit of local government nor did the area he ruled usually correspond to a precolonial political unit. Many chiefs were selected not because of royal birth but in return for their loyalty and recognized leadership aptitudes. The French changed very explicitly the nature of the powers of the traditional authorities. They were reduced to paid officials of the colonial administration and did not necessarily serve in the areas of their upbringing or family origin.

Under the French colonial system, the scope for local initiative was very limited. Even the governors-general were instruments, not initiators, of colonial policy. The principal source of colonial legislation was the French Chamber of Deputies in Paris, or more usually, the Ministry of Colonies which issued decrees. The indigenous chiefs were not local government authorities as they were in British Africa. They had no responsibility for police or the judiciary, and all taxes they collected went directly to the French commandant who turned them over to his superiors. Colonial laws were applied uniformly throughout the federations. It must be recalled that in British Africa, the colonies and protectorates were separately administered and its governors and legislative councils enjoyed considerable independence from the Colonial Office in London. Indeed, the governor in British African possessions was the principal source of legislation, and the British and African agents of local government were given considerable responsibility and administrative latitude.

Assimilation on the intellectual plane was never abandoned entirely, but it was seldom a two-way street. The French had no intention of assimilating African civilization. African culture was studied assiduously but not copied on any scale. Even the famous European cubists, who were inspired by African sculptural forms, made little effort to appreciate the social or spiritual purposes they served. The French sought to turn the black African intellectual into a black Frenchman. This was the rock upon which association foundered. The new évolué simply did not want to become associated with the traditional elites and their seemingly primitive lifestyle.

The Second World War had a great impact on French colonial policy. Because much of France was occupied by the enemy, the Free French movement under Charles de Gaulle had to rely heavily on the human and material resources of the colonies. In gratitude, de Gaulle held a conference in early 1944 in Brazzaville, capital of French Equatorial Africa. Although denying the possibility of future self-government, he abolished the status of sujet, under which nearly all Africans were liable to forced labor and summary administrative justice without a trial. All Africans were henceforth to be citizens of "Greater France," with limited voting rights.

The Brazzaville Declaration touched off a revolution of rising expectations. If Africans could not achieve independence, they would agitate for greater representation in the government of France itself.

After the Second World War, French West and Equatorial Africa were allowed to send deputies to the National Assembly in Paris and to the newly created Assembly of the French Union. France knew that its overseas colonies had the potential of outvoting the mother country. Consequently, three categories of citizenship were created. Only the "overseas citizen" could enjoy full rights equal to those of French citizens. There were few Africans who had the educational and cultural background to qualify. The old, nineteenth-century prepartition colonies now became Overseas Departments, and those won by conquest in the late nineteenth century had a lesser status. The peoples of the latter areas could be represented only in the Assembly of the French Union, which was little more than an advisory body and vastly inferior to the French National Assembly, in which the real power lay.

The period between 1946 and 1956 witnessed the emergence of political parties under the mantle of the Rassemblement Démocratique Africain (RDA). RDA sections were organized in most of the colonies, and the movement itself became affiliated closely with the French Communist Party. This practice of an African political party affiliating with a metropolitan party, or even of forming party branches in other colonies, was unknown in the British possessions.

The French demonstrated greater indecision in their colonial policy after their stunning defeat in Vietnam in 1954 and the onset of a fierce and costly civil war in their colony of Algeria. At home, the French government had become unstable and the postwar economic revival had slowed. In reaction to the rising tide of anticolonialism throughout the world and United States pressure, they reluctantly granted independence in 1956 to their Tunisian and Moroccan protectorates, and gave Togo, a United Nations Trust Territory, the status of an autonomous republic within the French Union. Meanwhile, they had to cope with civil strife and strikes in their territories of Ivory Coast, Guinea, and Chad.

Before 1956, French-speaking Africans, unlike their counterparts in the

British possessions who demanded complete independence, called on France to live up to its colonial policy of giving the overseas territories a greater voice in Paris. If France were to accede, it would mean that the people in the overseas territories would eventually be able to outvote Frenchmen in France itself. In other words, France ultimately would be governed by Africans and Asians. This was the irony of the assimilationist ideal. When the chips fell, France failed to concede that all men are equal in their rights. The French then did what Afrikaners in South Africa had already begun to do. They destroyed the concept of a single nation with common citizenship and put the Africans into smaller political units. For France this was easier to do because Frenchmen and Africans were separated from each other by an ocean.

This act was implemented in 1956 through a legislative *loi-cadre* (frame work law). The two great federations were balkanized, or broken up, into a number of internally self-governing territories, each with its own relationship with France. Each territory henceforth was responsible directly to Paris, rather than to Dakar or Brazzaville, the two former federal capitals.

Many Frenchmen, faced with the growing menace of Communism at home, feared that a Marxist coup in either federal capital could sweep millions of Africans and vast natural resources into the Communist bloc. The destruction of the federations might reduce this possibility. But it also meant an end to the splendid pan-African unity of the RDA and the beginning of nationalism and fatal divisions among French-speaking Africans. For example, Houphouet-Boigny of the Ivory Coast opposed any restoration of the federation for fear of Senegalese domination. On the other hand, Leopold Senghor of Senegal supported the federal concept, because Senegal otherwise would have to main-tain alone the extensive old federal installations at Dakar.

De Gaulle, when he became president of the Fifth French Republic in 1958, confronted the African territories with a referendum in which each had to choose either total independence or the status of "autonomous republic" within a Franco-African Community vaguely similar to the British Commonwealth. Under the latter, external affairs would continue to be controlled by France. All the territories but Guinea voted for limited autonomy. Guinea's Sekou Touré, opting for independence, defiantly stated that "we prefer poverty in freedom to riches in slavery."[4] The others feared that independence would spell an end to the substantial economic assistance that France had been pouring into its colo-nies since the end of the Second World War. Nevertheless, when France amended its constitution in 1960 to permit complete sovereignty with the French Com-munity, nearly all the territories quickly declared their independence.

---

[4] Edward Mortimer, *France and the Africans: 1944-1960* (New York: Walker Publishing Co., Inc.), p. 316.

PORTUGUESE CENTRALISM

In the nineteenth century, Portuguese colonial theory vaguely resembled French assimilationist thought. The old colonial towns of Luanda, Benguela, and Lourenço Marques had a municipal system of government, with councils somewhat similar to those in the old British and French enclaves. Employed Africans who could demonstrate a proficiency in the Portuguese language and culture were eligible for the status of *assimilado*. For assimilados there were no legal barriers to interracial marriage, social intercourse, or political participation. They had almost complete equality under Portuguese law. However, educational opportunities in these small, stagnant enclaves were even less adequate than in the British and French possessions, and consequently assimilados never represented more than one-fifth of one percent of the African population. Most assimilados were, in fact, *mestiços,* or people of mixed race.

As late as 1900, much of Angola and Mozambique were beyond the reach of Portuguese colonial authority, even though over the previous four centuries the Portuguese had occupied a few coastal and offshore enclaves and from time to time had penetrated a number of African interior kingdoms. During the frenetic period of European imperialism in the 1880s and 1890s, Portuguese plans for linking Angola and Mozambique into a transcontinental empire ran up against Cecil Rhodes's dream of a British corridor from Cape Town to Cairo. Portugal, one of the weakest nations of Europe and a diplomatic client of Great Britain, was forced to accept the British spheres of Northern and Southern Rhodesia and Nyasaland, which together geographically prevented a Mozambique-Angolan connection.

The outlines of twentieth-century colonial policy were laid down between 1899 and 1918 by several Portuguese officials, notably António Enes and Eduardo da Costa. Like the French, they backed away from the earlier liberal and assimilationist conceptions. Circumscriptions, the basic unit of local government, were laid out after the Colonial Reform Act of 1907. Considerable responsibility fell to the local Portuguese *administrador* of the circumscription and his chiefs of post. They enjoyed enormous powers over the local populations and could control administration, try cases, imprison, and coordinate labor and military recruitment. No real encouragement was given to the traditional authorities and their institutions. Over the years they were severely undermined. Indeed, the village chief, or *regulo,* became a uniformed colonial official and little more than a mouthpiece. The old nineteenth-century colonial towns continued to hold a special status. Elsewhere, the administrador and his *chiefs de postos* ruled supreme.

The traditional African rulers offered stiff resistance to this oppressive form of colonial government, and Portuguese control over Angola's hinterland was not fully secured until the second governorship of Norton de Matos in 1921-24.

After 1926, the Portuguese dictator, Antonio de Oliveira Salazar, sought to bring the overseas colonies under Lisbon's closer economic and political control. The Colonial Act of 1930 provided for the unification of administration in the hands of the state and reversed three decades of trends towards decentralization and local autonomy. Henceforth, greater power would reside in Lisbon, specifically in the Overseas Ministry. It was the overseas minister who directed the administrative, political, and financial life of the colonies. Most laws or decrees of the Council of Ministers originated from his office. The governors-general in each possession, usually military figures, supervised the administration, prepared budgets, and advised on legislation. Like the governors in French Africa, they could not legislate. Laws or decrees were handed down to Luanda and Lourenço Marques, the capitals of Angola and Mozambique.

In 1951 Salazar, with the stroke of a pen, converted the colonies into "overseas provinces" of metropolitan Portugal. The Salazar regime argued that there was no such thing as "native policy," that in legal theory no distinction existed between a Portuguese and an African. In reality, the difference was quite great.

Salazar saw Portugal and its provinces as a vast and unified pan-Lusitanian community. Africans saw it quite differently. In Angola, small nationalist currents appeared after World War II among urban assimilados and mestiços. The Portuguese brutally repressed all dissent and in a bloody revolt in 1961, nearly fifty thousand Africans died. The armed struggle for liberation began in February 1961 in Angola, in 1963 in Guinea-Bissau, and a year later in Mozambique. By that time, most of the British, French, and Belgian colonies had gained independence and for the most part, rather peacefully.

Portugal, an economically depressed nation with a small population, found it increasingly costly and unpopular to wage war against the guerrilla forces. In 1973 Africans in Guinea-Bissau had secured most of the countryside, declared their independence, and soon gained recognition from over eighty nations. A successful military coup in Portugal itself in April 1974 led to a radical change in government and a program of decolonization. In 1975 Angola, Mozambique, and Cape Verde were abruptly given their independence. But long-standing rivalries between three nationalist factions in Angola ushered in a period of civil war.

THE GERMAN IRON FIST

German rule in Africa was short-lived and was confined to Togo and Cameroun in West Africa, Tanganyika in East Africa, and the territory of South West Africa. African subordinates of the German governors and their district officers often were selected without regard to traditional procedures. In East Africa, they initially assumed control of the old Zanzibari coastal administration, which placed a *liwali* in charge of each town, with *akidas* serving as their assistants in outlying rural areas. Later they gave the akidas responsibility for tax collection and judicial matters, and made them the principal intermediaries between the German district officers and the *jumbes,* or village headmen and clan elders. Akida were recruited not from the traditional ruling cadres but from the coastal aristocracy of Arab and Swahili traders. Later they were drawn from graduates of the coastal colonial schools. The colony itself was divided into districts, under the watchful eye of the governor and his district officers.

The German government replaced the private chartered companies as rulers in the 1890s, after the companies had proved their inability to quell local African resistance. The German military officers also encountered formidable opposition. At first, German rule was cruel and brutal. But the genocidal suppression of the Herero Rebellion (1903-1907) in South West Africa and the Maji Maji Rebellion (1905-1907) in Tanganyika led to sweeping reforms, including the establishment of a Colonial Office and a civilian administration.

German rule in Africa came to an end in 1919 after the peace treaty concluding World War I. Its colonies were placed under the supervision of the League of Nations. Tanganyika was entrusted to Great Britain, Ruanda and Urundi to Belgium, South West Africa to the Union of South Africa, and Togo and Cameroun were divided among the British and French.

BELGIAN PATERNALISM

Belgian policy represented a kind of compromise between British and Portuguese colonial theories. The Belgian Congo was born in an age of imperialism and therefore was never influenced by the liberal, egalitarian currents of the eighteenth and early nineteenth centuries as were Senegal and the Gold Coast.

From 1885 to 1908 the Congo was a personal possession of King Leopold and euphemistically was called the "Congo Free State." In fact, there was nothing free about it. Most of the state was run like a socialist collective farm, and the remainder fell under semistate, monopolistic, concessionary companies. Forced labor, akin to slavery, abounded.

The Charter of 1908 laid the basis of a colonial policy under which the Congo would be governed until independence in 1960. In 1908, after world protest against the atrocities of King Leopold's agents, the Congo Free State was abolished and sovereignty passed to the Belgian government. Some historains have described the post-1908 Belgian colonial policy as "apologetic," in retribution for the maladministration of King Leopold's Free State. In theory, Belgium's monarch remained the chief legislator, though most authority rested with the governor-general, who held greater powers than his counterparts in the French possessions. Nevertheless, the governor-general received his orders from the Colonial Ministry in Brussels.

In the period before 1908, the Congo Free State attempted to recognize chiefs and to use them in the administration. But the Belgians were fairly ignorant of indigenous government systems and they appointed chiefs without consulting traditional electors. Precolonial aristocratic titles were retained, and many of the old kingdoms never completely lost their sense of identity. Real local power rested firmly in the hands of the Belgian district and provincial commissioners. This form of direct rule continued through the post-1908 days of the Belgian Congo. The chiefs gradually lost their political *raison d'être* and by 1918 the entire internal structure was rapidly disintegrating. Efforts subsequently were made to identify the real chiefs and to determine the true source of indigenous authority. A form of local government then was developed which divided the population among the traditional chiefs who ruled in accordance with local custom. Every African was assigned to an administrative unit and was required to carry an identity card when traveling beyond his or her unit. In this way, the colonial regime, like those in British Kenya and South Africa, gained more complete control over population movement. Many Africans gravitated towards the urban and mining areas and mixed with people of different ethnic backgrounds and customs. By 1931, the government exempted them from customary law, and built carefully designed, new towns with modern amenities. These *centres extra-coutumiers,* or noncustomary centers, were also an attempt to discourage the growth of a "Congolese" national identity and to separate the urbanites from the more conservative rural populations. After World War II, there were a growing number of évolués, the equivalent of the assimilado. By 1958, more than twenty-six percent of the colony's population lived outside the traditional villages. Of the colony's entire population, only one-sixteenth were considered évolués.

In the postwar era, the Belgians provided the Congolese with a relatively good standard of living and extensive vocational training. They reasoned that one could separate economic advance from political advance and that if you paternalistically gave the African basic health care, housing, and primary education, his needs would be satisfied and he would not demand political self-determination. Thus, the Belgians were explicitly paternalistic and never asked their subjects to make political decisions nor gave them a higher education and training in business or public administration.

The Africans had only to look across the Congo River to Brazzaville and the French Congo to grasp the meaning of self-determination. After 1956, the French Congo became more autonomous, and the civil service underwent a slow but steady process of Africanization. It was not until 1957 that the Belgians permitted any African participation in urban government.

In 1954 the Catholics had lost control of the government in Belgium to a coalition of Social Democrats and Liberals. The Catholics no longer controlled the powerful Ministry of Colonies. Some Catholic elements reacted by organizing Africans in the Belgian Congo against the colonial regime. This was easy to do because most schools were under the Catholic Church, and most Congolese nominally followed the Catholic faith. The population rapidly became politicized, and party activity began, which the government found difficult to contain. Violence erupted in 1959; and in the same year the National Congolese Movement, led by Patrice Lumumba, a young postal clerk, scored well in territorial elections.

Little Belgium feared a protracted, costly, and divisive civil war akin to the French conflict in Algeria. Almost overnight, it decided to give the Congo independence in June 1960, without first training an indigenous cadre to operate the vast and complex bureaucracy. Indeed, the Congo did not have an African transitional government until a month before independence. On the eve of independence a plethora of political parties appeared, each based on certain ethnic groups or regions. The Belgians always had inhibited the development of a national "Congolese" consciousness. For example, people in the city of Elizabethville in the Katanga province saw themselves more as Katangans than as Congolese. This, together with the size of the colony (as large as the United States east of the Mississippi River) and poor communications, prevented the rise of strong, national political parties.

An uneasy alliance was forged between the conservative president, Joseph Kasavubu, who favored a loose Congolese federation, and the radical prime minister, Patrice Lumumba, who demanded a strong central government. Not surprisingly, within days after independence the nation began to disintegrate under pressure of internal power struggles. The national army, under stern colonial-minded Belgian officers, mutinied; and the Congo's richest province (Katanga) under premier Moise Tshombe, seceded. Europen neocolonialism, inter-ethnic hostility, and bloody civil war all followed.

LAW AND JUSTICE

During the colonial era, traditional courts in Africa were absorbed into the legal system of the governing European powers. A wide, often bewildering variety of courts was formed, ranging from customary "native" courts operated by local chiefs and their elders to the civil and criminal courts of lay magistrates, to high courts under professional judges.

The powers, membership, and jurisdiction became subject to periodic review by European administrative officers. In British Africa, a conscious effort was made to preserve as much of the precolonial legal system as possible. For example, in Northern Nigeria, the Native Courts Proclamation (1902) gave a legal basis to the emirates' existing system of indigenous Muslim courts. It recognized and upheld the judicial council of the leading emirs as well as the alkali courts. Between 1914 and 1917 Lugard introduced native courts to Southern Nigeria. But as institutions alien to the southern ethnic groups, they operated less effectively. In British Africa, alongside the native courts were magistrates' courts, presided over by European officers and dispensing noncustomary law. They ranked from the lowest district officer's court to the high court of the colony or protectorate. Appeal from the highest native court was normally directed first to a district court. Cases were tried in the various courts, depending on the magnitude of the offence. The European courts tried "serious offences" like murder, failure to pay taxes, rebellion, and breaches of colonial laws or ordinances. Cases equally serious in African eyes, particularly those involving adultery or sorcery, were heard in the native courts, by which traditional customary law was applied.

The degree of survival of customary law and African judicial leadership depended on the colonial regime. The British gave encouragement. By contrast, the French abolished the official judicial powers of the chiefs after 1912, and only occasionally were they allowed to preside in courts concerned with "personal" law.

The colonial era led to rapid urbanization and demographical mobility. Peoples of different ethnic and cultural backgrounds, and thus of different legal experiences, found themselves living and working in a common political unit. Large-scale plural societies could not rely on a given set of customary laws because of the multiplicity of traditional legal norms. In Lagos, Nigeria, for example, the norms of the Islamic Hausa might conflict with those of the non-Islamic Igbo. There were severe problems of applying laws to an urban and industrial society, regardless of their ethnic basis, which had evolved in a rural, noncapitalist, nonliterate setting. In addition, written laws were needed to deal quickly with changing situations and institutions.

Gradually, local divergences of law were obliterated. Colonial laws from the beginning gave a certain legal unity to the multitude of constellations of ethnic groups and their legal systems. This was particularly true in the non-Muslim areas, for Islamic law itself had given some precolonial polities a legal uniformity transcending local laws.

Africans never completely abandoned their ties to the traditional laws of their own societies, particularly if they continued to be relevant to their lives and to serve as effective instruments of social control and cohesion. For example, customary law permitted polygymy; European laws did not. People often chose to be bound by both and not uncommonly, civil marriages received the additional sanction of customary rites. Also, many families continued to use traditional law in matters of inheritance.

Colonial governments had considerable difficulty enforcing their laws when these went against local customs. In some areas, customary laws were codified by European administrators and reinterpreted in terms of Western values. In South Africa's native reserves, white functionaries administered justice in "native commissioner's courts" according to the European conception of "native law custom." This did not always benefit the local people. Colonial justice, whether within the context of European or customary law, was not necessarily more consistent or impartial. European administrators sometimes failed to recognize that customary law in precolonial Africa was not a separate system, divorced from other institutions. The courts of precolonial Africa aimed at restoring community solidarity rather than at strictly adhering to the law. Laws thus were often flexible; European judges in the colonial era were more likely to imprison or fine the guilty individual instead of conceding that responsibility for one's offence should be borne collectively by the extended family. Punishment now seemed more important than reconciliation or rehabilitation.

In the colonial era, racial or cultural distinctions were reflected in differences in penalties. Formerly, social and political status were important criteria, particularly in the highly stratified societies. For example, during the heyday of the Atlantic slave trade, free people, especially those of aristocratic origin, were usually at a judicial advantage over their servants or slaves. Some customary laws perpetuated certain lineages in power. The colonial powers elevated the formerly servile populations to judicial equality. In the colonies of large white settlement, laws were formulated to ensure the domination of the Europeans over the indigenous groups. Everywhere in colonial Africa, Africans living in a traditional milieu were subject to a different set of laws. One of the greatest dilemmas for the colonial powers was devising separate legal structures for the Westernized African on the one hand and the so-called "native" on the other. It should be recalled that in French Africa sujets were under a "native justice" in which the tribunal was presided over by a European administrator assisted by two "native" assessors, who judged according to local custom. Before 1946, sujets were bound by the *indigénat,* or sanctions enforced by the police for a variety of misdemeanors. The indigénat empowered the French administrator to jail any African sujet without trial for up to fourteen days. Portuguese administrators in their colonies held similar powers of summary trial and imprisonment, and by law, adult African males were obliged to work at least six months a year.

Africans living in urban areas tended to be more cosmopolitan and Westernized, and gradually new laws were devised for them. Evolués and assimilados in Portuguese, Belgian, and French Africa, if they were citizens, were subject to both the advantages and disadvantages of European law. This special status often involved onerous obligations in return for limited advantages. In Belgian Africa, literate but not necessarily Westernized Africans were issued a *carte du merite* which entitled them to be judged in a territorial tribunal beyond the pale of customary law.

The colonial era witnessed the imposition of written laws in the form of proclamations, decrees, charters, ordinances, codes, and constitutions. While they may have brought a refreshing legal uniformity to the highest level of colonial government, they were regarded by many Africans as being rigid and formalistic. In some instances they conflicted with Muslim and customary law at the local level. Each European power had its own legal traditions, for instance French civil law, English common law, and Roman-Dutch law. The European scramble for African territory led to a rather arbitrary and hasty drawing of colonial boundaries. Often they cut across traditional ethnic lines and boundaries of former African states. This problem will be discussed later. What is important here is that a single ethnic group, let us say the Hausa, suddenly found itself straddling the Anglo-French boundary. Consequently, Hausa in French Nigeria were bound by one set of colonial laws and their relatives in British Nigeria by another set.

Some precolonial states were dismantled, and others became provinces of still larger political units. The scale of government and political activity expanded considerably, and administration generally became far more efficient. With improved transportation, regional government and courts of law came within closer reach of the people. In British Africa, kings and paramount chiefs, who in precolonial days rarely traveled beyond the walled confines of their palaces, were now required to tour their districts. To facilitate administration, traditional forms of authority initially were retained. But over time, they became increasingly anachronistic and unable to cope with modern demands. This was even true of the native courts in British Africa. By independence, much of the substance of political power and judicial authority had disappeared from the traditional political systems.

If one were to establish a balance sheet for law and justice in the colonial period, the positive contributions would slightly outweigh the negative, particularly in the British possessions. For Africa to evolve into modern ethnically plural nations, modern, uniform, written laws were essential. The colonial era also left a legacy of judicial autonomy, and of the separation of the judicial, executive and legislative elements. No longer were African monarchs and paramount chiefs above the law. New laws, more secular in nature, derived not from God or the ancestors but from legislators and professionally trained judges. People could now appeal beyond the king or chief to higher courts of law. The colonial powers also introduced, perhaps grudgingly, the concept of popularly elected assemblies or legislatures. This was not new for some of the more egalitarian societies, like the Igbo. But it was a liberating factor in societies dominated for centuries by entrenched privileged aristocracy.

Major constitutional reforms followed on the heels of the Second World War, expanding the franchise and increasing African participation in the legislative and executive branches. Africanization in the judicial branch moved at a slower pace. The British sought to export and impose their Westminster version of parliamentary government with its multiparty system. While the British continued to work towards a federal concept in East and Central Africa and Nigeria, it has been seen that the French worked against it in their possessions. Finally, colonial governments, especially British, introduced to Africans the concept that civil servants should be nonpolitical. Like judicial officers, civil servants were forbidden to engage in partisan political activity.

THE ROLE OF THE MILITARY

European military officers, after conquering African territory in the late nineteenth century, stayed on to provide the theory and framework for colonial administration. Indeed, they exercised considerable influence in the formulation of colonial policy. In the process of conquering the Sokoto Caliphate, Captain Frederick Lugard was appointed high commissioner of Northern Nigeria (1900–1906) and then served as governor-general of Northern and Southern Nigeria between 1914 and 1919. His *Political Memoranda* became the essential handbook for all British colonial officers. In the early years, his most trusted military subordinates served as provincial and district officers.

After about 1906, colonial administration in the British and German possessions became more geared to the civilian. The process of demilitarization in the French and Portuguese areas was much slower. In the rebellious sections of French Equatorial Africa and Chad, military rule persisted until after the First World War. In French West Africa in 1917, a famous military figure, Joost Van Vollenhoven, served as governor-general before returning to active military service. His writings greatly influenced subsequent educational and administrative policies. French colonial practice before the close of World War II strongly reflected the authoritarian attitudes of military commanders. In the early years of the twentieth century, colonial rule was made effective largely by the progressive extension of military control. In Portuguese Africa, military officers remained influential until the mid-1920s when pockets of African resistance finally were eliminated.

The modern armies of Sierra Leone, Ghana, and Nigeria are descendants of the Royal West African Frontier Force (RWAFF), created by the British Colonial Office in 1897 in response to French military rivalry in the hinterlands of the old colonies of Sierra Leone, Gold Coast, and Lagos. The Frontier Force, consisting mainly of Hausa recruits, was a conglomeration of the early enclave constabularies, dating back to the 1860s. After 1900, local regiments were established in the enlarged protectorates of Sierra Leone, Gold Coast, and Nigeria, and fell under the WAFF umbrella. This structure remained intact until the eve of independence in the late 1950s.

In regions of East Africa in the early 1900s, British troops consisted mainly of Sikh volunteers from the colonial Indian army. The major British force, the King's African Rifles (KAR) was established in 1897 and based in the East African Protectorate.

Military forces in Southern Rhodesia originated from the privately financed British South Africa (Company) police, which first saw action in the Matabele rebellions in the 1890s. It later became a military organization and the major element of the Rhodesian defense network. The white Rhodesian forces were multiracial, but blacks were rarely used in combat positions.

South Africa left the Second Boer War with more than 100,000 imperial troops on its soil. Many stayed behind and were used from 1905 through 1906 to suppress the Bambatha revolt in Natal. In 1913, the Union government was again obliged to call in British imperial troops to quell a white miners' strike on the Witwatersrand. Shortly afterward, Prime Minister Jan Smuts established a Union Defence Force, staffed mainly with Afrikaner officers. The UDF over the years was used to suppress a number of African strikes and demonstrations in both South and South West Africa. Like Southern Rhodesia, only whites were allowed to carry arms. Africans and coloreds were conscripted but acted as porters, laborers, and other noncombatant employees.

In the Congo Free State, the Force Publique was formed in 1885 and later under the Belgian Congo, it became both a military force and a gendarmerie (police force). The Portuguese, unlike the other colonial powers, counted more heavily on metropolitan soldiers.

From the very start, educated Africans were strongly biased against colonial armies because of the part they had played in the nineteenth-century imperial conquest and because of their role in the twentieth century in suppressing African rebellions. As a symbol of alien rule, they failed to attract those Africans fighting for political self-determination. European military officers deliberately avoided recruiting from among the Western-educated, urbanized populations for fear that in suppressing their own ideals, they would be disruptive. Alternatively, they looked to politically less sophisticated and predominantly illiterate ethnic groups with a precolonial martial ethos. For example, the British in East Africa avoided the educated Buganda and Kikuyu and recruited among the "physically stronger, more robust, and warlike" Kamba and Muslim Acholi. In West Africa, they preferred the "warlike" Tiv, the Hausa, and the "primitive" Dagomba to the more Westernized Yoruba, Igbo, Fante, and Asante. This discriminatory practice created deep ethnic divisions among the colonial forces and between them and the African nationalists.

The British paid their soldiers relatively well and were able to rely on volunteers during peacetime. By contrast, the French resorted to conscription and often forced their troops to engage in onerous public-works projects. In wartime, France depended on African troops much more than the British did. African political leaders, like the Senegalese deputy Blaise Diagne, took advantage of that dependence by demanding franchise and citizenship concessions in return for their cooperation in recruitment.

The European powers first saw their colonial military forces as necessary instruments in the conquest and "pacification" of African territories. Later, they were regarded as vital to the Allied war efforts against the Germans and Italians. After World War II they became an element in the Europeans' global military strategy against the Communist threat or, in the case of the Portuguese, as a deterrent to African guerrilla activity. For example, Africans in the King's African Rifles and Hausa in the West African Frontier Force served in the war against the Asante Confederacy in 1900. During World War I, black Belgian, Portuguese, British, and South African troops fought the Germans in Africa, and nearly 181,000 blacks from French Africa served in Europe.

European dependence on their colonial armies, as well as on Africa's natural resources, increased in the Second World War. British West African troops were sent to Burma, India, the Middle East, North and West Africa, and for the first time, to Europe. Freetown, Accra, and Maiduguri in Northern Nigeria became vital staging points for the Allies en route to North Africa, the Middle East, and the Far East. French Equatorial Africa, under the black governor-general, Felix Eboué, gave crucial support to de Gaulle's Free French forces throughout the war. In the postwar period, the Kenya police were organized in 1953 as a General Service Unit and were used against the Kikuyu-inspired Mau Mau rebellion. By the end of 1965, the Portuguese had nearly 100,000 soldiers in Africa, an army equal to all the forces of the black states south of the Sahara.

The armed forces in British Africa were organized regionally but recruited territorially. By contrast, French colonial forces, though also regionally organized, did not allow any of their units to identify with a given territory.

World War II forced the British and French to reconsider their colonial policies. First, their depleted treasuries could not sustain a strong military presence overseas. Second, both powers, particularly France, owed a great moral debt to African leaders for their wartime military support. Third, the two European wars destroyed the myth of the superior white monolith. African troops saw whites fighting against themselves, they shared muddy trenches with their white counterparts, whites tolerated violence by blacks against whites, Africans serving in other parts of the colonial world came into contact with others suffering from European domination, and in Europe, Africans became angered at the high standard of living enjoyed by their colonial masters. After the Second World War, ex-servicemen found it difficult to find jobs at home which could match their skills acquired during wartime. Many of them participated in postwar demonstrations against colonial regimes, and in Kenya they joined the Mau Mau rebellion.

Those who remained in the colonial armies after the war tended toward political conservatism. For example, Idi Amin, who in the 1970s was military dictator of Uganda, first won recognition in the 1950s as a soldier in the King's African Rifles fighting against African nationalists in Kenya. Likewise, Jean-Bedel Bokassa, autocratic emperor of the Central African Empire in the 1970s, fought to preserve French colonial control over Indochina in the 1950s.

The officer corps were "Africanized" at an extremely slow pace, particularly in the French and Belgian territories. The rate suddenly accelerated on the eve of Independence, and many of those promoted to senior positions were poorly educated but had long, dedicated military service. Concurrently, Western-educated younger men out of the best European military academies were recruited as junior officers. From the start, this led to promotion obstacles for the junior officers and to tension between them and the seemingly more "backward" old-timers who had advanced more because of experience and loyalty than because of expertise.

Just before independence, colonial armies and police in all but Portuguese Africa, were generally small, well disciplined, conservative in lifestyle, and apolitical. Military allocations were extremely modest and never placed a great strain on colonial budgets. Clearly, the military were no longer as crucial to colonial administration as they were earlier in the century.

chapter 5

Economic Horizons

THE PREDOMINANCE OF AGRICULTURE

Throughout the colonial era, agriculture remained the livelihood of most Africans. However, the colonial era set into motion a shift from economic structures based on subsistence peasant agriculture to an export-oriented cash-crop economy. African production continued to stay mainly at a subsistence level, though higher than in precolonial days. Africans in many regions grew steadily fewer garden crops for their own needs and concentrated on cash crops in order to buy European imports and to pay taxes demanded, in cash, by the colonial regimes.

The cash crops were determined not by African dietary requirements but by the needs of consumers in Western Europe. For example, Senegal and the Gambia proved to have excellent land for peanut cultivation, and consequently peasants began to spend more time growing peanuts than rice, their traditional staple. Rice production eventually declined to the point at which it had to be imported from French Indochina. Likewise, the Asante transformed their small vegetable patches into cocoa groves to meet British consumer demands for chocolates. The various colonial governments did very little to encourage the production of food crops, paying more attention to the expansion of cash crops for the overseas markets.

Each colony concentrated on the production of a limited range of cash crops. Exports were narrowly based upon a few agricultural products whose value rose through the boom of the 1920s, dropped in the Great Depression of the 1930s, and surged upward after World War II. This trend towards monoculture was encouraged in some regions by multinational corporations. They distributed new or improved strains of seeds and guaranteed the purchase of the crops. For example, the British Cotton Growing Association vastly boosted cotton cultivation in Northern Nigeria after 1902 by introducing an improved American variety of cotton seed, building cotton ginneries, and buying the local crop.

By the onset of World War I, each colony was known for the export of certain crops: Senegal and Gambia, peanuts; Ivory Coast, coffee and timber; the Gold Coast, cocoa; Nigeria, palm oil, peanuts, and cocoa; Liberia, rubber; and Uganda, coffee and cotton. The production of food crops for domestic consumption increased because of new fertilizers, insecticides, and seeds. But it failed to keep pace with the growth in population and cash crop production, with the result that food prices rose faster than income. From the 1920s on, prices paid in world markets for cash crops did not rise as rapidly as those paid for imported manufactured goods.

In some colonies, African peasant agriculture had to compete with European agribusiness. African farming remained relatively small in scale, with individual holdings rarely exceeding five acres. Scattered plots, shifting cultivation, and hand labor persisted. European agriculture was extensive, far better capitalized, and more efficiently managed. In Liberia, the Firestone Rubber Company of the United States established enormous rubber plantations in the late 1920s and 1930s. Rubber plantations also emerged in German Togoland and German Cameroun, as well as in King Leopold's Congo. Great timber plantations were planted in the Ivory Coast, peanut plantations in Senegal, and in Kenya the British Brooke Bond Company laid out extensive tea plantations. Plantation enterprise also became important in Mozambique (with cotton, sugar, copra, and sisal) and in Angola (mainly coffee). In Uganda and much of British West Africa, farsighted colonial governors laid down policies prohibiting or discouraging European agriculture of any kind.

Estates were another type of European agribusiness. They were owned and operated by individual farmers who usually lived on them. Estates were most common in South Africa, Southern Rhodesia, Kenya, and Tanganyika during the era of German rule. In Kenya, Africans were prohibited from growing certain commercial crops, especially coffee, tea, and sisal, which were cultivated by the European settlers. Nearly everywhere, European farmers saw labor-intensive African agriculture as a threat to their own labor supply.

In some areas, African peasants competed successfully with their European counterparts. African coffee growers in the Ivory Coast were far more successful than the Europeans in attracting and utilizing indigenous labor. In Tanganyika coffee was introduced by missionaries to the Chaga cultivators in the Mount Kilimanjaro foothills. British administrators, against the advice of local white settlers, helped the Chaga in 1924 to form the Kilimanjaro Native Planters' Association. The Chaga soon became some of Africa's most prosperous farmers and produced some of the best coffee. In Uganda, the collapse of world cotton prices in the 1920s ruined the plantations but failed to deter the growth of the peasants' production.

In the colonial era scientific experimentation in agriculture began; before 1945 it had been largely limited to improvements in export-oriented cash crops. Advancements had been comparatively meager in the peasant agriculture geared to domestic consumption. Colonial governments from the earliest days had established experimentation stations and botanical gardens; two of the most prominent before World War I were the Amani Institute (1902) in German East Africa and the Aburi Gardens (1892) in the British Gold Coast. All agronomic research in French West Africa was devoted to peanuts. A Senegalese institute conducted research into oil-producing substances and introduced superior peanut seeds. However, too much attention was given to peanut research and not enough to the development of other crops. In the Belgian Congo, the Institute National pour l'Étude Agronomique du Congo Belge (INEAC) coordinated all the biological research (plant and animal) carried on in the colony. It developed new strains of palm nuts and experimented with a wide range of forest products.

Some progress in tropical and temperate agriculture was also made by missionary stations and private entrepreneurs. In the Kenyan highlands, Lord Delamere invested his own capital and energy in introducing new crops and livestock and in improving strains of old ones. Africans took similar initiatives. A few farmers were responsible in 1879 for introducing cocoa to the Gold Coast. The crop later became one of the major exports of West Africa and the mainstay of the Gold Coast's economy. Dioula traders of the western Sudan also seized opportunities afforded by cocoa. They moved southward into the forest belt of the Ivory Coast and invested their earnings from precolonial trading into the crop's cultivation. In Northern Nigeria, Hausa traders used their precolonial marketing skills to become efficient middlemen in the peanut trade. They encouraged peasants to grow peanuts for export by paying good prices for them.

The expansion of cash-crop agriculture gave former slaves and nonaristocratic peasants an opportunity to liberate themselves economically from dependence on their former masters. It is argued that this commercialization drove a wedge into African society, separating those operating in the cash-crop economy from the traditional subsistence farmers. This bifurcation acquired racial overtones in South Africa where the growth of commercial agriculture widened the gap between whites and non-whites. Farm income, housing, and overall living standards improved far faster for whites than for blacks and coloreds. This was in part the result of enormous increases in white agricultural productivity and the fact that whites operated within the context of large individual, not communal, land holdings. By this century, whites had secured, mainly through conquest, much of the country's most fertile lands. After World War II, government subsidies to white farmers increased as special tariff policies were enacted to protect agriculture from cheap imports. In contrast, African agricultural productivity stagnated. Explosive population growth, low technology, and restraints on territorial expansion imposed by the native reserve system, led to overgrazing and soil erosion. Livestock management through pasture rotation proved difficult in societies adhering to communal land tenure and abhoring the idea of fencing. Nevertheless, in overall agricultural output, sub-Saharan Africa in little more than a half-century of colonialism had an agricultural revolution the likes of which had never before occurred.

Unfortunately, this revolution came at the expense of the natural ecosystem. European concessionaries, in search of timber, steadily encroached on the rain forest, converting it in some areas to open grassland. In West Africa, the present line between lowland rain forest and savanna woodland is not a natural one but rather has been created over the century through continuous cutting and burning. African farmers set fire to forests in order to expand crop cultivation. Fire was also used to kill game and stimulate fresh undergrowth for domesticated animals. Since at least 1875, wild game have been decimated through destroying their natural habitats by cultivation and destroying their breeding haunts. Improved hunting techniques with firearms has also been a major contribution.

At the same time, the colonial era saw an increase in domesticated livestock populations. Under conditions of nomadic pastoralism prevailing in East and West Africa, herds began to exceed the carrying capacity of the vegetation. Many pastoralists found they either had to become cultivators or abandon uncontrolled open-range grazing practices and submit to fencing. The agricultural revolution of the colonial era proved to be a double-edged sword. It set into motion environmental problems which in many cases would not become serious until the 1970s.

THE EXTRACTIVE INDUSTRIES

African minerals from earliest times have been an important resource to the continent and to the world beyond. Much of the splendor of Egypt and Kush rested on the gold and precious stones from south of the Nile. African gold of the western Sudan flowed into European royal treasuries during the Middle Ages. From at least the eleventh century A.D., copper streamed out of central Africa destined for sheiks in the Arabian peninsula and western India. African royalty, too, adorned themselves with jewelry fashioned from local ores and stones.

Africa's full mineral potential had not begun to be realized until the colonial era, when sophisticated technology enabled engineers to probe and mine deep beneath the earth's surface. Modern mineral extraction, extremely expensive and technical, lay beyond the reach of most small prospectors. Consequently, mineral exploitation became the preserve of a few highly capitalized European and American firms.

During the colonial era, most mining was in central and southern Africa, primarily in the Belgian Congo, Angola, Northern Rhodesia, and South Africa. In British West Africa, gold mines flourished in the Gold Coast, and coal and tin was extracted in Nigeria. The French, on the other hand, overlooked the mineral potential of their territories. France viewed its West and Equatorial African holdings mainly as agricultural resource areas and did very little to explore for minerals.

The expansion of mining industries in South Africa led to a rapid broadening of the economy's hitherto narrow base. Diamonds, gold, and coal became major industries. The government greatly encouraged mining and heavy industry after the First World War. This stimulus found fullest expression in 1928 with the establishment of the Iron and Steel Corporation of South Africa (ISCOR) as a public utility. From the early 1930s, ISCOR was phenomenally successful and contributed enormously to the nation's industrial development.

Before the turn of the century, Cecil Rhodes had founded the huge DeBeers Corporation and the British South Africa Company. The process of corporate amalgamation of the extractive industries reached a new peak in 1917 when Ernest Oppenheimer formed the sprawling Anglo-American Corporation of South Africa. Oppenheimer bought into DeBeers and the British South Africa Company, making him Africa's most powerful mining magnate.

In the Belgian Congo, four financial groups provided nearly two-thirds of the capital invested there. The largest of the four giants, Société Général, nearly monopolized mineral production and held controlling interests in transportation, banking, and power generation. Union Minière du Haut-Katanga, a subsidiary of Société Général, and Forminière were organized in 1906. The former was concerned with copper, the latter with diamonds. Forminière also had a major interest in Diamang, a Portuguese-based company founded in 1917 to mine diamonds in Angola. The impetus for mineral extraction in the Congo lay with King Leopold, who, lacking the necessary capital and expertise, turned to private enterprise and granted sweeping concessions in return for a percentage of the profits. The Guggenheim family of New York City was instrumental in providing much of the capital. They received from King Leopold ninety-nine-year rights to minerals of all the Congo save the area reserved for Union Minière. The Guggenheims also secured huge diamond concessions in the Kasai region. By the start of World War II, the Belgian Congo's mining base had expanded to include cobalt, uranium, tantalum, columbium, tungsten, and a number of other important minerals.

The Belgian Congo was not the only source of minerals for the West. One of the largest deposits of the rare mineral chromium was discovered in Southern Rhodesia. Full-scale exploitation of neighboring Northern Rhodesia's rich copperbelt came after 1924 in response to rising world demand. All these areas proved to be vital during the Second World War. By 1945 mining had become the keystone of the economies of South Africa, Northern Rhodesia, and the Belgian Congo, and together these countries were regarded as the capitalist world's most important non-Western sources of strategic minerals.

Mining and agricultural development did not promote much growth in the manufacturing sector except in areas of white settlement. It remained colonial policy to process raw products in Western Europe. In this way the European economies provided jobs for otherwise idle workers. On the other hand, white settlers in Kenya, Southern Rhodesia, and South Africa gained a large financial interest in their own economies and plowed profits from mining and agriculture into local manufacturing. As capital matured in South Africa after 1924, manufacturing industries replaced mining and agriculture as the largest contributors to the national income. But mining and agriculture continued to be the major earners of foreign exchange. In Kenya and Uganda, local Asians and Europeans developed small textile industries and in Kenya and Southern Rhodesia, dairies and meat processing became important parts of local industry.

Although the colonial era nearly eliminated traditional Africa metalurgical industries, other local crafts flourished. For example, the Kente weaving industry in Asante expanded, and the leatherworkers of Northern Nigeria had never been busier. In many areas, the volume of traditional industrial production grew. As in the Western industrialized nations, there were appreciable declines in the proportion of the population engaged in home industries, and in their share of total industrial production.

TRADE, MARKETS, AND TRADERS

Cash crops and mineral production facilitated the expansion of trade and commerce. Overseas as well as internal trade and market activity grew considerably during the colonial era. The value of West African overseas trade alone increased nearly fifteen times between 1906 and 1910. Growth rates subsequently moderated until the 1955–1959 period, when volume jumped nearly tenfold.

Throughout the colonial era imports seldom exceeded exports and consequently government budgets usually balanced. Tariffs and subsidies were used to reserve as much of the colonial markets as possible for their own countrymen. However, much of the postwar economic growth in British Africa resulted from a gradual liberalization in trade policy. Foreign competition became more intense as markets were penetrated by Americans, West Germans, Japanese, and others. By 1960, Britain's share of overseas trade was twenty-five percent less than in 1945. France, on the other hand, continued to dominate trade in its own colonies. After 1954 it followed a policy of generous price supports for African produce in an effort to achieve closer integration of its colonial economies with that of metropolitan France. The French assured a colonial market for themselves by purchasing African produce at prices above world levels. Portugal pursued a similar policy, though even more neo-mercantilist. Until the 1960s nearly all colonial financial and commercial transactions were in the home country.

Most of the overseas trade of colonial Africa was monopolized by a small number of European and British trading companies, which were often successors of the royal-chartered companies of the late nineteenth century. By

1930, the bulk of export-import and wholesale-retail trading in West Africa lay in the hands of three firms: the British-controlled United Africa Company (UAC), and two French concerns, Compagnie Française d'Afrique Occidentale (CFAO) founded in 1887 and Société Commerciale Ouest Africaine (SCOA) founded in 1906. These companies and others like them were outgrowths of the amalgamations of many smaller firms. For example the Royal Niger Company, bought by W.H. Lever, was amalgamated in 1929 to form the United Africa Company Ltd. The U.A.C. later became a subsidiary of the giant multinational called Unilever, owned by British, Dutch, and American interests. Overnight, the heavily capitalized United Africa Company was transformed into the largest single firm in the West African import-export trade. In Nigeria alone, it controlled forty percent of the import-export business. Through its Unilever connection U.A.C. spread in the 1930s into French West Africa and Portuguese Guinea. Prices eventually were coordinated among the giants in order to minimize competition and maximize profits.

After World War One in Equatorial Africa, the old concessionary companies gave way to larger industrial and plantation firms, financed by large European investors. Plantation agriculture in Gabon and the French Congo was greatly stimulated by the construction in the 1920s of the Congo-Ocean railway, connecting Brazzaville with the port of Pointe Noire. In the 1930s, the French government also gave generous subsidies to European planters cultivating cotton and palm products.

In East Africa, MacKenzie Ltd., founded in 1877, became one of the area's largest commercial firms. It concentrated on shipping as well as on tea and sisal production. Another large firm, the British East Africa Company, founded in 1906, was involved in cotton ginning in Uganda and estate agriculture in Kenya and Tanganyika. It later went bankrupt and was bought out by Mitchell Cotts, a London firm.

The big foreign companies and their monopolistic practices were formidable competition to the small African, mixed-race, and European traders. Until 1920, trade boomed and nearly everyone prospered. Then the economic depressions of 1921 and 1929–1935 eliminated much of this residual competition. Many of the great African mercantile families found it impossible to compete with the big European and British companies, which enjoyed the support of colonial governments and their affluent overseas stockholders. This retarded, but did not entirely stifle, the growth of an African bourgeoisie. In the decades after 1920, some Westernized Africans founded newspapers; others established bakeries, fleets of taxis or trucks, auto repair shops and small cafés. In the non-Muslim areas of West Africa, traditional market women expanded their retailing operations and became prosperous and influential members of their communities. Petty traders made money on the growing volume of locally manufactured goods such as cloth, blankets, woodcarvings, and in the sale of garden crops, livestock, kola nuts, and the like.

Offices of the Singer Sewing Machine Company, one of the early multinational corporations in the British Gold Coast Colony (now Ghana). Accra skyline is in background.

Control over small-scale retail and middleman trade in imported goods passed gradually into the hands of non-European immigrants. Syrians and Lebanese had begun to set up small shops in West African coastal towns in the 1890s, and Asians of Indian origin established similar retail operations in East and southern Africa at the turn of the century. Africans placed themselves at a competitive disadvantage by spending large portions of business profits on their extended families. The Asians and Lebanese, fully aware of modern bookkeeping and accounting, plowed their earnings back into inventory expansion. Like the larger European companies, they had well established sources of goods overseas, and it was easier for them to obtain credit from local banks.

These immigrant firms, almost all individually or family-owned, tended to hire only their own relatives or friends. Similarly, the European companies employed highly paid expatriates from their own countries. Corporate profits were either reinvested or remitted to overseas stockholders. Very little capital remained in Africa for reinvestment. Overall, French entrepreneurs invested less in their colonies than the British did. French-speaking consumers were comparatively less affluent, and the region was less densely populated. Corporate profits in such French colonies as Upper Volta, Niger, Chad, and Ubangui-Chari were far less than in British Gold Coast, Nigeria, or Sierra Leone. The British colonies tended to produce more, and therefore consumers had more money to spend. Nearly three-quarters of West Africa's exports came from British possessions, mainly from the Gold Coast and Nigeria.

Between the wars, transformations were made in the purchasing and marketing of export crops. African farmers in the more fertile areas formed their own producers' and cooperative societies. In some cases, they competed with established African and foreign middlemen and sold their produce directly to European companies. The cooperative movement was particularly successful in Nigeria and Tanganyika. It fared less well in Kenya and Uganda where Asians dominated the processing and marketing of many crops.

Government-operated marketing boards entered the picture during the Second World War. The British established them to ensure government control over supplies of essential raw materials. After the war the boards were expanded and granted monopoly powers to fix prices paid to producers for their crops. The idea was to guarantee the farmer a price floor, regardless of weather or world market conditions. Although the postwar commodity boom persisted far longer than anyone expected, the annual prices set by the marketing boards were invariably lower than world prices. Rather than return the accumulated money reserves to the farmers, the colonial governments used them to finance the development of infrastructure—roads, harbors, irrigation projects, and others. Reserves remaining at the time of political independence were turned over to the new governments, to be spent at their discretion.

CURRENCIES AND MONETARY SYSTEMS

Modern currencies were quickly introduced into the colonial economic systems in order to stimulate the production and export of cash crops and the importation of European manufactured goods. The monetary system of British India, based on the rupee, was formally adopted in Britain's East African possessions in 1905. Fifteen years later, as trade was directed more toward the home country, the three East African governments established a Currency Board, empowered to issue coins and notes. The connection with the rupee was then severed, and in 1922 the shilling became the unit of currency. In British West Africa, a wide variety of English coins circulated until 1912 when dstinctive currencies were established for each colony and protectorate. In French Africa this was not done until 1945.

Colonial currencies were tied to the monetary system of the home country, or metropole, to give them greater respectability and stability, and to ensure metropolitan control over as much trade with their colonies as possible. In fact, colonial monetary units mirrored those of the metropole in both name and value: Portuguese Africa's was the escudo; French-speaking Africa's, the franc; and British Africa's, the shilling.

The circulation of European currencies led to the introduction of modern banking institutions. In British West Africa, currency issuance became the monopoly of the Bank of West Africa. Banking itself was almost the sole preserve of the Bank of British West Africa (1894) and Barclay's Bank (Dominion, Colonial, and Overseas) which entered West Africa in 1926. In French West Africa, the powerful Banque de l'Afrique Occidentale (1901) controlled currency issuance and monopolized banking operations before the Second World War. In East and Central Africa, banking was dominated by National, Grindlay's, and the Banque du Congo Belge. The European-based banks usually transferred their reserves to their home countries. Consequently, the savings deposits of Africans were expatriated overseas instead of being available as loans to local entrepreneurs.

In South Africa, banking had been monopolized from the late 1860s by the more strongly capitalized British imperial banks. Small, locally based financial institutions were eliminated by such giants as the Standard Bank. A multitude of British institutions established branches in the Orange Free State and the Transvaal after the diamond and gold rushes. Until World War I, the Standard Bank, the National Bank, and the Bank of Africa controlled the issuance of notes and in so doing exerted considerable control over the country's monetary system. This changed after 1920. A government-regulated, central reserve bank was created and assumed the sole right of note issuance.

Despite the efforts to monetize African economies, the barter system remained an important form of exchange in the remote areas of the continent until after 1945. Where modern currencies were used, Africans continued to favor metallic coins over paper notes.

TRANSPORTATION AND COMMUNICATIONS

Modern transportation and communications were among the major legacies of the colonial era. Road and railway networks surpassed footpaths, creeks, and rivers as the main arteries of transportation. In West Africa, railroads completed the re-orientation of trade from the trans-Saharan routes to the Atlantic sea lanes. Africa's rapid economic growth would have been impossible without the development of efficient, inexpensive transportation and communication networks. Nearly all of them were publicly financed by loans from European governments and were built in anticipation of demand, not in response to it.

Markets and trade greatly benefited from the introduction of modern modes of transportation. Freight costs dropped considerably and the distinction between local and long-distance trade became less apparent. Produce could now profitably sell over a far greater distance than the immediate locality, and goods no longer had to be carried by slow-moving porters or pack animals. The revolution in transportation and communications is illustrated best by the fact that one train of average capacity could carry the load of thirteen thousand porters at one-twentieth the cost and seven times the speed. By telegraph, messages traveled at lightning speed between major administrative and trade centers and to the financial and commercial centers of the industrialized world. Talking drums, messengers, and ships were no longer essential to the transmission of information. These developments permitted the more effective administration of larger political and economic units. Trade and governance could now expand widely in volume and scope.

For transportation, colonial authorities initially concentrated on railroad development. Many of Africa's present networks were begun before the onset of the First World War. Railroad construction in sub-Saharan Africa began in the Cape Colony of South Africa in the early 1860s. From the 1870s and 1880s it rapidly expanded to the interior diamond and gold fields. In French West Africa railways began in Senegal in 1882, then in Guinea and Dahomey in 1900, and in the Ivory Coast three years later. The British built lines in 1896 in Sierra Leone and Nigeria. By 1911 the seaport of Lagos was linked by rail to the peanut and cotton center of Kano in the north. In the Gold Coast, two lines to the old Asante capital of Kumasi were completed in 1898; one from Sekondi through the gold-producing region, and the other from the old surf port of Accra into the burgeoning cocoa lands of Asante. In East Africa, the Uganda Railway extended from the ancient Swahili port of Mombasa to Kisumu by 1901 and ultimately to Kampala, Uganda's capital, three decades later. The Germans in neighboring Tanganyika developed a series of excellent surveys for an ambitious railroad and harbor infrastructure based on Dar es Salaam. Rail laying for the Central and Usambara lines began in 1893, and by 1914 the former had reached Kigoma. It was extended by the British to Arusha in 1929. By then, Dar es Salaam and Mombasa, serving as vital rail termini, had surpassed Zanzibar as the gateways to East Africa's interior. Between 1890 and 1898 King Leopold's concessionaires in the Congo employed nearly seven thousand overseas laborers to build a railroad from the lower to upper Congo River. A private British firm built the Benguela Railway which ran from the copper mines of the Congo's southern Katanga province across Angola to the former Atlantic slaving port of Benguela. Some of the railroads turned a profit, stimulated exports, and generated capital for investment in ancillary projects. In human terms, the construction of these lines took the lives of literally thousands of workers, from Africa, India, China, Europe, and the Americas.

Attention shifted in the 1920s to the construction of vehicular routes to act as feeders for the railroads. Unlike the latter, they were usually financed out of colonial budgets. These new roads opened the way to bicycles, which soon became an important transportation mode for workers and peasants.

Railroads also led to the concentration of shipping into the larger, deepwater ports. Into the pages of history passed such precolonial ports as Benin's Gwato, Dahomey's Whydah, Ivory Coast's Grand Bassam, the Niger Delta's Calabar and Bonny, and many more. After the 1920s colonial governments spent large sums on modern dock construction. Man-made structures were necessary in a continent so lacking in natural deep-water harbors. The vibrant new ports were impressive: in French West Africa, Dakar and Abidjan; in British West Africa, Sekondi-Takoradi, Lagos, and Port Harcourt; in French Equatorial Africa, Libreville and Pointe Noire; in the Belgian Congo, Matadi; in Portuguese Africa, Lobito-Benguela and Beira; in South Africa, Durban, Port Elizabeth, East London, and Cape Town; and in East Africa, Dar es Salaam and Mombasa.

Shipping from the colonial ports was dominated by a small number of firms which received generous government subsidies. The bulk of freight in West Africa was handled by either the Elder Dempster Line or the German Woermann Line. French shipping was mainly in the hands of a few Marseilles firms, and in East and southern Africa the powerful Union Castle Line predominated. Shipping companies coordinated their activities by forming monopolistic conference lines and fixing freight rates among themselves. The companies usually cooperated with the larger trading firms and gave them preference in shipping freight. Smaller independent lines found it extremely difficult to compete. The capital necessary to establish a profitable operation was so great as to exclude virtually any African participation.

African endeavor was more successful in the development of a local press. Most newspapers in colonial Africa before World War I were subsidiaries of European chains, and their news reflected Western opinion and events. Few Africans were literate and therefore the papers' readers were mostly Europeans. This began to change in the postwar period with the astounding growth in African literacy rates. Local presses appeared in the 1920s in colonies with sizeable Western-educated elites. African-owned newspapers blossomed in Senegal, the Ivory Coast, Togo, the Gold Coast, and Nigeria. The Nigerian press magnate, N. Azikiwe, founded the *West African Pilot* in the late 1930s. Within another decade he built a vast newspaper chain which included the *Pilot,* the *Daily Comet,* and the *Guardian.* In the late 1940s and early 1950s, supporters of the Gold Coast nationalist leader, Kwame Nkrumah, set up the Accra *Evening News,* the Sekondi *Morning Telegraph,* and the Cape Coast *Daily Mail.* These papers were politically oriented, and their editorial pages attacked colonialism's injustices and contradictions.

African journalism developed much earlier in South Africa. The father of black newspapers was John Tengo Jabavu, who founded *Imvo* in 1884. *Imvo* became an overnight success as an influential instrument of African protest and remained in operation through the 1970s. In 1903 the American-educated John Dube began *Ilanga Lase Natal* (in Zulu and English). By 1976 its circulation had exceeded 150,000.

A turning point in the history of the black press in South Africa was reached in 1932 with the establishment of the *Bantu World.* Within four years it had bought up four African papers including *Imvo* and *Ilanga.* The *Bantu World* became the most widely read African newspaper in the country. It was complemented in the 1950s by the appearance of the magazine *Drum,* which published the works of many of South Africa's leading writers and music critics. By 1961 it had a distribution throughout the continent.

Unfortunately, the black community lost a large measure of journalistic independence in the early 1960s when the white-owned Argus newspaper chain purchased a controlling interest in the Bantu Press Ltd. holdings. The *Bantu World* was converted from a weekly to a daily and became less political and more entertainment-oriented.

The most surprising feature of the press in British and French Africa during the colonial period was the degree of its journalistic independence. Many African editors and owners of papers were actively involved in nationalist movements and used their publications to promote independence. Only rarely did colonial governments engage in massive censorship or attempt to close a newspaper because of its anticolonial views.

African influence in broadcasting journalism was far more limited; and broadcasting, almost always a government-owned activity, developed more slowly. South Africa was the scene of early radio. The African Broadcasting Company was formed in 1927 by domestic motion picture and theatrical interests. It was a private monopoly, catering almost exclusively to the urban English-speaking population. The Afrikaner resented this and in 1936 the company's license was not renewed. In its place emerged the government-sponsored South African Broadcasting Corporation (SABC), which would provide service in English and Afrikaans languages. Broadcasting soon became a major element in the English-Afrikaner struggle for political and cultural hegemony. At first a symbol of English cultural dominance, the South African Broadcasting Corporation gradually fell under Afrikaner control and became an instrument of Afrikaner political and cultural objectives.

One of the earliest stations was Radio Bantu, founded in South Africa in 1940, with programming in three African languages. The station, under strong white influence, avoided sensitive political issues and concentrated on traditional music and light comedy.

Large-scale broadcasting in French Africa began during the Second World War when de Gaulle's Free French Movement constructed a powerful transmitter at Brazzaville in Equatorial Africa. Its major wartime role was to broadcast news to partisans in Nazi-held France. After the war, the Brazzaville station beamed to much of French colonial Africa, and it remains today one of the continent's most powerful stations. Radio had only a limited direct impact on the African masses, because few people could afford to purchase sets or to pay the annual government licensing fees. Moreover, only the largest towns had the electricity necessary for reception.

Civilian air transportation was quite late in developing. Before World War Two, the only significant passenger airlines based in sub-Saharan Africa were government-owned Mozambique Airlines (1936), Angola Airlines (1938), the

Rhodesia and Nyasaland Airways (1933), and South African Airways (1934). A conscientious program of airport construction did not commence until the height of the War when bases were needed for ferrying men and materiel to the North African and Italian fronts. Large military airstrips were hastily built outside Freetown, Sierra Leone; Monrovia, Liberia; Accra, Gold Coast; Maiduguri, Nigeria. They were also established in Kenya, the Belgian Congo, the Rhodesias and South Africa. Civilian air transportation in the postwar period assumed responsibility for many of these bases, and the larger national airlines of the mother countries extended their routes, pioneered in the late 1920s, to the major cities of their colonial possessions. For example, the British Overseas Airways Corporation (formerly Imperial Airways) expanded in the British territories; Air France and Union de Transports Aeriens (UTA) in the French; Portuguese Air Transport (TAP) to Portuguese Africa; Sabena to the Belgian Congo and so on. The route between Africa and the Americas fell to Pan American Airways, a private firm based in the United States. In some cases, airlines established subsidiaries or management arrangements with nominally African lines. BOAC's East African Airways (1946) serviced mainly Kenya, Uganda and Tanganyika; Central Africa Airways (1946), the Central African Federation of Northern and Southern Rhodesia and Nyasaland; and Ethiopian Airways (1945) became affiliated with Trans World Airlines of the United States in 1946 and flew overseas.

LAND AND LABOR

By right of conquest or treaty, the European powers assumed from the traditional African authorities ultimate sovereignty over their land. Many kings, chiefs, and priests lost their constitutional right to allocate land and to control its exploitation. In reality, in the areas where traditional authorities had considerable power, land allocation continued to be under their control as long as it did not conflict with colonial objectives. After the 1890s Great Britain declared millions of square miles of land as "crown lands" and placed them under the nominal control of the British monarch. In the Gold Coast as elsewhere, efforts to place so-called unoccupied lands at the disposal of the colonial government were fiercely resisted by local leaders. It was an issue which in 1897 brought Western-educated Africans and traditional chiefs together into an organization called The Aboriginals Rights Protection Society. Their successful petition to the British crown a year later established the principle that West African colonial governments must not have the power to alienate land in Africa to Europeans. Consequently, British West Africa was closed to permanent white settlement. The same principle prevailed in French West Africa, though it was not always conscientiously applied. All "vacant" land was declared state property in 1904 and reserved for peasant farming. Yet in time European companies obtained concessions in Guinea for banana plantations and in the Ivory Coast for timber and coffee. The French also alienated a considerable amount of land in Gabon, Middle-Congo, and Ubangui-Chari to private concessionaires in return for payment of a rental fee and a percentage of their gross profits. There, and in King Leopold's neighboring Congo Independent State, European companies gained full rights to exploit the natural resources, and Africans lost the benefit of selling, under free market conditions, the crops they grew on their ancestral lands. All production henceforth belonged to the holder of the given concession.

In Kenya, Southern Rhodesia, and South Africa, Africans lost not only their crops but their right to occupy the lands of their ancestors. In 1901 a British Order-in-Council legalized the alienation of land in the fertile and temperate highlands of Kenya to white settlers. A year later, much of Kenya was declared "crown lands," for public, not private use. The Foreign Office, however, violated this principle by issuing ninety-nine-year leases of African land along the railroad. They did this to enable the colonial government and the British-built Uganda Railway to achieve financial self-sufficiency. The principle of crown lands was further abused in 1915 when a new ordinance permitted the lease of urban lands for ninety-nine years and extended agricultural leases to nine hundred ninety-nine years. Nomadic Masai pastoralists and sedentary Kikuyu cultivators in the so-called "white highlands" were evicted from their lands and forced into reserves, which in time became overpopulated. A land commission in 1932 in effect denied Africans access to any lands in the white highlands. Little was done to change this until 1959, even though the British government had pledged that "native interests shall always be paramount in Kenya."[1]

Land in neighboring Uganda received different treatment. The Buganda Agreement of 1900 created a permanent landed aristocracy by converting communal lands into privately held, freehold tracts and awarding them to loyal chiefs. This European-style land tenure system was applied later to other Ugandan kingdoms. Unlike Kenya, the productive land remained in African hands and the protectorate did not fall victim to permanent white settlement.

Southern Rhodesia more closely resembled the Kenya pattern. African reserves were first established in 1894 and officially designated in 1924 as Tribal Trust Lands. As in Kenya and South Africa, the reserves encompassed the most densely populated and often least fertile lands. In time, they became pools of surplus labor for the benefit of white farmers and industrialists. The Land Apportionment Act of 1930 set up "native purchase areas" for Africans wishing to acquire their own farms on a freehold basis. Finally, the Native Land Husbandry Act of 1951 sought to convert all the lands in the reserves from communal to individual freehold tenure.

---

[1] George Bennett, *Kenya: A Political History* (London: Oxford University Press, 1963), p. 61.

In the Union of South Africa, the idea of territorial segregation as a national policy was applied legislatively in 1913 under the Native Land Act. It established a series of native reserves in which the traditional principle of communal land ownership prevailed and where Europeans were barred from purchasing land. Africans were forbidden to acquire land in the remaining eighty-six percent of the country. The latter was set aside for exclusive white settlement and exploitation. From an economic point of view, native reserves in colonial Africa were woefully inadequate in terms of natural resources and territorial extent. They condemned Africans to a condition of underdevelopment. Because no provision was made to expand the reserves as population increased, many Africans had to seek employment in the white-controlled areas. The 1913 Land Act remained unaltered until 1936 when more land was promised but little was actually added. Through these acts of parliament, the whites constructed a legal framework around their occupation of South African lands and laid the groundwork for *de jure* racial segregation. The nearly three hundred years of struggle between blacks and whites for the land had been brought to a close as far as the government was concerned.

Africans gravitated towards the towns in search of a livelihood. Under the 1923 Urban Areas Act they could purchase land only on the outskirts of the white towns, in special "native locations." Amendments in 1937 and 1957 specifically barred them from buying property in "white" areas outside the locations in order to prevent the growth of African vested interests in white-governed towns.

In many regions of the continent, land alienation provided a fundamental source of grievance. Indeed, "land rights" remained one of the most potent emotional questions of the colonial era. Among Africans, it generated feelings of unity, common purpose, and identity, and was a major element of protest.

Forced labor, so much a part of the colonial scene, was actually rooted in the precolonial past. In the empires and kingdoms of Africa, rulers compelled common folk to devote a portion of their time to work on public projects. They could also be called upon to serve in the armed forces. The servile population toiled in the mines and labored on the agricultural estates of their masters. In 1901 the French and British abolished the legal status of slavery. Actually, domestic, or household slavery historically had been comparatively benign and humane. It was the bondage of the prisoners of war in precolonial Africa which was so brutal, for few of them found their way into the compounds of their masters. Commonly, they lived in remote, segregated villages and worked in the fields. All people born after 1901 were free, but slave owners were not forced to liberate immediately people already in bondage. The Europeans feared such a requirement might create economic chaos. In Northern Nigeria in the old Sokoto Caliphate, the British reasoned it would also alienate the Fulani aristocracy, whose support was so essential in the formative years of colonial rule.

The French also balked at the idea of rapid liberation. During the period of conquest, their African mercenaries were allowed to take captives from conquered villages. Denying the mercenaries their booty risked losing necessary military collaboration. Moreover, the French colonial administration had earlier retained liberated slaves to meet its own manpower needs. "Liberty villages" were established supposedly as refugee settlements for liberated slaves. In practice, they became reservoirs of forced labor for French commandants. Even though these villages had been eliminated by 1910, domestic slavery, or servitude, persisted in much of French Africa until the Second World War. The Germans, too, displayed a rather nonchalant attitude toward involuntary servitude. Every child born after 1906 was free, but those already in bondage remained so for years afterward.

Forced labor, institutionalized in the precolonial monarchies, was applied on a far wider scale during the colonial era. While domestic servitude gradually died out, forced labor thrived. Compulsory labor was practiced most widely in the Portuguese possessions. There, colonial authorities argued that Africans could only become "civilized through work." Portugal itself never had an industrial revolution or a humanitarian movement. Its labor laws were consequently harsh and archaic. Labor recruitment practices bordered on slavery, and workers were in effect "bought" by white plantation managers and mining companies. The colonial authorities often acted as recruiters and supervisors of contract labor for private employers. The situation improved somewhat after 1926 when forced labor was limited to public works projects and punishment for crimes. Nevertheless, the practice was not entirely abolished until 1960.

Forced labor was also common in the neighboring Congo. After freeing the slaves from the Arabs in the 1890s, King Leopold's state retained them in compulsory employment for more than seven years. Missionaries and other foreign observers revealed numerous atrocities against African laborers being committed by the King's concessionaires. Thousands of Africans were compelled to work on the European rubber plantations without wages and under conditions reminiscent of the worst forms of ante-bellum slavery in the American South. By 1906 world attention was focused on this murderous situation and sweeping reforms followed. King Leopold lost his exclusive right to the Congo in 1908 when his responsibilities were transferred to the Belgian parliament. Even though labor practices became less savage, Africans continued to be compelled to cultivate certain cash crops, serve in the militia, and to donate their labor for public works.

The Germans in their colonies also resorted to forced labor practices. In German East Africa, the Maji Maji rebellion of 1905 was partly in protest against the compulsory planting of cotton and the use of former Arab slavers as plantation overseers. The rebellion was ruthlessly suppressed by machine guns and scorched-earth techniques, but it did force a reassessment of colonial labor policy and the creation of a civilian administration.

In French Equatorial Africa, peasants were told to gather rubber or risk flogging, bodily mutilation, or imprisonment. Also in the early days of colonialism, the French authorities in West Africa forcibly conscripted labor for use on privately owned plantations. The French in West Africa were more inclined than their British neighbors towards forced labor because the former ruled over a territory larger in area and less densely populated. With the exception of the coastal colonies, it lacked a labor base sufficient for the construction and maintenance of public projects. The interior colonies also were too poor to afford salaried laborers.

Under French colonial laws, every male between age eighteen and sixty was compelled to contribute a certain number of days of labor to the state. The obligation could either be fulfilled in person or, in some cases, one could purchase a replacement. During the two world wars the French and British conscripted thousands of Africans into the military, to serve overseas or to work in local mines or on state-sponsored projects. Many Africans deeply resented this, and in various areas the colonial governments found themselves quelling riotous protests.

In British and French Africa the actual recruitment of labor remained the responsibility of the traditional authorities, in order to minimize indigenous resistance. The chiefs usually bypassed men from the upper ranks of society and drew mainly from the formerly servile class.

Forced labor in French Africa, though abolished in 1946, had encouraged many men to escape it by migrating to other territories. This was particularly true in West Africa where the development of commercial agriculture in the southern forest zone further encouraged the redistribution of population toward the coast.

The colonial era accelerated earlier migratory patterns and created new ones. There was a large increase in the seasonal migration of laborers, especially from poorer colonies such as Niger, Upper Volta, and Sudan (Mali) to the more fertile colonies of the Gold Coast, Nigeria, and even to Senegal and the Ivory Coast. Climatic zones in West Africa are such that the unproductive dry season in the savanna coincides with the peak season of crop production in the southern forest. The major demand for labor is agricultural and therefore seasonal. Migration to the Ivory Coast accelerated from the 1950s when the colony's plantation economy and light industries grew rapidly. Labor became scarcer in the north, and the Sudan, Niger, and Upper Volta colonies fell further behind their coastal neighbors in economic development.

Initially, most migrant laborers in Africa were seasonal and on temporary contracts. Over the years, the rate of return to home declined in some areas as employment opportunities expanded, especially in the urban centers. In 1927 Union Minière de Haut-Katanga in the Belgian Congo was the first to change its labor policies from emphasis on migratory to permanent labor. Mining companies on Northern Rhodesia's copperbelt followed in the 1940s. By contrast, South African patterns of oscillating migration increased. By 1936 the South

African Chamber of Mines employed over 300,000 blacks, of whom forty percent were from the Transkei and Ciskei Native Reserves, twenty-five percent from Portuguese Mozambique and nearly fifteen percent from Basutoland. White farms also required a large seasonal labor force and also recruited over a wide area. This prevented agriculture in the reserves from developing because many able-bodied men were absent from their farms for varying periods.

In West Africa, labor became more stabilized as a result of land in some areas shifting out of the hands of the community and into individual ownership. Peasants could now sell their holdings and invest the money elsewhere. Previously, under conditions of communal land tenure, migratory labor was more oscillating. Migrants had periodically returned to their farms in order to ensure that the local authorities would not allocate them to a more diligent member of the community.

At this point, the question might be asked why Africans were so anxious to enter the cash economy. Certainly, it was partly the prospect of earning money for food, clothing, shelter, and luxuries. Some were target workers, who labored only long enough to earn sufficient money to pay a bride price back home or to acquire a bicycle or some other specific object. They also were driven into the capitalist labor market in order to pay taxes demanded by colonial regimes. In Kenya, Southern Rhodesia, and South Africa, taxes, plus the dispossession of their lands, forced many Africans to sell their labor power to Europeans. Kenya followed South Africa in enacting a Masters and Servants Ordinance which stated that if a worker broke his contract by leaving before the agreed time, he risked imprisonment. In both countries, laws stipulated that Africans residing on European lands could pay their rents only in labor, not in cash. This was because many European farmers were experiencing shortages of labor.

The colonial regimes attempted to control the increasing migration, particularly to the urban and mining centers. The pass system, which had been in effect in South Africa since the early nineteenth century, was adopted in other colonial areas. This system aimed at directing and controlling migrant labor for the benefit of white employers and complemented the native reserve system. Africans outside the reserve and not in white employment were considered vagrants. With the pass, which was in effect an identity and employment document, a person could be tracked down, punished, and possibly returned to his employer.

Colonial governments at first actively discouraged the formation of labor unions for fear they would put an end to one of the colonial era bulwarks: cheap labor. Until the 1930s neither the British or French recognized the right of Africans to form trade unions or to strike as a legitimate means of coercing employers to improve working conditions and wages. After the 1920s, as wages failed to rise commensurately with the cost of living, colonial governments were faced with numerous strikes.

Trade unionism on a massive scale began in South Africa in 1919 when Africans formed the Industrial and Commercial Workers Union (ICU) under the leadership of Clements Kadalie. Its branches spread like wildfire through South Africa, the Rhodesias, and Nyasaland. At first whites tolerated the ICU but the 1924 elections brought to power a coalition government strongly influenced by the Labor Party and the Afrikaner Nationalist Party. Almost immediately, efforts were made to strengthen the position of the white, mainly Afrikaner, workers. The Industrial Conciliation Act of 1924 provided for the registration and regulation of trade unions. Africans were denied entrance to the registered unions yet could not petition to have their own unions registered. Most Africans also were excluded from the definition of "employee." The ICU continued to grow and reached a membership exceeding 200,000 by 1928. It may have grown too fast, for factions began to develop within the organization, and new government legislation weakened its effectiveness. Within two years the union had nearly collapsed, its various branches quarreling among each other and its membership falling away.

The Native Labour Act of 1953 further damaged the position of black workers by preventing white unions from accepting any nonwhite members. Wage differentials also remained racially biased. In 1948 the government reaffirmed a policy established in 1924 ensuring that white workers would be paid at higher rates than nonwhites doing similar work. The principle of job reservation was enshrined in the Industrial Conciliation Act of 1956 which set aside certain types of work for whites only. The position of the black worker was further eroded that year with the creation of the all-white Trade Union Council of South Africa (TUCSA). The fact that nonwhites continued to be denied equal labor rights was revealed in 1961 statistics indicating that only 1.9 percent of the African population was recognized as having any union affiliation.

Trade unionism in tropical Africa did not become a potent force until after World War II, when inflation and inadequate urban housing began to cause considerable hardship. The Trade Union Congress of the Gold Coast was almost indistinguishable from Nkrumah's Convention Peoples Party. They shared common goals and almost identical membership. The trade union movement in Nigeria was not linked as closely to the struggle for independence and lacked the unity of purpose so evident in the Gold Coast. In French West Africa, trade unions at first were affiliated with those of the home country. In 1957 the majority of these unions joined to form the Union Général des Travailleurs d'Afrique Noire (UGTAN), under the leadership of Sekou Touré. For the first time, union activity was firmly in African hands. Throughout French Africa, the Overseas Labor Code of 1952 guaranteed workers and their trade unions minimum wages, work hours, and collective bargaining akin to that of workers in France. Trade unionism in East Africa did not become a powerful force until after 1953 with the formation of the Kenya Federation of Labour under the dynamic leadership of Tom Mboya.

TAXATION AND REVENUE

Since the early nineteenth century, the major economic objective of the colonial powers was to stimulate the exportation of raw materials and the importation of European manufactured goods for local consumption. Export production was needed to provide a tax base capable of covering the cost of colonial administration. In colonial West Africa this was achieved largely through African peasant farming, in East and southern Africa through white estate agriculture, and in central Africa through European concessions. Europeans reasoned that if Africans had to pay taxes in cash, they would be forced either to produce commercial crops for export or to sell their labor to those prepared to do so. To the British mind, and to a lesser extent the French, economic development should be supported out of customs and excise duties, local taxes, and if necessary, supplemented by loans serviced from local revenues or floated on the London or Paris stock markets. The British, especially, adhered to their mid-Victorian belief that the colonies must be financially self-supporting and should not be a burden to the budget of the home country.

The taxation rate in French West Africa was higher than that of their British neighbors because the former possessed fewer known resources and a smaller population. Direct taxation, already a feature of precolonial Muslim states, was retained in much of Islamic British and French West Africa. After the First World War British colonial authorities encountered stiff resistance when the practice was extended to the non-Muslim southern and western regions of Nigeria. The Aba Womens' Riot of 1929–1930 was one of the most vehement expressions of this opposition. It was reminiscent of the Bambata Rebellion of 1906 in Natal, which was triggered by attempts to introduce a poll tax on the Zulu. Indeed, resistance to direct taxation dated to the Hut Tax War in Sierra Leone in the 1890s.

Throughout colonial Africa, indirect taxes were levied on crops, minerals, and overseas trade. To handle the rapid growth in revenue, colonial governments established regularized treasuries and modern accounting procedures. Colonies were expected to, and usually did, balance their annual budgets. In British West Africa huge sterling reserves were built up and then drained to help finance the Second World War. After the war, monetary reserves were restored.

From 1904 to 1957 nearly all the colonies of French Africa were linked into one of two federations: French West Africa or French Equatorial Africa, with their respective capitals at Dakar and Brazzaville. Responsibility for revenue and taxation in the various component colonies rested with the federation government. After the Loi Cadre of 1956, the federations were liquidated and fiscal responsibility was transferred to each colony, now renamed a territory. Fiscal responsibility always had prevailed in British West Africa where each colony handled its own budget. In East Africa, Kenya and Uganda had enjoyed a free trade and customs arrangement since 1917. After the war, the move towards closer economic union gathered further momentum. In 1932 the postal services and customs of Kenya, Uganda, and Tanganyika were united. This led to the formation of the East African High Commission in 1948. The commission assumed from the three governments responsibility for posts and telegraphs, railroads and harbors, customs, currency, and other noneconomic services. In central Africa, the economic resources of the Rhodesias and Nyasaland were in many ways complementary: Northern Rhodesia had industry and mining; Southern Rhodesia, agriculture and manufacturing; and Nyasaland, manpower. A Central African Federation was created in 1953 but Southern Rhodesian whites soon came to dominate it. Most of the wealth was produced from Northern Rhodesia's copperbelt, yet most of the revenues collected from the three states went toward development in Southern Rhodesia. By 1963 the federation had collapsed.

Before the Second World War, total British capital investment in West Africa was considerably greater than the French. This was reversed in the postwar period, even though after 1940 both colonial powers had abandoned the principle of colonial self-sufficiency and had undertaken the financing of most investments, particularly in the development of transportation infrastructure in urban areas. Dakar became the third largest port in the entire French empire. Abidjan also rose from obscurity and became a major West African port.

British public investment was made primarily through machinery set up by the Colonial Development and Welfare Acts of 1940 and 1945. After 1946, the French operated out of the Fonds pour l'Investissement pour le Development Economique et Sociale (FIDES). It is said that FIDES invested more capital in French West Africa from 1946 to 1960 than the total public and private contribution in the 1903–1946 period. The postwar era marked the commencement of a new chapter in African economic development, one in which the metropolitan governments extended direct assistance to their colonial possessions.

POPULATION, DISEASE AND HEALTH

The colonial era marked the beginning of an explosive population increase. For example, between 1898 and 1963 the African population of Rhodesia (Zimbabwe) grew from 450,000 to just over four million. Even more dramatic was the growth in the African population of the Union of South Africa. Between 1911 and 1960 it climbed from four million to nearly eleven million. By contrast, declines accelerated in the populations of the bushmen and pygmies. These two groups, which formed the majority of sub-Saharan Africa's population before 1 A.D. were a tiny minority centuries before the colonial era.[2] Standards of health care, including sanitation, greatly improved in some areas, and there were

[2] Colin McEvedy and Richard Jones, *Atlas of World Population History* (London: Penguin Books Ltd., 1978), p. 209.

successful vaccination campaigns to reduce the incidence of such infectious diseases as measles, smallpox, and yellow fever. Prophylactics against malaria reduced its morbidity, but the conditon itself continued to be widespread. Birth rates slowly climbed, while death rates dropped dramatically, particularly among infants. Medical research and services grew enormously after World War II, with emphasis on prevention. This all is reflected in the rate of population increase, from only 0.6 percent in 1900-1930, to 1.3 percent between 1930 and 1950 and to a colossal 2.5 percent by 1960. Despite the dramatic increase, little attention was paid to the problem of overpopulation or demographical maldistribution. Family planning programs were virtually nonexistent, and few demographers seemed alarmed that the unevenness of the population was becoming more marked as people moved into the urban areas. Urban life-expectancy rates soared and people had more to eat, yet the nutritional level of many Africans actually declined. Kwashiorkor, a severe form of malnutrition, became more prevalent in Sahelian regions. In the areas of mineral extraction, especially in Northern Rhodesia and South Africa, the incidence of tuberculosis rose significantly. In the burgeoning cities, the rate of venereal disease soared. Ironically, nutritional levels were found in some cases to be higher among subsistence farmers, nomadic pastoralists, and hunters and gatherers than among those producing commercial crops for European markets. The so-called "primitive" societies often had better nutrition and a lower incidence of iron deficiency than populations living on a predominantly cereal or high carbohydrate diet. The colonial era brought better health care. Much still had to be done in the area of nutrition.

The colonial era was also marked by the growth of large European residential populations, especially in regions of cool climate, rich soil or large mineral deposits. Immigration to the Portuguese possessions was stimulated by government subsidies. Elsewhere, whites were lured by cheap indigenous labor and the prospect of high profits.[3]

By 1960, there were nearly 215,000 Portuguese settlers in Angola and 160,000 in Mozambique. The white population of the Union of South Africa advanced from 1.2 million in 1911 to more than 3.0 million five decades later. On the eve of independence in the Belgian Congo there were 110,000 Europeans, in East Africa they numbered over 92,000 and in the Federation of Rhodesia and Nyasaland the census revealed some 308,000, most of them in what is today called Zimbabwe.[4]

Commercial opportunities brought Indians to East and South Africa. In the Union of South Africa alone, they numbered over 477,000 by 1960. The growing presence of these non-African populations heightened racial tensions and intensified patterns of geo-political segregation.

[3] L.H. Gann and P. Duignan, *White Settlers in Tropical Africa* (Harmondsworth: Penguin Books Ltd., 1962), pp. 159-170.

[4] Leonard M. Thompson, *Politics: The Republic of South Africa* (Boston: Little, Brown and Company, 1966), p. 30.

chapter 6

Patterns of Culture

THE IMPACT OF CHRISTIANITY AND ISLAM

Classical African religions survived the colonial era, but in many cases they were strongly influenced and modified by Christian and Muslim concepts. Converts from the old faith took some traditional beliefs with them which resulted in a gradual mixing of ideas. There was a weakening of the belief that animals, plants, stones, and the like possessed a conscious life and were inhabited by spiritual forces which could influence man's destiny. Ancestor veneration persisted but with less intensity. Witchcraft, sorcery, and sacrifices waxed and waned, depending on the degree of colonial trauma. The influence of traditional ritual leaders—divine-right monarchs, magicians, rainmakers, and cult priests and priestesses generally declined. The humiliating defeat of these leaders had a demoralizing and traumatic effect. Many priests and priestesses had promised European defeat if the people would only take up arms against the whites. One after another they failed and their credibility was reduced: the Mwari priests in Matabeleland and Mashonaland in 1896, the Maji-Maji priests in Tanzania in 1905, and so on. When local gods and their intermediaries failed, people lost confidence. Some groups fled to other areas. For example, a number of Muslim Fulani families emigrated from the disintegrating Sokoto Caliphate to the Nile Valley rather than face the prospect of Western civilization and British rule. In a few isolated cases, people committed suicide or engaged in deadly human sacrifice. In 1897 Oba Ovonramwen of Benin forced the death of many of his subjects through human sacrifice in desperate hope this would invoke the ancestors into intervening against the imminent British conquest. Many in Africa, however, turned to the white man's god and to the missionaries. Christianity provided through its educational institutions, a method for coping with the political and economic conditions of colonialism.

The Christian missionaries were in a sense a revolutionary force in colonial Africa. They appealed to the downtrodden and social outcasts—the lepers, former slaves, and nonconformists. These people had nothing to lose by embracing the new faith. They gained inspiration, hope, and confidence from the notions of equality and brotherhood and from the idea that one must not fatalistically accept his or her station in life as beyond human control. The missionaries placed emphasis on the individual rather than merely on the collectivity. They also told Africans that life could be separated into spiritual and secular spheres. This concept ran counter to traditional patterns of authority, and not surprisingly many rulers initially resisted missionary intrusions.

Christianity also reduced people's fear of magical and supernatural forces. It encouraged people to innovate and to question things that previously had been regarded as under the control of spiritual entities. Missionaries looked the other way when colonial engineers built roads through "sacred" or "evil" forests. Local rulers, who often gave missionaries land in areas supposedly occupied by malevolent forces, were shocked to discover that their churches and schools thrived where people formerly had feared to tread.

With financial support from home and through profits made from their own local business enterprises and farms, missionaries built churches, schools, and medical clinics. Their knowledge of modern medical science undermined somewhat the traditional healers, even though the latter's herbal medicines and psychological counseling techniques often were remarkably effective. In a sense, Christian teachings were a force for continuity in that they supported the traditional African view that a connection existed between physical and spiritual illness. It may be for this reason that Africans never have become completely divorced from precolonial patterns of faith-healing and magical thought.

European missionaries often demanded total conversion. They encouraged converts to cut themselves off from "pagan" customs, to adopt Christian names and Western clothing, to reject ancestor veneration and old taboos. Traditional musical instruments and art, particularly sculpture, were confiscated and sometimes shipped off to European ethnographic museums or sold to private collectors.

Clearly, Christianity presented a serious challenge to African civilization and to indigenous faiths. By 1905, nearly every sect and denomination in America, Britain, and Europe had established itself in tropical Africa. Some missionaries argued that Christianity was a "civilizing" force which inoculated Africans against both traditional "primitivism" and the inevitable force of Western secularism.

Most Africans, even enthusiastic Christian converts, never completely abandoned their traditional beliefs and practices. According to Michael Crowder and J.F. Ade Ajayi, "Ethical and aesthetic values continued to be shaped to a large extent more by the traditional values of the old religions than by Christianity."[1]

[1] J.F.A. Ajayi and Michael Crowder, eds., *History of West Africa* (New York: Columbia University Press, 1974), p. 516.

Some rituals continued to be important even though the participants no longer believed in their ritual basis. Though ceremonies were increasingly divorced from the religions that produced them, they continued to reaffirm community solidarity. Festivals still were held at planting and harvesting time, sacrifices were offered to appropriate fertility deities, and people occasionally sought the advice of traditional religious leaders when problems could not be solved by other means. Some ethnic groups, the Igbo for example, continued to believe that every person possesses a personal *chi,* or spirit, which affects his life. Christianity only gradually became integrated into local culture and as it did, both it and the traditional religions lost a degree of their orthodoxy.

Almost from the beginning of the modern colonial era, many Africans attempted to form their own, independent church movements. The process of church separatism began in 1892 when the so-called "Ethiopian" church was formed and sought links with the African Methodist Episcopal Church, founded in the United States by black Americans. Separatist churches represented African efforts to localize Christianity, and to remove Christian teachings from the abstract formalism imposed by the growing number of European missionaries. Some separatist churches were "break-aways" from established mission churches; others were started completely independent of preexisting religious groups. Most of them tolerated a large measure of traditional African beliefs and practices, especially polygamy, ancestor worship, and the extended family. They tried to incorporate African ideas of worship into Christian liturgies, in other words, to fit Christianity into the African context. An important feature of these churches was the emphasis on healing and divine revelation through visions and dreams. Adherents continued to believe that supernatural forces lay at the base of physical and psychic malaise. They were convinced that sorcery and witchcraft were still potent activities and should be neutralized or destroyed.

Separatist church movements were in part a reaction to the spreading social disequilibrium and transformations. Colonialism injected Western values into African society. The increasing monetization and commercialization of the economy led to indigenous capital accumulation and a stronger emphasis on materialism and individualism. This resulted in social upheaval as new groups, notably women and the formerly nonfree people, moved into positions previously denied them. This, along with urbanization, led to intense competition and to a weakening of family ties. Messianic movements, among other things, sought to reestablish old norms and community and family cohesion.

There were a wide variety of independent churches, ranging from those which were modernizing and desirous of emulating missionary forms and organization, to others which were prophetic, faith-healing, and atavistic-millennarian. The latter promised a divine intervention which would drive whites away and place their wealth and power in black hands.

Break-away churches were in part a reaction to colonialism and the domination of Europeans over religious, economic, and political life. They were most prolific in areas of intense political suppression and where Europeans had settled in large numbers. Break-away churches were attractive to African nationalists because in most colonies they, as well as the established churches, were the only legally permitted vehicles for attacking colonial rule. Separatist church movements were linked to the emergence and growth of African nationalism. They were a school for nationalist leadership, providing a platform for addressing and organizing large numbers of people. Georges Balandier, an authority on the subject, saw separatist church movements as a transferral of political reactions to the level of religious activities. He viewed religion as a smokescreen for politics.

Separatist churches grew rapidly in number and size from the early years of the First World War to the mid-1930s. In some cases, they were viewed as a threat to colonial rule, and their leaders were suppressed. In Nyasaland (now Malawi) John Chilembwe, an American-educated separatist church leader, attacked the colonial practices of taxation and military recruitment, and established a number of independent churches and schools with strong political overtones. In 1915 he was killed while leading an abortive rebellion against British rule. The same period witnessed the growth of the Watchtower movement. In the 1920s and early 1930s, domestic servants from Nyasaland carried the movement to the rural Shona in Southern Rhodesia. There, it became a significant political and religious movement. In Northern Rhodesia, immediately after World War I, millenarian preachers of the Kitawalan movement predicted the imminent end of the world and the total collapse of colonialism. The Kitawala movement was an offshoot of the Watchtower movement which was an African-organized branch of the Jehovah's Witnesses. The only major separatist church movement in French West Africa was Protestant and founded by a Liberian, William Wade Harris. Between 1913 and 1915, the year of his expulsion from French possessions, he won nearly 100,000 converts, mainly in the Ivory Coast. In the early 1920s Simon Kimbangu led a break-away church movement which he centered in lower Zaire. His followers refused to pay taxes to the Belgian regime and threatened to withhold their labor. Fearing a major uprising, Kimbangu was arrested and remained in prison until his death in 1951. Kimbanguism continued to win adherents on both sides of the Congo River. The movement itself was a reaction to a combination of traumas brought on by colonialism: forced labor, the death of more than half the Bakongo population from sleeping sickness, and the weakening of Bakongo ethnic particularism. At the other end of Zaire, in Katanga region, the Mwana Lesa (son of God) movement began in 1925 after first appearing in Northern Rhodesia. Its leader was deported to Northern Rhodesia where he was hanged in 1926. These movements and others like them were doomed to failure because of their provincial nature and their appeal to emotionalism and notions of a romanticized past which could never be recreated.

The missionary Christian churches experienced different rates of growth in different colonies and in different historical periods. Missionary activity was not encouraged in French-speaking Africa and thus grew slowly. Modern French history was marked by bitter conflicts between Catholics and anticlericals, and government tended to be distrustful of church involvement in state affairs. In English-speaking Africa, missionaries were not permitted in heavily Muslim areas without the consent of local African rulers. Elsewhere they were welcomed by colonial authorities. Protestant missionary activity had steadily gained momentum in Great Britain since the evangelical revival of the late eighteenth century. In the Belgian Congo after 1908 the government subsidized the Catholic mission schools which may have accounted for the preponderance of Catholicism over Protestantism from the 1920s onward. In British West Africa, the number of converts quadrupled between 1895 and 1914. In the Belgian Congo, the rate of conversions soared after World War I. Generally, the major attraction of mission Christianity was its ability to provide Africans with a modern education, the ability to read and write, and thus an avenue for upward social and economic mobility.

The advance of Islam was equally impressive, particularly in East and West Africa. Between 1900 and 1960 the Muslim population in Africa more than doubled; in number of converts it may have exceeded the growth of Christianity. In East Africa, Islam spread rapidly between 1890 and 1930 from the coastal Swahili towns and large interior communities into the rural areas. In West Africa, it moved southward from the savanna lands. Only in central, equatorial and southern Africa did Islam grow slowly.

The colonial era ironically accelerated the spread of Islam. European rule put an end to inter-ethnic warfare and ushered in a period of unprecedented peace. This enabled Muslim traders and clerics to circulate more widely and to penetrate areas, such as the Mossi states, which in precolonial times had been closed to them. In West Africa laborers from the Muslim savanna zones sought cash employment in the densely populated forest and coastal belts and brought Islamic ideas with them.

Islam enjoyed several advantages over missionary-imposed Christianity. First, it was seen to be more of an indigenous African religion and was free of association with European colonialism. Its propagators were Africans, while by 1900 most Christian missionaries were Europeans and Americans. Muslims tended to live among the local people, to mix with them socially and in business, and to follow a similar lifestyle, whereas Christians initially lived in separate areas and maintained an essentially European way of life. Second, Islam accommodated more traditional social and religious institutions, particularly of magic, divination, polygamy, and communalism. It placed more emphasis than Christianity on social cohesion and less on competition and individual achievement. But Islam in most cases lost its puritannical, reformist, and revolutionary zeal, so evident in the nineteenth century. In English-speaking Africa it became a force for conservatism and in Northern Nigeria and on Zanzibar island, Muslim leaders spurned nationalism and modernization. In French-speaking West Africa,

Muslims played a significant role in nationalist movements, especially in Senegal, Mali, and Guinea. British colonial authorities viewed Islam as a force for stability and status quo; in Northern Nigeria they assisted in the construction of mosques and Qur'anic schools.

In any case, Islam as a religion did not stagnate. The Tijaniyya brotherhood grew into the most influential single order in West Africa. Alongside it flourished newer brotherhoods: The Isma'ili in East Africa and in West Africa the Muridiyya, the Hamaliyya, and the education-oriented Ahmadiyya. The latter came closest to being a missionary movement.

By the twilight years of colonialism, Islam had taken its place as the largest single religion in Africa, but its impact was far more subtle than that of Christianity. The latter had left a more visible impression and had made a much greater social, cultural, and political impact. Islam moved into African society in a more piecemeal manner and in some cases laid deeper roots as a result. Some historians have suggested that in West Africa, Islam advanced more widely and more profoundly in a half-century of colonialism than in the previous ten centuries of precolonial history. Syncretic tendencies were tolerated by Muslim clergy, and thus there was less need than in Christianity for separatist movements. Separatism, however, was not totally absent. The Muridiyya, the Hamaliyya, and the Ahmadiyya were in a sense separatist in that they deviated from orthodox Islamic traditions. Some of their objectives were secular, and the Muridiyya openly criticized orthodox religious leaders and their close relationship with colonial authorities. The Ahmadiyya missionaries, however, were apolitical and devoted much of their effort towards modernizing Islamic education, translating the Qur'an, and publishing texts. Humphrey J. Fisher stated: "Moslem separatism . . . is an attempt to maintain a balance between the faith and the practical circumstances in which the faith exists. If the faith seems too foreign, it will be adapted; if it seems too acclimatized, it will be reformed."[2]

EDUCATION

Education was closely linked to religion in the colonial era. Before the 1960s, the educational policies of the British, Belgians, and Portuguese were strongly influenced by Christian churches and missionaries. A majority of the schools outside French Africa were initiated and operated by missionaries.

Before the post-World War II era, the European colonial powers placed their greatest emphasis on primary education. Instruction was usually in the vernacular language. In German East Africa, Swahili was introduced by the colonial authorities as the medium of instruction and remained so during the subsequent British

[2] Humphrey J. Fisher, "Separatism in West Africa" in James Kritzeck and W.H. Lewis, eds., *Islam in Africa* (New York: Van Nostrand-Reinhold Publishers, Inc., 1969), p. 129.

period of rule. The French gave no official support to mission or Qur'anic schools and discouraged American and British educational penetration by requiring all missionary teachers to hold degrees from French institutions. The French government exerted considerable control over curriculum, and education was highly centralized and uniform. Colonial secondary schools almost mirrored schools in France. The philosophy, structure, and curriculum of metropolitan French education were applied almost undiluted to the colonies. Thus, education in Indochina differed little from education in Senegal or some other overseas French possession. Everything was centralized in the Ministry of Education in Paris.

The British, by contrast, left the operation of most schools to private initiative but supervised them through a system of grants-in-aid and periodic inspections. Departments of education in the various colonies had a large measure of independence from London. In all systems of colonial education, outside the Muslim areas, schools were instruments for Westernization. School uniforms were of European style. History was emphasized but was taught so as to extol the virtues of Western Christian civilization and to justify European conquest of Africa and the resultant benefits of colonialism. African history was almost totally neglected in favor of studies in the origins and growth of Anglo-Saxon or Gallic civilization. The French paid considerable attention to their own culture and its purported universal qualities. But unlike the British, the French made almost no concessions to the ethnic differences of the pupils. Little attention was given to a pupil's tribal origin or to the distinctiveness of his or her own culture.

Everywhere in colonial Africa, educational emphasis fell on fostering literacy —not so that Africans could read a farmers' almanac and the like but in order for them to read the Bible and become active Christians or to better serve the needs of the colonial bureaucracies. Most courses beyond basic grammar bore little relationship to the requirements of economic development. Nonpractical courses led to unemployment among school-leavers, especially those coming out of the primary schools. The students were victims of educational systems designed to produce clerks, teachers, and clergymen, rather than self-reliant mechanics, progressive farmers, engineers, and business managers. The only technical and vocational training available was confined to government departments such as public works and transportation. Colonial education, particularly at the secondary level, was elitist in nature in that it placed greater stress on white-collar occupations than on manual labor.

The British paid very little attention to education in the Muslim areas, where Qur'anic schools continued to flourish and missionary enterprise was discouraged. This created enormous contrasts in educational attainment between Muslims and Christians. In Nigeria, for example, in 1960 only nine pecent of the children in the predominantly Muslim northern region were in primary schools in contrast to more than ninety percent in the eastern and western regions. This

Anglican cathedral, Kampala, Uganda, with cemetery for European missionaries in foreground.

imbalance created serious regional and political cleavages in the postindependence period.

After World War I, the spotlight began to beam on secondary educational needs. A report by the American-based Phelps-Stokes Fund Commission in 1924 urged colonial governments to assume greater responsibility for education and to open secondary schools. Already in 1922 the Makerere Technical School was set up in Uganda; two years later Achimota College in the Gold Coast was established to provide education from kindergarten to university level. Dr. J.E.K. Aggrey, an American-trained Ghanaian educator, was instrumental in the 1920s in prodding the British colonial governments into devoting more attention to the educational needs of Africans. Also in 1924, Fort Hare College, a South African institution for nonwhites founded in 1916, turned out its first graduating class. A decade later, the Yaba Higher College was founded in Nigeria.

Secondary school students in French Africa tended to be better educated than their English-speaking counterparts, but there were fewer openings in their schools. Senegal led the way, and the 1920s and 1930s saw an expansion in the Lycée Faidherbe, the Dakar Medical School, the Lycée van Vollenhoven, and the prestigious Ecole Normale William Ponty, founded in 1903.

Secondary school education in the colonial period, especially in French West Africa, was almost as good as that in France. However, there were far fewer institutions, and these were concentrated in Dakar and environs. The French, Belgians, and Portuguese did not educate nearly as many Africans for elite

Achimota College, founded in the British Gold Coast in 1924 as a co-educational institution which for years provided education for the African elites, from kindergarten through high school.

roles as did the British. Even in British Africa, secondary education did not begin to expand, quantitatively, until after the Second World War.

In areas of large white settlement, particularly in Kenya, Southern Rhodesia, South Africa, and the Portuguese territories, education tended to be racially segregated and unequal. In Portuguese Africa, there were two systems, one for traditional Africans and one for Europeans and Westernized Africans, or assimilados. The former was officially the responsibility of the Roman Catholic missionaries, and the latter was a state education system, replicating the one in Portugal. Government high schools, few in number, served Portuguese and assimilados only. In South Africa, most educational facilities had been racially segregated for decades. This *de facto* situation became *de jure* after 1953 with the passage of the Bantu Education Act which placed all African primary and secondary education, formerly in the hands of the churches and missionaries, under state control. The Extension of Universities Act (1959) launched an era of racial and ethnic segregation in higher education. Until then, all but the so-called open universities (i.e. University of Cape Town and University of the Witwatersrand) were closed to nonwhites. Henceforth, nonwhites could attend a white university only by special permission, and few were subsequently granted. The act called upon the government to establish five universities to accommodate nonwhites according to their ethnicity: Turfloop in the Transvaal for the Sotho, Fort Hare for the Xhosas, University of Zululand for the Zulu, University of the Western Cape for the coloreds, and University of Durban for Asians.

By 1959, South Africa had made enormous strides in university education, but almost exclusively for the benefit of whites. In 1916 Victoria College in Stellenbosch and the South African College in Cape Town became independent universities. The six others were transformed into constituent colleges of the University of South Africa, eventually attaining the status of independent universities: the University of the Witwatersrand in 1922, the University of Pretoria in 1930, the University of Natal in 1949, the University of the Orange Free State in 1950, and Rhodes University and the Potchefstroom University for Christian Higher Education in 1951. Victoria College and the South African College, became the University of Stellenbosch and the University of Cape Town, respectively. In 1946, the University of South Africa, formerly a supervising body, introduced correspondence courses. Within a decade, it became the largest university in sub-Saharan Africa, serving people of all races. With the exception of the University of South Africa, each university in the country catered to either Afrikaans or English speakers. There were certain ethnic and language proclivities at all levels of South African schooling.

The secondary schools, technical, and teacher-training colleges of colonial Africa fostered many future African nationalist leaders. Before the close of World War II, Fourah Bay College was the only institution in English-speaking tropical Africa offering a degree recognized by British universities. In French-speaking Africa, the School of Pharmacy at Dakar was the only equivalent. From the 1920s, a growing number of Africans began entering American, British, and French universities. They eventually returned to Africa, and one of their strongest demands was for colonial governments to spend more money on education and to establish national universities in Africa. The British and French were first to respond to these demands. The former did this by drawing upon the Colonial Development and Welfare Acts and the latter by receiving funds from the Investment Funds for Economic and Social Development, or FIDES. The results were impressive in comparison to the years of neglect. The number of children attending schools in British tropical possessions grew by nearly 400 percent between 1945 and 1960, with increased attention given to primary and university education. Colonial government budgets also began to grow. For example, before World War II, Nigerian expenditures on education ranged from 1 to 4.3 percent of the budget. Between 1946 and 1960 it often exceeded ten percent.

The postwar period witnessed the rise of African university colleges. The University College of the Gold Coast was established in 1947 and the College of Technology at Kumasi in 1951. The University College of Ibadan in Nigeria opened in 1948 and secured association with the University of London. University colleges were founded in Dakar and Tananarive (Madagascar) in 1950, and scholarships for education in French universities increased. In 1950, Makerere in Uganda became a university college, linked with the University of London. The Royal Technical College of Nairobi in Kenya was established in 1956. On the eve of independence, in 1961, university colleges were founded in Nairobi and Dar es Salaam (Tanganyika) as complements to Makerere College. The multiracial University College of Rhodesia and Nyasaland was established in Salisbury in 1953.

The Belgians and Portuguese lagged far behind in providing higher education. The Belgian Congo in the late 1940s and 1950s boasted the highest literacy rate in tropical Africa but did not send a single student to university level until 1952. In 1954 Lovanium University was established on the outskirts of Leopoldville, mainly to train Catholic priests. This was followed by the opening of the State University of Elizabethville in Katanga two years later. Just before independence in 1960, in the entire nation there were only thirty Africans with university degrees.

Colonial education produced a new, Westernized elite, from a system heavily influenced by religion: Catholicism in French, Belgian, and Portuguese Africa, and Anglicanism in the British territories. Great strides were made in the postwar period in overall growth in enrollment, but course content changed little. Scant attention was given to engineering, medicine, business administration, or even to vocational arts. Emphasis continued to be placed on classical education, concentrating on grammar, history, geography, theology, law, and pedagogy. Pupils still left school knowing more about the Seine and Thames Rivers of France and England than about the Niger or Zambezi, and more about King George and Napoleon than Usuman dan Fodio or Samory Touré.

Critics argued that colonial education was too academic and too closely tied to a western curriculum. It was designed to open African minds to European culture but did little to advance understanding of one's own heritage. Western education was in great African demand by the close of the colonial era, because it was viewed as the only means of achieving elite status outside of being born into an aristocractic family. Nonetheless, it did contribute to a strong alienation of its students from traditional rural life.

On the positive side, colonial education resulted in a phenomenal increase in literacy. It also introduced common languages, the European languages and Swahili, which helped to break down ethnic and regional barriers, contributed to the growth of a modern national consciousness, and enabled the political mobilization of the masses. Secondary schools, particularly Makerere, the Ecole Normale William Ponty, and Fort Hare, attracted students from different colonies and therefore provided a forum for pan-African sentiment. In addition, colonial education gave the peasant and formerly servile populations an unprecedented opportunity for economic advancement. Emphasis gradually shifted towards individual advancement and meritocracy, and that in turn helped to trigger the post-World War II social and political revolutions and to speed the collapse of colonial rule.

Sub-Saharan Africa had come a long way down the road to mass literacy. At the turn of the century 99.9 percent of the population was illiterate. By 1960 that percentage had been reduced to approximately 85 percent, a modest though substantial drop when one considers that much of that reduction had been achieved in the short decade before the close of the colonial era.

SOCIAL ORGANIZATION

The colonial era marked the beginning of a sweeping and fundamental social transformation, giving birth to new social categories and classes. Africans became more mobile, both geographically and occupationally. Positions once held to be hereditary, such as weaving, dyeing, leatherworking, woodcarving, and the like were opened to everyone. Opportunities for capitalist enterprise gave increased economic independence to women. In many regions of non-Muslim West Africa, the economic position of women underwent a greater change than that of men. Igbo women became economically and politically powerful, and in 1929 they led a successful rebellion in Aba, Nigeria, against British taxation. All along the West African coast, women gained ascendancy over urban markets in their capacity as petty traders. By the 1950s, women had also begun to dominate the markets in the Belgian Congo, Northern Rhodesia, and in Nyasaland. This placed considerable strains on marital relationships and contributed to a rise in promiscuity.

One of the first acts following imperial conquest was the manumission of the nonfree populations. The majority of freed people remained in the compounds of their former masters or nearby. Others migrated to mission stations, to their original homeland, or to towns if wage labor were available. Most significant was that manumission led to an overall redefinition of social relationships, to a form of clientship or towards an accelerated formation of kinship. The stigma of servile origins often persisted for decades, though in varying degrees in different societies. The Osu slave system of the Igbo was abolished by the British but not forgotten by the people; in Ruanda and Urundi the ethnic Tutsi continued to dominate the Hutu and Twa. In remote regions, blacksmiths and woodcarvers remained separate from the rest of society. With the expansion of cash-cropping, trade, and market activity, one could increase his or her personal wealth. As a result, economic differentiation became more important to stratification and the process of class formation was hastened.

The colonial era also spawned an administrative-clerical-professional bourgeoisie. A new, indigenous elite structure became prominent as a growing number of Africans attended colonial schools, became Christianized and Westernized, took jobs in the civil service, and joined such professions as law, medicine, education, or the clergy. Literacy became an important social index. The traditional elites (nobility), while in some cases losing real political power, retained considerable social prestige, particularly in the rural areas. However, the new elites, along with the European overlords, formed a more powerful reference group for the society as a whole than did the old elites.

In the post-Second World War era, the long-established coastal elite families in Senegal, Sierra Leone, Liberia, Ghana, Dahomey, and Nigeria, known variously as Creoles, evolués, and assimilados, began to lose their influence in the face of an expanding number of Western-educated youths of poor "up-country" origins. Together, they jockeyed for social and political influence and based themselves mainly in the urban areas.

Economic development in the colonial era led to greater occupational specialization and the emergence of a subelite consisting of self-employed mechanics, bricklayers, tailors, truck drivers, and the like. Below the subelite appeared a new strata, the urban proletariat. This was a landless, dependent class of laborers who in some cases felt less secure than the nonfree peoples of the precolonial era. They had fallen into a confusing and dangerous autonomy, with a loss of kinship reinforcement.

Many of these groups had left their rural extended family environments to find their way alone among the large and impersonal public and private urban organizations. Their decision to leave home significantly transformed the family from the larger kinship units to the much smaller, nuclear family. Traditional value, belief, and behavioral systems were less important, and the subelites and proletariat fell under the influence of norms set by the colonial and new indigenous elites.

Voluntary associations and clubs began to substitute for the lineage and extended family. Many recruited on a nontribal basis and thus weakened ethnic allegiances. They also softened the trauma of urbanization and modernization by resocializing the urban newcomers and teaching them new mores. In other words, they served the same acculturative functions as the traditional family did.

URBANIZATION

Colonialism brought forth a new kind of urbanization in Africa. During the first quarter of the twentieth century, many of the old colonial coastal towns and surf ports, which had been built for slave and palm-oil trading, began to stagnate; for example, Saint Louis in Senegal, Grand Bassam in the Ivory Coast, Elmina and Cape Coast in the Gold Coast, Whydah in Dahomey, Badagry, Bonny, and Calabar in Nigeria, and Benguela in Angola. Towns with superior harbors or a favorable geographical location were rejuvenated, notably Freetown, Accra, Lagos, Luanda, Cape Town, Lourenço Marques, Dar es Salaam, and Mombasa. In addition, numerous old interior towns and cities grew in population, largely because they served as rail-transportation crossroads or termini. Among them were Ouagadougou and Bamako in French West Africa's savanna, Kumasi, Kano, and Ibadan in British West Africa, Leopoldville (old Kinshasa) in the Belgian Congo, and Bulawayo in Southern Rhodesia. Such traditional towns were transformed into modern commercial and administrative centers. Mining activity gave birth to industrial and financial cities, the largest and most typical of which were on the South African rand and along the copperbelt north of the Zambezi; Kimberley and Johannesburg in South Africa, Kitwe and Ndola in Northern Rhodesia, and Elizabethville in the Katanga region of the Belgian Congo. Johannesburg mushroomed from nothing in 1886 to 166,000 at the turn of the century.

The growth of entirely new cities and towns, some as administrative centers, was a major feature of the colonial era. Important examples were Nairobi in Kenya, Salisbury in Southern Rhodesia, Blantyre in Nyasaland, Conakry in French Guinea, Kaduna in northern Nigeria, and Niamey in French Niger. Large population centers grew up wherever colonial authorities chose to situate their railheads, docks, hospitals, schools, and administrative offices. These were what attracted and retained people.

The French and Belgians made the greater effort in creating carefully planned new towns, as centers of political authority and as reflections of European con-

Old clock tower, built by a nostalgic British colonial official to remind him of London's Big Ben. Kumasi, Ghana.

The French-designed city of Dakar, administrative center of the French colony of Senegal and eventually capital of French West Africa. It is laid out along lines of modern planned cities of metropolitan France.

ceptions of spatial layout and architecture. The Belgians planned and laid out over 180 new towns in their possessions and endowed them with modern ameni- ties. Both the French and the Belgians emphasized radial-concentric layouts with broad, tree-lined avenues. By contrast, the British in many areas left the old urban centers intact and built European-style, government residential areas on the periphery for their own personnel and offices. This practice re- flected British conceptions of indirect rule and recognized the preexistence of large flourishing cities. Many urban areas, particularly in British Africa, grew rather haphazardly and became shanty-towns. The French, on the other hand, governed territories less densely populated and generally lacking urban centers.

In precolonial cities, social relationships, rather than geometric order were major criteria for building placement. The reverse was true of the European-built and designed colonial cities. Spatial structure was no longer the key to social and behavior patterns. The colonial cities were physical reflections more of political and economic networks than of social concerns and organization.

After the Second World War, even Dakar, Abidjan, Brazzaville and other French colonial cities witnessed the development of outer suburbs of unplanned sprawls. These *bidonvilles,* as they were called in French Africa, suffered from appallingly low housing and sanitation standards. Residential structures in these shanty-towns were crudely fabricated from a mélange of discarded oil drums (*bidons*) and sewer conduits, wooden packing-crates, and strips of corrugated iron. As the twentieth century progressed, urban diets deteriorated and housing became more overcrowded.

Urbanization greatly accelerated after the Second World War. This spectacular urban explosion was in response to increased government spending on infrastructure (roads, harbors, schools) and the multiplication of government bureaucracies to administer it. It was also a result of the rapid development in commercial facilities and the availability of power, light, water, communications, and subsidiary services which all were unavailable in the rural areas. Unfortunately, all this was not matched by comparable growth in public amenities and services. Urban demands for skilled and semiskilled wage labor brought rural people to the urban areas in search of quick wealth. Between 1940 and 1960 most towns doubled in population and many major cities nearly trebled. The figures speak for themselves:

Dakar: 1921, 32,400; 1931, 54,000; 1960, 300,000

Abidjan: 1929, 5,400; 1939, 22,000; 1949, 48,000; 1960, 168,000

Accra: 1931, 70,000; 1948, 135,000; 1960, 325,000

Lagos: 1870, 41,236; 1880, 62,000; 1910, 74,000; 1931, 126,608; 1951, 230,000; 1960, 500,000 est.

Ibadan: 1890, 200,000 est.; 1921, 238,000; 1952, 459,196

Leopoldville: 1940, 46,884; 1946, 110,280; 1951, 221,757; 1959, 301,000

Dar es Salaam: 1931, 23,000; 1948, 69,000; 1957, 128,000

Luanda: 1940, 61,000; 1960, 250,000

Johannesburg; 1936, 519,268; 1970, 2,000,000

This astounding growth resulted in unstable populations of oscillating migrants whose roots and ethos were still essentially rural. In the first quarter of the twentieth century, towns and cities drew immigrants most heavily from the immediate hinterland, and they thus were made up predominantly of one ethnic group. After World War II, peoples from villages and farms further afield and from differing ethnic and cultural origins flooded into urban centers and settled in quarters consisting mainly of their own kin. In fact "strangers" were often constrained by indigenous African urban authorities, as they had been for centuries, to reside outside the city walls in *sabon garis,* or "strangers towns," as the Hausa called them.

Lineage fragmentation is always inevitable in the process of urbanization, but at least these ethnic quarters, *sabon garis,* or *zongos* provided a measure of communal solidarity. There was a tendency for unmarried men to migrate to the cities so that many urban areas gained a preponderance of young bachelors but few wives, children or elderly. Juvenile delinquency, prostitution, alcoholism, and unemployment, almost all unknown in precolonial times, became widespread urban phenomena by the late 1940s. On the positive side, cities provided opportunities for acculturation, communication across ethnic lines, wage employment, and an opportunity for people of rural origin to forge a new life, free of the traditional social and economic restraints.

Cities and towns in colonies with large European settlements were often legally demarcated between "ville indigène" and "ville blanche." In the mid-1950s Portugal built numerous black *colonatos,* or cooperative new towns on the periphery of white agricultural areas. White new towns, notably Cela, were established to accommodate poor immigrants from Portugal. Efforts to slow the movement of rural blacks to the cities failed and from the late 1950s, shantytowns, called *senzalas,* appeared on the outskirts of the predominantly white and assimilado Angolan cities.

There was a tendency almost everywhere for the African section or "ville indigène" to be separate from and economically and politically subordinate to a European center. This was carried to its greatest extreme in South Africa. Patterns of urban racial segregation have existed there since the seventeenth century, when Cape Town was under the rule of the Dutch East India Company. The white view of Africans in urban areas as "temporary sojourners" was carried northward from the 1840s to the Afrikaner towns of the Transvaal and Orange Free State. Before the Second Boer War, South Africa was overwhelmingly a rural country. In 1870, there were only twenty towns with a population of over 1,000. But the agony of rural poverty after the Boer War (1902) propelled Boers and Africans to the towns in what some historians regard as the Boers second Great Trek. An urban poor white problem was created, because most Boers lacked the necessary skills and education yet continued to harbor a strong prejudice against menial labor. The "temporary sojourner" status now was advocated more strongly as a pretext for denying economic and political rights to Africans in the so-called "European" cities.

Laws to regulate urban Africans date from an Act in 1923. But the flow continued, particularly after the Second World War when an industrial boom attracted peoples of all racial and ethnic backgrounds. In the 1946 census, urban Africans, for the first time in history, outnumbered urban whites. The African population of Johannesburg alone had increased by 150,000 in six years, and

eleven squatter camps had sprung up on the city's outskirts. Even the Nationalists, who came to power in 1948 and placed segregation on a more rigidly legal
footing, failed to check the permanent settlement of increasing numbers of
Africans in towns and cities. In 1950 they passed the Group Areas Act which
zoned towns into areas for the exclusive residence of specific racial and ethnic
groups. A law in 1952 extended the system of influx control (for instance,
through identity books) to all urban areas and forbid blacks to remain in an urban area for more than seventy-two hours without obtaining a special permit.
Four years later the industrial magnate, Sir Ernest Oppenheimer, convinced the
government to build planned African townships with public amenities. Thus
began the rise of an enormous black satellite city, called Soweto, on Johannesburg's periphery. Revised labor regulations in 1959 tightened controls over the
employment of Africans in urban areas and made them applicable to African
women as well.

The 1960 South African census revealed that the urbanization rate for
Africans continued to be much faster than for whites, who were by then outnumbered in all the large cities. Between 1951 and 1961 the number of Africans
in urban areas increased by forty-five percent. In Johannesburg alone, the
African population grew by thirty-six percent during that period while the
white population declined by fifteen percent. Soweto had expanded from
225,000 in 1956 to an estimated 400,000 by 1961. South Africa had been
no more successful in stemming the urban tide than those colonies which had
few or no legal influx controls.

Similar though far less comprehensive and restrictive segregationist measures
were adopted in Southern Rhodesia, Kenya, and the Belgian Congo during
colonial times. But by the time of African majority rule, they were almost all
abolished.

From an architectural point of view, the colonial era was marked by a transformation in structural form and building material. There was an accelerated
movement away from the predominantly circular or rondavel, mud-walled,
thatched-roofed dwellings and the burnt mud-brick, dome-on-box, adobe-type
structures of the Muslim zones. Corrugated iron roofs replaced thatch, and clay
bricks and cement blocks were now favored over the mud or wattle-and-daub
materials that required continuous maintenance. The rich architectural diversity
of precolonial days, when each culture enjoyed its own distinctive styles, was
submerged into a European-inspired uniformity. Before the European conquest,
strong distinctions existed in layout and architecture between a city like Zanzibar
and the Buganda capital of Mengo, or between Kumasi and Kano. Cities built by
the European colonialists, though beautifully planned, with broad tree-lined
streets and public gardens, were remarkably similar, especially those conceived
by the French. The accent in the colonial era was upon rectangularity and order.
By 1960, round dwellings had almost completely disappeared from the major
towns of tropical Africa.

THE DECLINE OF ART

Christianity and Islam, where it had penetrated, tended to weaken sculptural artistic traditions. Muslims were opposed to the making of graven images, and Christian missionaries looked upon African masks and sculpture as symbols of primitivism, superstition, and paganism. Many carvings were destroyed; others were taken to Western Europe by missionaries, military men, and colonial administrators, and sold to private collectors who in some cases donated them to museums. Much of the art of the Congo region found its way to the Musée Royal du Congo Belge in Tervuren, Belgium. Enormous quantities of West African art ended up in the British Museum in London, the Pitt Rivers Museum at Oxford University, the Musée de l'Homme in Paris, and the Museums für Völkerkunde in Berlin.

The flood of traditional African sculpture into the studios of European modern artists at the turn of the century had a profound effect on the rise and development of so-called "modern art." Europeans described African art as "primitive and tribal." Much of Africa's traditional art was regional and not limited to any one ethnic group. The "primitiveness" of its form strongly influenced the modern cubist movement and its early exponents. Cézanne, a pre-Cubist, once stated, "You must see in nature the cylinder, the sphere and the cone."[3] All three elements were forcefully revealed in African sculpture. By 1907, African sculpture had been collected by the great artists Vlaminck, Derain, Modigliani, and Picasso. Picasso made his own discoveries of African art in the Trocadéro, and they inspired him to paint his famous Les Demoiselles d'Avignon.

An interest in African art for its own sake and on its own merits arose after the First World War. Gradually, Americans gained an appreciation for it and in the late 1950s and early 1960s, a number of museums began to acquire large collections. Among the most active museums were: the Brooklyn Museum, the Museum of Primitive Art, and the Museum of Natural History in New York; the Denver Museum; and the Robert H. Lowie Museum of Anthropology at the University of California (Berkeley). From the beginning of the colonial era in this century, so-called "primitive" artifacts had begun to attract the attention of artists and critics. In the 1950s, educated Africans and enlightened Western anthropologists recognized the desirability of establishing museums within Africa itself. William and Bernard Fagg were instrumental in developing the national museums of Nigeria; Father Joseph Cornet in founding the Institute of the National Museums of Zaire, and others in setting up the Musée de Dakar in Senegal.

Ironically, as Western interest in African art increased, the quantity and quality of the art slowly declined. The weakening of traditional ritual authori-

[3]Ladislas Segy, *African Sculpture* (New York: Dover Press, Inc., 1958), p. 29.

ties and the secret societies led to a corresponding decline in the plastic arts, because such art served a specific purpose or function. As traditional institutions were destroyed or transformed and the old patrons of the arts died, the original purpose and meaning of the art forms were lost.

THE MUSICAL SYNTHESIS

Musical traditions were more affected by the penetration of Western culture than art. In British West Africa, Africans had begun to experiment with Western music from the turn of the century. Colonial military and police units developed uniformed brass bands, and in off-hours, the players composed their own variations on European themes.

Neo-folk music first took the form of "highlife music." This was a synthesis of colonial regimental music, Christian hymns, and traditional dance music. Highlife flourished first among the Fante people along the Gold Coast. It gradually spread to other towns in Nigeria, Sierra Leone, and the Gambia. Percussion lost some significance as trombones and acoustical guitars became popular instruments of the fledgling brass and guitar bands and dance orchestras. In the 1930s and early 1940s, highlife music permeated the smaller towns of the British West African interior. E.T. Mensah's "Tempos" band of the Gold Coast traveled widely and set the musical pace for other groups in the towns of British and French West Africa. From the war years onward, highlife musicians, exposed to black American servicemen, borrowed freely from black American ragtime, Latin-American jazz, particularly from Brazil, and West Indian tunes. Syncretic musical traditions were far less developed in East and Central Africa, with the exception of towns along the coast which had for centuries been exposed to music from the Middle East and India. Elsewhere, sharp dichotomies existed between traditional music and the music dominated by white settlers and colonial officials.

Syncretic music did not come into vogue in French-speaking Africa until the early 1950s, largely because European musicians had dominated the nightclub scene. Thereafter, it spread with the speed of a brush fire. The Luba in the Belgian Congo led the way with so-called "Congo music." This quickly radiated to French Equatorial and West Africa. Young musicians also experimented with African variations of Latin-American rhumbas. In the mid and late-fifties, highlife bands drifted away from Jamaican calypso and towards a style influenced by American bebop and modern, New Orleans-inspired jazz. In Nigeria, these imports at first encountered tough competition from "Juju music" which originated in the 1930s. As the decade of the sixties opened, West African towns were the scene of flourishing, big bands and smaller guitar groups.

Syncretic music during the colonial era did not take hold among the older generations or among the millions of people living beyond the major towns.

Traditional music remained a strong and compelling force with the overwhelming majority of Africans. But among the urbanized youth, traditional music was increasingly being viewed as "bush" and "primitive."

DANCE AND DRAMA

Music, dance, and drama were brought together in the form of the comic folk-opera. This genre was most popular and best developed in Nigeria and the Gold Coast, and reached its zenith in the decade after the Second World War. Like the masquerade dance/drama, secret societies of old, the comic opera groups traveled widely and gave performances subtly laced with social and political commentary.

The upsurge of popular interest in the dramatic arts may be explained by the colonial emphasis on school and church-organized morality plays. Attention also was paid to the works of the great European playwrights, particularly Shakespeare and Molière. We must remember that in Nigeria the professional theater enjoyed a long history. The Yoruba Operatic Theater appeared as a new theatrical form in the early twentieth century. It thrived and in 1945, its founder, Hubert Ogunde, formed the African Music and Dance Research Party. Ogunde's movement was responsible for drawing many young people into the dramatic arts. In the same year a new professional theater group came into existence and emphasized folklore and nationalistic themes.

Modern theatrical traditions in French-speaking Africa date to the 1930s with the establishment in Senegal of the David Sorano National Theater at the William Ponty School. Here too, themes of traditional folklore became the major source for theatrical productions. In the late 1950s, Les Ballets Africains of Guinea went on a world tour and introduced to the West a new dimension of African culture.

African drama also flourished in the Union of South Africa. In 1944, the eminent musicologist, Hugh Tracey, and K.E. Masinga collaborated on a musical play, *Inkosi yaphezulu nenkosi yaphansi* (Chief Above and Chief Below), based on an old Zulu legend. In 1951 L.L.J. Mncwango (a Zulu playwright) completed *Manhla iyokwendela egodini* (She Will Surely Marry into the Grave). It dealt with sexual jealousy, violence, with witchcraft and the use of medicines expressing human emotions. Eight years later, Mncwango came out with *Ngenzeni* (What Should I Do? What Have I Done?), a love story set in the time of the famous nineteenth-century warrior and founder of the Zulu nation, Shaka.

Through the mediums of music, song, and dramatic satire, Africans of the colonial era were able legitimately to attack colonialism and express their yearnings for a return to political and cultural self-determination. The role of these peripatetic music bands and drama groups in mobilizing people behind African nationalism has been grossly underestimated.

LITERATURE AS PROTEST

The colonial era was a time when a large body of oral literature began to be committed to writing and in many cases translated by Europeans and Africans into Western languages. Traditional legends, myths, and tales were the major sources of inspiration for the emerging African writers. The Reverend Moses Lijadu's *Yoruba Mythology* (1896) was one of the earliest literary pieces written in West Africa. In 1918, a Gold Coast intellectual, Kobina Sekyi, wrote the first English-language novel, *The Anglo-Fante.* Two years later the South African, Sol. T. Plaatje, translated Shakespeare's *Comedy of Errors* into the Tswana language. In 1930, he wrote his first novel, *Mhudi.* This was followed a year later by Thomas Mofolo's historical novel, *Chaka,* which first was published in the Sotho language. Other prominent early works of fiction were J.L. Dube's *Insila kaShaka* (Shaka's Personal Servant) published in 1933 and B.W. Vilakazi's *Noma Nini* (1938).

In Portuguese Africa, modern literary traditions took root in the early 1890s. The African novelist, Pedro Machado, wrote *Scenas d'Africa* in 1892. Literature in the Portuguese possessions was spurred on by the establishment in 1926 of a "colonial literature competition." Out of this developed a small literary movement based in the Cape Verde islands, which published a magazine entitled *Claridad.* Most works were poems, and were in Portuguese, with occasional pieces in Creole. The movement spread to Angola under the inspiration of Agostinho Neto, a poet/physician/guerilla leader who became independent Angola's first president in 1975.

French-African literature was born in 1920 with the first original work of fiction in French: A.M. Diagne's *Les Trois Volontes de Malic.* The 1920s also saw the publication of *La Revue africaine,* a Dakar-based magazine, and Bakary Diallo's autobiographical novel, *Force-Bonté.* The modern literary movement took firm rooting in the mid-1930s with the founding of the Paris journal, *L'étudiant noir.* This was followed by the poem *Cahier d'un retour au pays natal* (1939) by the West Indian, Aimé Cesaire. Cesaire's poem marked the birth of "négritude," a literary and political movement against French assimilationist policies in Africa and the West Indies. Négritude's major founders, the Martinique poet, Aimée Césaire and the Senegalese, Léopold Sedar Senghor, were responding mainly to the cultural domination of France. Unintentionally, the trauma of French assimilationist policy forced the *assimilé* into a recognition of his own blackness and of the need of preserving Africa's own cultural identity in the face of aggressive Gallic intrusions. In *Paris in the Snow,* Senghor speaks of the devastation of traditional African civilization by white Europeans. He and other exponents of négritude expressed a love-hate relationship with French civilization. This is clearly revealed in Senghor's *Luxembourg* (1939). Négritude also influenced Frenchmen. Jean-Paul Sartre argued in *L'Orphée noir* that African poetry is "the true revolutionary poetry of our time."[4] In the 1940s and 1950s this was a valid remark.

African literature did not come of age until after the Second World War. Many French-speaking African intellectuals, particularly from Senegal where the full force of French education and assimilation was felt, spent considerable time in the salons of Paris. The Senegalese writer, Alioune Diop, founded in Paris the highly influential *Présence africaine,* a cultural review of the "Negro World." This publication quickly became the major forum for French-speaking writers.

Further stimulus to the literary flowering came through the Negro Writers and Artists Conferences of 1956 and 1959. Senghor had already published his *Chants d'ombre* in 1945. Camara Laye's first book, *L'Enfant noir* (Black Child), in 1953 represented one of the first autobiographical novels. A year later, a Camerounian, Mongo Beti, completed *Ville Cruelle,* followed by *Le Pauvre Christ de Bomba* (1956), which dealt with the failure of Christianity in Africa. In 1957 he published *Mission Terminée.* A year earlier, Bernard Dadié of the Ivory Coast came out with *Climbié* and the Senegalese, Sembène Ousmane, with *Le Docker noir.* Ousmane, a bitter critic of colonialism, placed his work in a Marxist setting dealing with class-struggle and focusing on the exploitation of the poor by the black bureaucratic bourgeoisie. "Uprootedness" (or *deraciné*) remained a pervasive theme of French-language novels written in the 1950s.

A similar postwar literary awakening took place in English-speaking Africa, particularly in Nigeria, the Gold Coast, and South Africa. The *Dertigers* (poets of the thirties) led by the Afrikaner, van Wyk Louw, gave way in the 1940s to a new, more serious, and realistic generation. Peter Abraham's novel *Mine Boy* was published in 1946. Abrahams became the first black novelist from South Africa to gain a major critical following in the West. Other prominent South African writers of global fame were the Afrikaner Etienne Leroux and the English-speaking Alan Paton and Nadine Gordimer. South African novelists of the 1940s and 1950s dealt primarily with racial confrontation and contrasting social structures.

In West Africa, the African novel in English was dominated in the forties and fifties by Nigerians. Cyprian Ekwensi led the way with his novel *When Love Whispers* in 1948. Amos Tutuola's *Palm Wine Drunkard* appeared in 1952, Chinua Achebe's *Things Fall Apart* in 1958, and his *No Longer at Ease* two years later. The Sierra Leonian, William Conton, published *The African* in the same year. Ezekiel Mphahlele, a South African in exile, published his autobiographical *Down Second Avenue* in 1959. The work deeply affected the thoughts and style of many English-speaking writers in West Africa. The major theme in English-language West African novels was the confrontation of cultures (Western and African) and the conflict between traditional and modern values.

[4] Frederick Michelman, "French-African Fiction," *Research in African Literatures,* II, No. 1 (1971), p. 8.

African authors looked to Europe rather than to Africa for their audience. Few Africans could afford to buy their works or had acquired a taste for written literature. Most publishing firms were European-owned and dominated by European editors. Indigenous writers therefore at times had to compromise their creativity by writing in a language other than their native tongue. Fortunately, Literature and Publications Bureaux were established in Nairobi and Lusaka after World War II and encouraged short works in vernacular languages. So did the Lovedale Press in South Africa, which had been publishing works by Africans since the 1930s. Many small, locally owned and managed presses arose in Nigeria in the 1940s and early 1950s. The most prominent vernacular press in Nigeria was the Gaskiya Corporation in Northern Nigeria which published history and literature in Hausa.

part **III**

THE INDEPENDENCE ERA

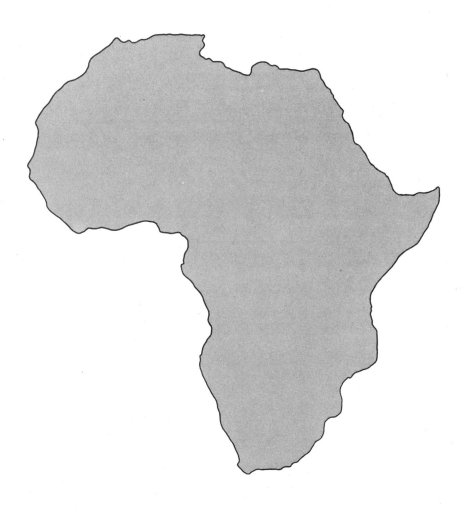

chapter 7

Patterns of Authority

THE STRUGGLE FOR INDEPENDENCE

The decade that commenced in 1957 is considered the decade of black African independence, a time when political sovereignty was restored to the African people after more than six decades of colonialism. After 1951 the British began to set into motion constitutions providing for a large measure of self-government for their various possessions. General, popular elections were permitted, and modern political parties promoted platforms and candidates. Colonial governments did little to stand in the way of this democratic process. Elections between 1952 and 1954 installed African majorities in the legislative and executive councils in Sierra Leone, Nigeria, and the Gold Coast. Executive councils by the mid-1950s were evolving into cabinets, headed by African prime ministers. In March 1957, the Gold Coast and the United Nations Trust Territory of British Togoland attained independence as the state of Ghana, with Kwame Nkrumah as prime minister. Ghana became the first black African nation to achieve independence in the twentieth century, and its success was an inspiration to all Africans. It marked the commencement of the independence era in Africa south of the Sahara. Nigeria, along with Somalia, which was a merger of Italian Somalia and British Somaliland gained independence in 1960. For Sierra Leone and the United Nations Trust Territory of Tanganyika, independence came a year later. Zanzibar, a British island protectorate, was given independence under its Arab sultan in 1963. His violent overthrow by the African majority in 1964 resulted in Zanzibar and Tanganyika joining to form the United Republic of Tanzania under the presidency of Julius Nyerere. Uganda became independent in 1962 and Kenya in 1963.

A similar process was taking place in the French territories, though before 1958 full independence was not contemplated. In the previous chapter it was stated that after the loi-cadre of 1956 the French devolved greater power and autonomy on the executive and legislative bodies in their newly created territories. In the referendum of 1958, only the territory of Guinea dared to opt for complete independence. Yet nearly all the others followed, at once, in 1960: in West Africa, the Ivory Coast, Senegal, Sudan (Mali), Upper Volta, Niger, Dahomey, and the Trust Territory of Togo; in Central Africa, Ubangui-Shari (Central African Empire), Chad, Congo, Gabon; and in the Indian Ocean, the island of Madagascar. East Cameroun, a United Nations Trust Territory under French supervision, also became independent and joined in 1961 with the U.N. Trust Territory of British Cameroons to form the Federal Republic of Cameroun. Nineteen-sixty was also the time of independence for the Belgian Congo and for the Belgian Trust Territory, which was given sovereignty as two nations—Rwanda and Burundi.

Independence was slightly delayed in Britain's Central African possessions because of Southern Rhodesia's powerful white settlers, who clung to the disintegrating Central African Federation. African majority interests prevailed north of the Zambesi River in Northern Rhodesia and Nyasaland, and in late 1964, these two former federal provinces became Zambia and Malawi under Prime Ministers Kenneth Kaunda and Hastings Banda. It should be recalled that the white-dominated government of Southern Rhodesia unilaterally and illegally declared its independence from the British crown in 1965.

The last cluster of British possessions to achieve independence were the High Commission Territories of Bechuanaland, Basutoland, and Swaziland. The first two gained independence in 1966 as Botswana and Lesotho. Swaziland followed two years later, along with the British island of Mauritius. Gambia, a small river-enclave surrounded by Senegal, secured independence in 1965. Spain, a minor colonial power, administratively combined Rio Muni and the island of Fernando Po to form in 1968 the independent state of Equatorial Guinea.

Independence came relatively later to the remaining colonial possessions. We should recall that Portugal stubbornly adhered to a colonial policy that considered its overseas possessions as integral parts of the "Portuguese nation." The liberation movement in Guinea-Bissau unilaterally declared independence in 1973 for that territory after occupying most of the hinterland. Mozambique and Angola won their freedom in 1975, after a protracted guerilla war and a revolutionary change of government in Lisbon. By 1976 the fascist Franco regime in Spain had ended, and Spanish forces withdrew from the Western Sahara colony in the face of an invasion from Morocco. Morocco and Mauretania then partitioned the territory between themselves in defiance of Algeria and the Algerian-supported, Polisario liberation movement. France ended more than three centuries of colonial involvement in 1977 when it gave their territory of Afar and Issas in the Horn of Africa its independence as the state of Djibouti. Djibouti became the forty-ninth member of the Organization of African Unity.

By late 1977, only two decades after Ghanaian independence, sub-Saharan Africa, with the exception of Namibia, had regained its political independence. In early 1978, Rhodesia's prime minister, Ian Smith, achieved a fragile internal settlement with three moderate African nationalists (Bishop Abel Muzorewa, Reverend Ndabaningi Sithole, Jeremiah Chirau) which aimed at African majority rule. The two liberation movements, the Zimbabwe African National Union and the Zimbabwe African Peoples' Union, which together formed the Patriotic Front, described the internal settlement as a "sellout." They vowed to continue the military struggle and won the unanimous backing of the Organization of African Unity. In Namibia, a former League of Nations Mandate under South Africa, talks for independence stalled over quarrels between the South African government and moderate African leaders on the one hand, and the Marxist-leaning SWAPO movement on the other. SWAPO (South West Africa Peoples' Organization), like the Patriotic Front, refused to accept an internal settlement.

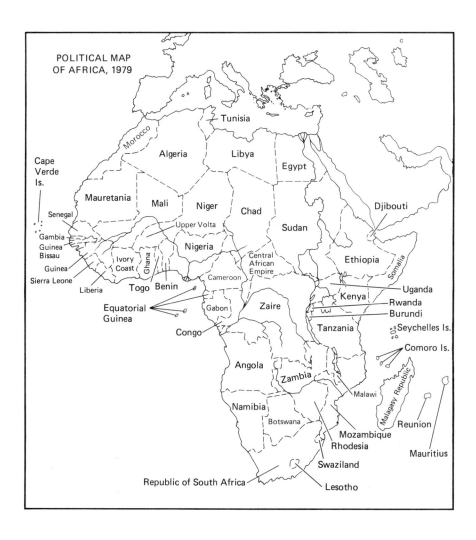

POLITICAL MAP OF AFRICA, 1979

At this point, the question of why the colonial powers after the Second World War transferred political authority to the Africans and ultimately granted them complete political independence must be asked. Part of the answer surely lies in the rapid postwar growth of African nationalism and its transition from an elitist movement to a mass movement. With few exceptions, African nationalists achieved independence in the late 1950s and 1960s without having to resort to violence or guerrilla activity. Power came not out of the barrel of a gun but through well organized, political demonstrations, strikes, and boycotts followed by adroit diplomatic bargaining. The British, French, and Belgians capitulated to the nationalists in large part because the Second World War had weakened their home economies. Having come through a costly and exhausting war, Europeans were loath to sustain the expense of maintaining a colonial empire. Providing economic assistance was one matter, for it contributed to a resurgence in trade between the colonies and the home country. But financing the expanding colonial bureaucracies was something else. Postwar European governments were more socialistically inclined and tended to be less sympathetic to colonial interests. Consequently, African nationalists found little difficulty in obtaining legitimacy and moral support from powerful European and American political parties, and from the United Nations and its espousal of the cause of self-determination for all peoples under colonial domination. In addition, the United States, the Soviet Union, and later West Germany and Japan, had become major world powers and were able to challenge the hegemony of the colonial powers over international trade and finance. It was therefore in the interest of the United States and the Soviet Union to support the cause of anticolonialism. Their burgeoning postwar industries required vast new supplies of raw materials, especially nonferrous metal ores. The United States after the war also found itself with a superabundance of domestic capital and was in a position to operate on a world scale—a condition Britain and France had found themselves in in the late nineteenth century, when they were poised for the scramble for African territory. However, the 1950s were unlike the 1880s and 1890s. Concepts of formal, territorial empire were no longer acceptable to the masses, who incidentally were now better educated and more politically sophisticated. The industrialized West therefore found that it had to return to the mid-nineteenth-century concept of "informal empire," of exploiting Third-World economies without bearing the cost, responsibility, and world censure for holding their political sovereignty. In other words, colonial and noncolonial industrialized nations reasoned that colonies could be granted formal political independence without drastically changing their economic relationship with them. The only need was to change collaborators. Before the Second World War, the British posed as the great power supporting the masses and their traditional rulers against the "detribalized," Western-educated middle class. Now, they would shift back to the early nineteenth-century practice of supporting the latter group and also of maintaining ties to the more influential chiefs.

The political and economic disruption of the colonial metropoles following the Second World War, the concomittant growth of powerful African nationalist movements, and the spread of Euro-Communism, encouraged the Soviet Union and the United States to make inroads to their own advantage. The United States, particularly, sought to assure the continuation of Western capitalist involvement in Africa. Indirectly, through NATO and the Marshall Plan, the Americans enabled the crumbling colonial powers to maintain a semblance of control and economic stability in their restless dependencies. At the same time, the United States and the Soviet Union in the late 1950s entered the preserves of the colonial powers by becoming major providers of military and economic aid. More will be said of this, in this and subsequent chapters.

THE NATIONALIST IDEAL

Let us return now to the phenomenon of African nationalism, the major engine of the independence struggle. Before 1945, nationalist membership in all the British colonies was small, and its leaders consisted largely of prosperous, Western-educated men who embraced Western morality and lifestyles yet who also displayed nostalgia for the "old African ways." In the British colonies, they called for a restoration of human dignity for the "Negro," equality before law, and greater civil liberties. Their demands took the form of programs of such limited and realizable goals as an increase in the proportion of elected members in the local legislatures, greater Africanization of the civil service, and an expansion of educational opportunities. During the twentieth century, urbanization and the revolution in transportation and communications brought peoples of different ethnic backgrounds together and gave rise to voluntary organizations, such as Bible classes and athletic clubs, which tended to recruit members on a non-kin basis. They formed interlocking networks of people, with branches in different towns within a given colony. This had the effect of creating a national consciousness and consensus, so that, for example, a Yoruba also might identify himself as a Nigerian. Colonialism, with its boundaries crossing ethnic lines and with its modern infrastructure, ironically contributed to the very forces which ultimately would bring about its downfall.

A crucial turning point was reached after World War II in the British possessions. Economic recovery was slow and many youthful school-leavers and "been-tos" (those who studied for higher degrees overseas) found themselves without employment. They resented the lack of progress made by the older intellectuals and agitated for more militancy including passive resistance, and a more broadly based nationalist movement. Labor unrest became a common feature of the colonial landscape and Nigeria, alone, had to cope with major strikes in 1945, 1947, and 1949. These "new nationalists" questioned the very legitimacy of the colonial system and demanded "self-government now," not in the distant future.

They were willing to go into the rural hinterlands to organize and politicize the semiliterate masses. In the Gold Coast, Nkrumah's break with the old nationalists under Dr. J.B. Danquah and his formation of the Convention Peoples Party in 1949, marked the beginning of modern nationalism in British West Africa. With the development of elective government, the old congresses of intellectuals and the ethnic cultural unions gave way to modern political parties. In French-speaking Africa, parties initially were extensions of metropolitan French parties but after the loi-cadre of 1956, political activity was territorially based within Africa itself. Both the British and French encouraged multiparty development. While political organization tended to be on a territorial, non-ethnic basis in the French possessions, its foundations in the British areas, particularly in Nigeria, were often along ethnic and regional lines. Indirect rule, with its accent on ethnicity, made it difficult for parties to build a national following.

African nationalists took advantage of the urban residents' restlessness and sense of alienation. They recruited them into their political movements and promised that independence would bring greater job opportunities. Ironically, colonialism had wrought the very social and economic change and loss of equilibrium that contributed to this urban malaise. The British colonial forces, short of men and money, tried to avoid violent confrontations and readily acceded to nationalist demands. At first, political leaders were detained. But by 1951 it had become obvious that detention conferred upon nationalist leaders a sort of legitimacy and charisma. In the Gold Coast, Kwame Nkrumah and his jailed partisans won the popular title of "prison graduate." From the early 1950s on in West Africa, the British governors entered into a period of diarchy, or shared rule, with the African nationalist leaders and elevated them to prime ministers. Thus, they were brought into the political establishment rather than driven into the hands of external, possibly Marxist, forces which were prepared to support urban guerrilla warfare. Where the nationalists were suppressed, as in Portuguese Africa, Rhodesia, and Southwest Africa, the white regimes had to face violent, externally supported resistance.

THE CHALLENGE OF PAN-AFRICANISM

The "nationalist ideal" both complemented and conflicted with dreams of pan-African unity. Pan-Africanism was at its inception an American phenomenon, fostered by Africans of the diaspora. Its origins can be traced to Philadelphia with the formation of the Free African Society (1789) and the Bethel African Methodist Episcopal Church (1794). Pan-African sentiment also was manifested through schemes to settle freed black Americans in Africa. The British government in 1792 took such groups living in Nova Scotia to West Africa and established the colony of Freetown, Sierra Leone. Paul Cuffee, an American of

African and American Indian ancestry, sailed groups of freed blacks to Sierra Leone in 1810 and 1816. Shortly afterwards, the American Colonization Society of Philadelphia established Liberia as a base for freed blacks in the United States wishing to live in Africa.

Unfortunately, most black Americans living in Liberia and Sierra Leone proved to be anything but pan-African in deed. They conquered and exploited the indigenous African populations with a ruthlessness comparable to the white colonialists elsewhere. They also established a kind of "pigmentocracy," in which skin color was an index to political and social status.

One of the earliest articulators of the pan-African concept was Edward W. Blyden, a Liberian of West Indian birth. In 1881 Blyden stated, "the African must advance by methods of his own. He must possess a power distinct from that of the European."[1] He abhorred the arrogant, light-complected, Westernized blacks and called for racial integrity. Blyden believed that the indigenous African was more racially pure and that the essence of his civilization and inner core of his personality must be preserved. Blyden was first to coin the expression "the African personality" and he emphasized that Africa must struggle for a separate personality. Also linked to pan-Africanism is the slogan "Africa for the Africans," first enunciated by a white missionary, Joseph Booth, in his book *Africa for the Africans* (1896). A year later, W.E.B. Du Bois, a black American of European and African ancestry, stated that "if the Negro were to be a factor in the world's history it would be through a pan-Negro movement."[2]

The idea of "Negro unity" transcending continental bounds was more specifically manifested in a series of pan-African conferences. The first was convened not in Africa but in London and was sponsored not by an African but by a Trinidad lawyer, H. Sylvester Williams. The meeting, in 1900, protested the European partition of the continent and the loss of African land and sovereignty. From the start, there were serious fissions in the pan-African movement. The Jamaican, Marcus Garvey, disliked light-skinned mulattoes and echoed Blyden's call for racial purity. Garvey called for a revival of the "back-to-Africa" movement and organized the Universal Negro Improvement Association to achieve his goals. Garvey savagely attacked European colonialism through his New York-based journal, *Negro World.* His "Negro Empire" was centered in New York and flourished in the 1920s. Du Bois and Garvey clashed over the "back-to-Africa" concept, and Du Bois founded the National Association for the Advancement of Colored People and his own journal, called *Crisis.* Garvey's Black Star Line, which was meant to transport blacks to Africa, encountered financial problems, and the movement itself was mismanaged and harassed by the United States government. Garvey was later jailed, deported, and died in 1940 a broken man in London without ever reaching the shores of Africa.

[1] Colin Legum, *Pan Africanism* (New York: Frederick A. Praeger Publisher, Inc., 1962), p. 20.

[2] Ibid., p. 24.

The Second Pan-African Congress was held in Paris in 1919, at the close of the First World War, and under Du Bois's leadership. According to the historian, Colin Legum, "The congress adopted a resolution which nowhere spoke of the Africans' right to independence."[3] Rather, "It proclaimed the need for international laws to protect the natives; for land to be held in trust; for the prevention of exploitation by foreign capital; for the right of education, and finally, it insisted that 'the natives of Africa must have the right to participate in the government as far as their development permits'."[4] These were utopian ideas, sadly out of touch with the realities of postwar colonial policy in Africa.

By this time, Western-educated Africans in the British West African colonies were beginning to advance their own ideas. The National Congress of British West Africa, founded in 1920, was the first pan-Africanist movement of its kind on the continent. Africans from Sierra Leone, the Gambia, Nigeria, and the Gold Coast, led by Caseley Hayford, called for equal opportunity and the "better and more effective representation" of their people in affairs concerning their well-being. The initial momentum of the movement was not sustained and with the death of Hayford in 1930 it soon collapsed. A major reason for its demise was the failure of its leaders to secure the support of the traditional rulers and the masses. The colonial governments of British West Africa were hostile to any African movement which sought to foster political unity among the various colonies. Colonial authorities had convinced most African chiefs that Western-educated Africans were a threat to the status quo.

The pan-African movement thus continued to flourish mainly outside Africa. In 1921 Du Bois convened another conference, which met in London, Brussels, and Paris, the capitals of the major colonial powers. Du Bois now came up against Blaise Diagne, the Senegalese Deputy to the French National Assembly. For the assimilated Diagne, the only unity in Africa should be between whites and blacks. He stated that "to isolate the black race . . . and to let it work out its own evolution is ridiculous . . . the evolution of our race . . . requires the co-operation of everybody." Diagne's thoughts are best summed up in his remark that "we Frenchmen of Africa wish to remain French."[5] Du Bois was undaunted. At the fourth pan-African conference, held in London and Lisbon in 1923, his group stated, "We ask all the world that black folk be treated as men." The fifth conference was convened in New York in 1927, still under Du Bois's leadership.

A great turning point in the pan-African movement came in 1945 with the sixth pan-African conference, held in Manchester, England. Fewer black Americans were present and the West Indian group, still strong, was led by George Padmore and C.L.R. James. For the first time, it was a meeting dominated by

---

[3] Ibid., p. 29.

[4] Ibid., p. 30.

[5] Imanuel Geiss, *The Pan-African Movement* (New York: Africana Publishing Corporation, 1974), p. 234.

Africans, by such young nationalists as Kwame Nkrumah, Peter Abrahams, S.L. Akintola, Jomo Kenyatta and others. From the meeting came the Manchester Manifesto, calling for "one man, one vote," "Equal and rapid economic, cultural, and social development of Africa" and a demand for "autonomy and independence" for black Africa. This was the last demonstration of Africa and Afro-American solidarity. Du Bois now played a very modest role and attended as a private person without any organizational representation. The pan-African movement no longer asked for financial assistance from white philanthropists. The movement had now become liberated, financially, politically, and socially. It had become more militant and rested firmly in African hands. The strategy of the pan-African movement would now be to organize the masses through trade unions and political parties, and to engage in a struggle for political power through nonviolent means, based on Gandhi's principles. Historians have emphasized that pan-Africanism was a race-conscious, not a racist movement. Africans criticized the system of colonialism, rather than the whites as a race.

The mantle of the pan-African movement now passed to Kwame Nkrumah, who returned to the Gold Coast after nearly a decade of study overseas. Once home, he realized that he first had to establish a national base from which to launch his pan-African objectives. Nkrumah, the pan-Africanist abroad in the 1940s, became a nationalist at home in the 1950s. The same held true for other leaders of the Manchester conference; Jomo Kenyatta became a Kenya nationalist, Nnamdi Azikiwe a Nigerian nationalist, and so on. Once Nkrumah had led the Gold Coast to independence in 1958, he turned his attention back to the pan-African ideal. In that year, he and his close associate and mentor, George Padmore, organized in Accra a meeting of eight independent governments—the first Conference of Independent African States. For the first time, North African Arabs and sub-Saharan blacks conferred together, and as one observer put it, "pan-Africanism had returned from the diaspora to the promised land."[6] George Padmore, a Marxist who had become deeply disillusioned with international Communism, succeeded in keeping pan-Africanism a purely African movement.

In Ghana, pan-Africanism acquired a solid base in a sovereign national state. But this may also have been its undoing. The pan-African movement, after Padmore's death in 1959, became too closely associated with one man, Kwame Nkrumah, and one nation, Ghana. Leaders of the emerging African nations were by no way united on the meaning and implications of pan-Africanism. Nkrumah envisioned the political amalgamation of independent African nations into a United States of Africa, under his presidency. He was convinced that this must occur very soon, before nationalist tendencies in each state could become too strong. Others believed he was too impatient. They preferred only loose economic linkages or regional federations at best. They pointed to the failure of

[6]Ibid., p. 420.

attempts at multistate groupings—the Mali Federation of 1959, the Council of the Entente (Ivory Coast, Upper Volta, Niger, Dahomey) of the same year, and the abortive Ghana-Guinea-Mali Union of 1960. They foundered in part on the rock of nationalism, but also because of the economic and political legacies of the colonial era.

By 1962, these differences of approaches had crystallized into distinct interest blocs. The states advocating each approach were known by the cities in which they had met to draw up their position. The "Brazzaville group" comprising the French-speaking states favored a loose clustering of independent states and the maintenance of their individual ties with France. A year earlier they had formed the African and Malagasy Union (UAM), which was built upon the foundations of various ties and traditions inherited from their common colonial past. The organization's political aspirations went no farther than an expressed desire to adopt a common stand on all issues affecting member states and external powers. The "Casablanca group" included states supporting unity with a strong, centralized, executive authority and an all-African military force. The philosophy of the "Monrovia group" fell between the other two groups and emphasized consultation among sovereign nations rather than the formation of continent-wide executive and legislative institutions.

In May 1963 representatives of thirty African states met at Addis Ababa, Ethiopia, and drew up a charter establishing the Organization of African Unity (OAU). The event was a major milestone in African history and in the history of international relations. Never before had so many African nations reached unanimous agreement on aims and objectives. The charter was designed to accommodate the approaches of the Brazzaville, Casablanca and Monrovia groupings but fell short of Nkrumah's call for a "Union Government of Africa."

The OAU charter pledged in vague terms to promote African progress and unity, to respect its members' sovereignty and territorial integrity, to eradicate colonialism, to remain nonaligned with respect to the Great Powers, to settle disputes peacefully by negotiation and conciliation, and not to interfere in members' internal affairs. The charter's preamble reaffirmed the principles of the United Nations Charter and the United Nations Universal Declaration of Human Rights.

The OAU has four main institutions and a number of specialized commissions. The Assembly of the Heads of State and Government, acting as the supreme organ of the OAU, considers resolutions prepared by the Council of Ministers, which in turn consists of the foreign ministers of each member state. Major decisions can be made only by the heads of the member nations or their representatives meeting at the annual assembly. The assembly also considers reports submitted by the secretary general and the OAU's specialized commissions and ad hoc organs. The Council of Ministers has an essentially executive function and is charged with implementing the assembly's decisions. In addition to the assembly, the council, and the general secretariat, is the Commission of

Mediation, Conciliation, and Arbitration. The OAU's major aim through these institutions is to achieve unity and cooperation through persuasion and consensus rather than through force and mandatory sanctions. It consecrated the principle of noninterference and created a loose confederal structure that emphasizes socioeconomic cooperation. The issue of regionalism or federation among various states was deliberately avoided. Nkrumah asserted that "regional groupings of any kind are a serious threat to the unity of Africa."[7]

After 1963 the Organization of African Unity, with its headquarters at Addis Ababa, was the major vehicle for African unity and represented the aspirations of the more moderate African heads of state. Nkrumah was disappointed that a larger step towards political union was not taken and that he was prevented from playing a major role in the organization itself. He became increasingly isolated, disillusioned, and impatient with the OAU's lack of progress. Ghana soon became a base for guerrilla activity against heads of African states who seemingly "betrayed" the cause of pan-Africanism. In 1966 Nkrumah was overthrown in a military coup and pan-Africanism as a political movement declined rapidly. Pan-African leadership passed to Presidents Julius Nyerere and Sekou Touré of Tanzania and Guinea, respectively, both of whom shared Nkrumah's political philosophy.

These leaders encountered their own, internal challenges to unity. Touré had to resort to dictatorial and repressive measures to maintain unity within his own nation, and Nyerere encountered difficulty in fully integrating Zanzibar into the Tanzanian republic. By 1977 Nyerere's dreams of East African unity were shattered by the disintegration of the economic federation of Tanzania, Kenya, and Uganda.

The pan-African movement temporarily returned to the United States in 1970 under the black American intellectual, Imamu Baraka (formerly Leroi Jones), who called for the establishment of a "Republic of New Africa." The Congress of African Peoples, held in Atlanta, Georgia, that year failed to draw up a clear blueprint. In July 1974 a poorly attended Pan-African Congress was convened in Dar es Salaam, Tanzania, but still no mechanisms were developed to implement pan-African ideas. Nor was it clear what role Afro-Americans and Caribbeans should play in the politics of African liberation and unity. Pan-Africanism did not die in Dar es Salaam, rather it shifted to the nonpolitical, cultural plane. This new trend was manifested in the Second World Black and African Festival of Arts and Culture (FESTAC) convened in Nigeria in early 1977.

Imanuel Geiss, a noted authority on the pan-African movement, has observed that "The triumph of African nationalism, which on the whole took place with startling speed and smoothness, simultaneously deprived the pan-

---

[7]Kwame Nkrumah, *Axioms of Kwame Nkrumah* (London: Thomas Nelson and Sons Ltd., 1967), p. 17.

One of many billboards throughout Zaire, praising the leadership of President Sese Seko Mobutu.

African movement of the opportunity to prepare itself mentally for the far more difficult post-independence period."[8]

In any case, the Organization of African Unity survived, and by mid-1977 its membership had grown to forty-nine nations, ranging in population from 220,000 (Djibouti) to more than 74 million (Nigeria), representing more than 350 million people from a wide diversity of historical, cultural, linguistic, and political backgrounds. Its creation and endurance is a remarkable testimony to the compelling African desire for interstate cooperation.

The OAU has nevertheless suffered from a multitude of problems, including shortages of funds, an unwillingness of some member-states to participate in vital OAU organs, and an extreme reluctance to become involved in the internal affairs of member-states. In the area of human rights, the OAU has been preoccupied with the issue of white racism in southern Africa. It has expressed moral outrage over human rights violations only when it is perceived to be politically advantageous and has remained silent when speaking out might trigger dissension with the organization or cause general embarrassment. For example, the OAU refused to act in 1972 against Burundi when more than 150,000 ethnic Hutu were exterminated by the ethnic Tutsi in a blatant act of genocide. Nor did they speak out against the mass murders in Uganda of more than 120,000 opponents of the fascist Amin regime, despite the find-

[8] Geiss, *The Pan-African Movement,* p. 439.

ings of the International Commission of Jurists that the Universal Declaration of Human Rights had been violated. The OAU also has failed to unite against Equatorial Guinea's policy of forced labor and its discrimination against the ethnic Bubi populations.

By 1977, Africa had the highest ratio of refugees to total population in the world, and this too has been a relatively neglected issue. There are refugees from the racial discrimination of South Africa and Rhodesia, from the religious discrimination against the Jehovah's Witnesses in Malawi, from the abrupt changes of government in Mozambique and Angola, from the political oppression in Guinea, from the ethnic persecution in Burundi, Equatorial Guinea, and Uganda, and from the prolonged drought and famine in the West African Sahel.

A few specific examples must suffice. An estimated 170,000 Hutu refugees from Burundi are scattered through Zaire and East Africa; there are another 250,000 or so refugees from Guinea; more than ten thousand refugees have come out of Rhodesia and South Africa; Idi Amin, the Ugandan dictator, abruptly expelled some 40,000 Asians; and more than 350,000 Portuguese fled from Mozambique and Angola when their possessions were nationalized shortly after independence.

A prominent African political scientist, has offered an explanation for many of Africa's refugee migrations. He observed that there is a definite tradition in Africa of punishing the group for the acts of an individual. This may stem from the African conception of collective responsibility.

The refugee problem in Africa is certainly not new. Slave trading and raiding from at least the fifteenth century caused major population displacements; the Zulu wars in the early nineteenth century uprooted tens of thousands of Sotho- and Nguni-speaking peoples in southern Africa, and the European conquests of the late nineteenth century unsettled many of those who resisted. Recall that the British conquest of the Sokoto Caliphate in 1903 provoked the *hejira,* or flight, of several thousand Muslims to the Nile Valley.

The Organization of African Unity has made little headway in resolving disputes over national boundaries, which were hastily delimited by European imperialists when the continent was partitioned. This has proven to be one of the most serious obstacles in the quest for African unity. The border disputes between Somalia on the one hand and Ethiopia and Kenya on the other are of long standing. On the grounds of ethnic relationship, Somalia called for the incorporation of the Ogaden in Ethiopia and the Northern Frontier District in Kenya (along with Djibouti) into a greater Somalia. These demands have long presented a problem for African unity, and OAU efforts at mediation have consistently failed. The Ogaden question festered until 1977 when Somalia invaded Ethiopia and militarily occupied the region. At the same time Ethiopia was fighting a losing battle with secessionist forces in its coastal province of Eritrea. Faced with becoming a landlocked, dismembered, and nonviable nation, the Ethiopian Marxist regime called upon the Soviets, who rushed in nearly $1 billion of military equipment, and the Cubans, who dispatched more than 12,000 soldiers. The Ogaden was easily retaken and the United States persuaded Somalia to withdraw to its national borders. The OAU, though condemning Somali irredentism, watched passively as Great Power rivalry returned to the Horn of Africa, for the first time since colonial days.

Assisted by its new Cuban and Soviet allies, Ethiopia in December 1978 re-captured Eritrea, ending a seventeen-year-old secessionist movement. This was viewed by many pan-Africanists as a victory for the forces of African unity. It also seemed to assure the future of Ethiopia as a coherent, viable state. Others viewed it as a triumph for the Soviet Union which by late 1978 had become the dominant maritime power in the western Indian Ocean (across which so much of the capitalist West's oil must pass) and a strong presence in the Red Sea leading up to Suez and Egypt. The United States had already begun to step up its arms sales to the Sudan, Kenya, Egypt and other nations around the rim of Africa's geographical Horn.

REGIONAL AND ETHNIC CONFLICTS

Civil war in four African states also has presented the OAU with serious prob-lems. The regional and ethnic conflicts in Zaire, Nigeria, Angola, and Ethiopia resulted in divisions among the member-states and gave rise to intervention by non-African states.

The crisis in Zaire (then Congo) in the 1960s between the central government and the secessionist Katanga province could not be resolved by the OAU and led to the intervention of the United Nations and outside powers. Again, the invasion of Shaba (formerly Katanga) province in 1977 by a refugee army was suppressed by a joint Franco-Moroccan force, called in at the request of Zaire's President Mobutu.

The Nigerian civil war (1967–70) also tested the movement for African unity. Though the OAU condemned the secession of Biafra, its mediation efforts failed. Tanzania, Zambia, and the Ivory Coast accorded official recognition to Biafra in the face of OAU insistence on the preservation of Nigerian unity. Outside powers became involved: the Soviet Union, Great Britain, and the United Arab Republic supported the Nigerian federal government, and France threw its weight be-hind the Biafrans. Nigeria was reunited, but by means of a violent war and not through the peacekeeping machinery of the OAU.

In the case of Angola, the OAU failed to achieve agreement among the three liberation movements—Roberto Holden's FNLA (National Front for the Libera-tion of Angola), Dr. Agostino Neto's MPLA (Popular Movement for the Lib-eration of Angola), and Dr. Jonas Savimbi's UNITA (National Union for the Total Independence of Angola)—on the establishment of a government of national unity. A destructive civil war ensued, which led to massive military intervention by the Russians and Cubans on behalf of the Marxist MPLA and by South Africa in support of UNITA. In 1976, the OAU meekly recognized the MPLA as the legitimate government of Angola, even though nearly a third of the country and a fourth of its population were under UNITA control. The civil war continued, disrupting the economies of Angola and Zambia, the latter being unable to ship its ores across the Benguela Railway to Angola's southern port of Lobito.

The OAU's efforts to settle the Rhodesian problem have also encountered problems. The Organization's African Liberation Committee over the years has found it difficult to obtain sufficient financial support from member-states, and the two liberation movements, ZAPU (Zimbabwe African Peoples' Union) and ZANU (Zimbabwe African National Union), have had to rely increasingly on external support, mainly from the Soviet Union. In face of OAU failures, Tanzania, Botswana, Mozambique, and Zambia in 1975 formed a pressure group called the "Front-Line States" to unite the two liberation movements into a single bloc, henceforth known as the Patriotic Front, to negotiate with the Rhodesian regime. As Joshua Nkomo, the leader of ZAPU, and Robert Mugabe of ZANU jockeyed for power between themselves, Rhodesia's prime minister, Ian Smith, in early 1978 negotiated an internal settlement with the moderate black leaders, Bishop Abel Muzorewa, Reverend Ndabiningi Sithole, and Chief Jeremiah Chirau. The Patriotic Front and the Front Line states were temporarily outflanked and became more dependent on Soviet military support in hopes of overthrowing Smith and the pro-Western, black nationalists whom they regarded as lackeys of the whites. Again, the OAU was unable to reconcile the various African nationalist factions.

CONSTITUTIONALISM: REPUDIATING
THE EUROPEAN LEGACY

A major obstacle to pan-African unity has been the diversity among states in political ideologies and government structures. As Africa moves farther from the advent of independence, variations in political systems have been more obvious.

France left its colonies with independence constitutions providing for a unicameral "national assembly" elected by universal suffrage from a single-voter roll. The executive head in each new state was a popularly elected president. France also bequeathed a strong sense of centralized administration, with comparatively little power at the level of local government.

Independence constitutions in the British possessions placed real political authority in the hands of a prime minister. The queen, as the sovereign, remained the constitutional head of state. Her official seal was placed on all legislative acts, but she had no actual power to veto or amend them. The queen was represented in each state by a governor-general.

As in the British Westminster parliamentary system, which served as the model for the independence constitutions, the prime minister would be head of the political party which held the majority in a representative legislature. The independence constitutions adopted the Westminster concept of a loyal parliamentary opposition as an essential ingredient in a multiparty political system. African parliaments were to be bicameral (with a few exceptions, notably Ghana), consisting of an upper chamber of citizens with hereditary claims to governance (mainly the traditional rulers) and a lower one of popularly elected representatives. The upper house, usually called the Senate, was designed to protect "tribal" and parochial interests and to act as a brake on the more radical modernizing elites. Each constitution contained a clause protecting the liberties of ethnic minorities. This was in contrast to the French constitutions which largely neglected minority rights.

The leaders of the newly independent governments in French-speaking Africa tended to have closer emotional ties to their former colonial master than did their English-speaking counterparts. This was a product of the colonial policies of assimilation and association. For example, Felix Houphouet-Boigny, president of the Ivory Coast, served as a deputy to the French National Assembly in Paris from 1946 to 1948 and was a minister of state in de Gaulle's government from 1958 to 1959. President Leopold Senghor of Senegal was a deputy to the French National Assembly from 1946 to 1958. Both leaders in the postcolonial era were influenced by their close personal bonds with France. As a result, during the French presidency of Charles de Gaulle and his

Legislative chambers, Nairobi, Kenya.

Arch of Triumph and eternal flame, symbols of Ghanaian nationalism built in Accra during the era of President Kwame Nkrumah.

successor, Georges Pompidou, most French-speaking states followed policies favorably inclined towards the French republic. Some historians argue that this "neo-colonial" relationship inhibited the French-speaking states from fully supporting programs aimed at greater African solidarity.

In the first five years of independence, the English-speaking nations revised their European-imposed constitutions and moved towards republican status within the commonwealth. Ghana initiated the trend in 1960 when Prime Minister Nkrumah was elected as "president" under a republican constitution. One by one, other states abandoned the British monarch as head of state and replaced her with a popularly elected president under a republican form of government. The problem was that once in power, the presidents sought to remain there permanently. Nkrumah again led the way, in 1964, with a new constitution vastly increasing his powers over the legislative and judicial branches. It made him "president-for-life" and head of the Convention Peoples' Party, which henceforth was the only political party allowed. The constitution represented a reversion to the traditional African conception of the head of state having an indeterminate tenure of office and commanding a national consensus.

African governments everywhere adopted new constitutions which greatly centralized the political framework, discouraged or destroyed multiparty systems, weakened legislative authority, and conferred sweeping powers on the president. Some historians suggest that this can be interpreted as a return to the precolonial situation in which there was little differentiation between executive, legislative, and judicial functions. As in the era immediately preceding the colonial conquest, African leaders seemed less concerned with limiting power than with strengthening it. Consequently, from the early 1960s, decision making became more concentrated, central bureaucracies increased in power at the expense of local government, and popularly elected institutions declined.

At the time of independence, personal charisma was viewed as an essential vehicle for the transfer of loyalties. The personalization of power was aimed at creating a sense of nationhood transcending ethnic or other sectional divisions within the country. The dynamic and magnetic personalities of the nationalist leaders did invoke strong feelings of nationality. Government heads argued that strong executive leadership was the only way to achieve unity and that legislative bodies, deeply divided by a multitude of conflicting political parties which by colonial legacy were usually regionally or ethnically based, engaged in endless and paralyzing debate. The departure of the alien colonial government tended to remove a major, albeit negative, force for unity. Prior to independence, nearly everyone was united on at least one issue—removal of the colonial regime.

Ironically, as the civilian leaders centralized and consolidated their authority, their regimes became more fragile and had to be held together by military coercion. Civilian leaders were convinced that strong leadership was a prerequisite for modernization, and they were impatient with regional limitations upon their authority. That impatience led them to suppress basic democratic institutions. Political parties declined as an institutional source of authority, and nations came to be ruled under a personalistic cabinet autocracy. African political systems succumbed to personal rule: Sekou Touré in Guinea, Leopold Senghor in Senegal, Houphouet-Boigny in Ivory Coast, Nkrumah in Ghana, Macias Nguema in Equatorial Guinea, Jomo Kenyatta in Kenya, Julius Nyerere in Tanzania, Kenneth Kaunda in Zambia, Kamuzu Banda in Malawi, Jean-Bedel Bokassa in the Central African Empire, Sese Mobutu in Zaire and so forth. Power, rather than becoming more institutionalized instead became more deeply personalized and thus less enduring.

Increasingly, African leaders believed they could strengthen the legitimacy of their regimes not through ballots but with sacred symbols and romantic awe, much as the precolonial rulers had done. They argued that in the precolonial past many Africans were subject to an authoritarian political order, under the control of powerful hereditary rulers with spiritual sanction. They therefore sought to combine political office with ritual or religious office as in the past. Nkrumah assumed the title of "Osagyefo," or redeemer, and constructed a throne, or "stool" similar to the traditional Asante stools. He ruled over "Ghana," a name taken from a distant ancient empire which had collapsed in the eleventh century. President Mobutu of Zaire added to his constitutional titles that of "Ngbendu wa za Banga," or the "cock that leaves no hens alone," in order to return to the precolonial concept of the ruler as symbolizing the fertility of the nation. Extreme paternalism had been a common feature of government in both the early empires and in the policy of the Belgian colonialists. The masses were not encouraged to make political decisions. Mobutu continued this practice and posed as the munificent father of his people. He called upon them to address him as "the Father of the Revolution," "the Guide," the "Helmsman," the "Chief," and the "Redeemer." In 1973, King Sobhuza II of Swaziland, who had been on the throne since 1922, went even further. He repealed the British-imposed constitution, abolished the legislature, and assumed absolute powers. This trend towards royal absolutism culminated in 1977 when Jean-Bedel Bokassa of the Central African Republic transformed the state into the Central African Empire and crowned himself "Emperor Bokassa I" in Napoleonic fashion.

The British and Belgians tended to leave behind government structures that allowed for a considerable degree of regional autonomy. Colonial administrations in the British areas had always encouraged feelings of regional identity. It should be recalled that indirect rule organized local political units along precolonial ethnic lines, and that the ethnic basis of national politics was intensified by the preferential treatment accorded the Fulani, Asante, Baganda, Lozi, and others. Consequently, from the advent of independence, African governments found it difficult to reconcile the requirements of central leadership with the demands of regional autonomy. In Uganda and Nigeria it resulted in attempts by the Baganda and Igbo, respectively, to transform their ethnic group into a separate, sovereign nation. More will be said of this later.

In Zaire (formerly Congo) the province of Katanga held a disproportionate share of the colony's minerals and hence its wealth. Naturally, the ethnic Lunda, who in precolonial times ruled over this area, did not want to share this wealth with the rest of the Congo, which was relatively impoverished and far less developed economically. The years following Congolese independence in 1960 thus were chaotic. Six provinces of the colonial administration were fragmented into twenty-one under a federal structure. Katanga feared that its wealth would be siphoned off to support the other provinces. With the help of Belgian businessmen and European mercenaries, Katanga seceded and proclaimed its independence. Rebellion spread from province to province like a brushfire and could be put down only by a United Nations force.

Prime Minister Patrice Lumumba became impatient and turned to the Soviet Union for assistance. President Kasavubu, constitutionally his superior and backed by the Western powers, called for Lumumba's resignation. The latter in turn repudiated Kasavubu and the government became paralyzed. Elements in the Western powers, fearing the Congo would become a Soviet satellite, brought about Lumumba's death in February 1961. President Kasavubu was unable to restore national unity, even though the United Nations forces ended Katanga's secession in early 1963. Peasant uprisings continued in Kwilu, Kivu, and Oriental provinces. Kasavubu, and Moise Tshombe whom he had ironically appointed as prime minister, eventually struggled among themselves for political power.

When Sese Seko Mobutu came to power in a military coup in 1965, he took several steps to crush ethnic subnationalism. He created eight de-politicized provinces and deprived them of their own legislatures; governors were appointed to posts outside their home areas and were rotated frequently, the provincial police were nationalized, and a single national party was established—the Popular Movement of the Revolution (MPR). Zaire was thus reunited, in Bismarckian fashion, but at a frightful price. Political opposition outside the MPR was suppressed, nearly all decision-making authority was transferred to the national capital, at Kinshasa, and local government atrophied. The national legislature in 1974 became a rubber-stamp body, and all real initiative and power passed to Mobutu and his self-appointed Political Bureau.

Some observers believe that the federal system of distributing powers between the central and regional governments was one of the major causes of political instability within the Federation of Nigeria in the early 1960s. In Nigeria, the independence constitution established three regions and a federal capital at Lagos. Considerable power was given to the regional governments, and political parties, as we have seen, developed along regional, rather than national lines: The Hausa/Fulani-dominated Northern Peoples' Congress (NPC) in the North, the National Convention of Nigerian Citizens (NCNC) in the Igbo South, and the Action Group in the Yoruba West. In other words, each region was allowed to maintain its ethnic political culture. The Northern region, the most populous of the three, had a commanding position in the central government. In the Federal Assembly, the balance of power rested on regional population figures. Thus, the more conservative northerners could block bills submitted by the socialistically inclined representatives from the Eastern region. A referendum in 1963 created a fourth, Mid-West region, but this failed to overcome the imbalance. Regional jealousies persisted and the results of the 1962 census, reconfirming northern domination, led to rioting, strikes, and deeper divisions. The federal government refused to intervene as the nation slipped into anarchy. In January 1966 the military staged a coup, suspended the constitution, banned all political parties, and thus ended less than six years of civilian rule. After a military counter-coup only months later, the North reasserted its hegemony and in May 1967, the Eastern region seceded and declared itself the independent nation of Biafra.

It should be recalled from the previous chapter that conflicts in Uganda between the central government and the kingdom of Buganda led to a constitutional crisis. In 1966 Prime Minister Milton Obote suspended the constitution and forced the nation's president, the kabaka of Buganda, into exile. A new constitution the following year abolished all four kingdoms in favor of a unitary national government. It provided for a unicameral legislature with Obote as president with almost unlimited authority. Divisions in the nation persisted and in 1969, Obote abolished all opposition parties and ruled as a virtual dictator. He surrounded himself with a secret service, designed to root out dissent. Gradually it began to probe into army affairs and in 1971, the army reacted with a successful military coup. Uganda thus had less than a decade of civilian government.

Nkrumah in Ghana encountered similar problems. The wealth of Asante and its importance to the national economy posed a threat to Nkrumah's programs. His major opposition always had come from the Asante, who resented being submerged in a greater Ghanaian nationalism. Nkrumah met this challenge by reducing the legal powers of the chiefs and de-stooling those who resisted. But Asante was simply too rich and populous to be dealt with in that manner. Nkrumah's inability to compromise with the Asante was a major reason for his overthrow by a military coup in early 1966. Ghana, which had held out so much promise as a fledgling democracy in 1957, had become one of the independent Africa's first dictatorships.

The above case studies serve merely to highlight one of the most important problems in the history of African politics, that of the centralization of power. It was a problem most prominent in the former British possessions. Regional/ center conflicts plagued many African nations following independence. The problem was not only of an ethnic or economic nature. It also reflected tensions between traditional authorities at the local level and the modernizing elites at the center. The traditional authorities, especially the chiefs, who had enjoyed a revival under British indirect rule, now felt threatened and alienated by the modernist politicians who had assumed control of the central governments after independence. Guinea, Tanzania, and Ruanda simply abolished chieftaincy. In most French-speaking areas, the chiefs were reduced to figureheads before independence. The British independence constitutions did not take into full account the waning political power of the traditional authorities and therefore left the new governments with a major impediment to nation-building.

BUILDING A NATIONAL ETHOS

It would be fair to say that regardless of their actions, most African nationalists were sincerely interested in building a modern nation-state. They believed in the need for a "national-belief system," or ethos around which everyone might rally. Nkrumah, Mobutu, and Nyerere have devoted considerable attention to this.

The people of Zaire, under the extreme paternalism of Belgian rule, found their pride, identity, and culture weakened. Mobutu believed that political independence had not resulted in cultural liberation. Consequently, in 1972 he launched a policy of "psychological decolonization" and called it "Authenticité." The country's name was changed from the Congo to Zaire, municipalities and streets assumed African names, and thus Leopoldville reverted to the precolonial name of Kinshasa, Stanleyville to Kisangani, Elizabethville to Lubumbashi, and so on. All Zaireans were to address each other as "Citizen" and to renounce their Christian names in favor of African ones. Authenticity also called for a return to traditional values. Citizens were expected to dress in a modest, dignified manner, preferably non-Western in style, and to spurn skin-lighteners and hair-straighteners. Mobutu aimed to inculcate the masses with his concepts through party cells and the youth league of the party, the MPR (Popular Movement of the Revolution). The bureaucratic elites would learn through an MPR ideological school, the Makanda Kabobi Institute, which Mobutu called "a school of life" and which resembled Nkrumah's Winneba Institute in Ghana in the 1960s. The MPR and its organs, like Ghana's Convention Peoples' Party, became the major vehicles for implementing this national ethos. Mobutu also followed the general trend in Africa of merging the party and the state into a single, indivisible entity. By 1974, he had presented himself in the manner of a traditional African king: as the embodiment of the state, the interpreter and disseminator of its values, and the symbol of the personality of society. Mobutism in the 1970s, like Nkrumahism in the 1960s, was the consecration of the cult of personality and called for total obedience, submission, and subordination. As Mobutu's major ideologue expressed it in 1974, "Authenticity will merge traditionalism with modernism. For Christianity it was the Church which gave it its structure. For Mobutism, it is the party, MPR. Like the clergy, the cadres of the MPR will relay the thoughts of the president-founder to the masses."[9] A decade earlier, Nkrumah in his philosophy of Consciencism, stated: "Consciencism is the map . . . which will enable African society to digest the Western and the Islamic and the Euro-Christian elements in Africa, and develop them in such a way that they fit into the African personality." He concluded, "The cardinal ethical principle of philosophical consciencism is to treat each man as an end in himself and not merely as a means. This is fundamental to all socialist or humanist conceptions of man."[10]

Tanzania probably has been the most successful country in developing and implementing a national ethos as an instrument of nation-building. Most of the credit must go to President Nyerere, who, beginning with the Arusha Declaration of 1967, laid down a set of basic socialist beliefs for all citizens:

> That all human beings are equal;
>
> That every individual has a right to dignity and respect;
>
> That every citizen is an integral part of the nation and has the right to take an equal part in Government at local, regional and national levels;
>
> That every citizen has the right to freedom of expression, of movement, of religious belief and of association within the context of the law;
>
> That every individual has the right to receive from society protection of his life and of property held according to law;

[9] Address at New York University by Nguza Karl-I-Bond, April 15, 1974.

[10] Nkrumah, *Axioms of Kwame Nkrumah*, p. 27.

That every individual has the right to receive a just return for his labor;

That all citizens together possess all the natural resources of the country in trust for their descendants;

That in order to ensure economic justice the state must have effective control over the principal means of production; and

That it is the responsibility of the state to intervene actively in the economic life of the nation so as to prevent the exploitation of one person by another or one group by another, and so as to prevent the accumulation of wealth to an extent which is inconsistent with the existence of a classless society.[11]

Nyerere has argued that "the ideal society is based on human equality and on a combination of the freedom and unity of its members."[12] He adds, "There must be equality because only on that basis will men work cooperatively."[13] Nyerere's ideas have worked moderately well, in one of the world's poorest nations, with over 120 ethnic groups, none of which is large enough to dominate the others. In a nation like Nigeria, with rigid class structures and with several powerful ethnic groups vying for wealth and power, such ideas seem almost utopian.

As a means of implementing a national ethos and in minimizing internal factionalism, most African nations in the mid-1960s adopted a one-party system of government. In Tanzania, for example, the Revolutionary Party of Tanzania (RPT) (1977) is the only legal party in the nation, and all political competition must take place within the RPT framework. A two-party system has been suspect in Tanzania because it was regarded as symbolic of class and ethnic antagonism. In 1965 Tanzania launched an experiment in competitive elections within the single party. Members of TANU (Tanganyika African National Union) contested the same seats against each other. The experiment worked quite well, and the one-party system gained wide acceptance among the population.

Kenya, on the other hand, preferred a one-party structure, but not by constitutional fiat. In 1969, President Kenyatta suppressed the opposition Kenya People's Union (KPU) and detained its leaders. However, the government party, the Kenya African National Union (KANU) was allowed to factionalize so that in the 1970 elections a degree of choice in candidates was offered to voters.

We already have seen that in many nations, once a one-party system is established, the party and the state are merged. In Mozambique, under the constitution, the president of the party Liberation Front for the Independence of Mozambique (FRELIMO) is also president of the Marxist Republic. The su-

---

[11] Julius K. Nyerere, *Essays on Socialism* (London: Oxford University Press, 1970), p. 15.

[12] Julius K. Nyerere, "Freedom and Development," in *African Aims and Attitudes,* Martin Minogue and Judith Molloy, eds. (London: Cambridge University Press, 1974), p. 64.

[13] Ibid., p. 64.

preme body of FRELIMO is the Congress, which is mandated to meet every five years. The highest organ is the Central Committee which elects the president of the party and the powerful Standing Political Committee.

In single-party states, the executive, administrative and legislative cadres are intertwined. The one-party states tend to become monolithic and absorb the youth movements, trade unions, and the cooperatives. Opposition is permitted, but only within the context of the party organs and within the general framework of the national ethos, as defined by the party.

The one-party system of government has worked democratically only in a few nations. In 1977, Freedom House, a nonpartisan foundation which monitors global freedom, placed Africa in an unfavorable light. Of the thirty-seven "least politically free" nations in the world, eighteen were in Africa and of the twenty least free in civil rights, eight were African.

At the beginning of 1978, only four African nations had functioning multiparty electoral systems—the Gambia, Botswana, Mauritius, and Senegal. After years of one-party rule, a Senegalese law in 1976 made it possible for three parties to exist, and national elections in early 1978 were among the most free and peaceful on the continent in over a decade. A few other nations showed signs of returning to a multiparty system. In the same year, Upper Volta's electorate voted overwhelmingly to return to civilian rule and to a three-party structure.

Beset by a multitude of conflicting ethnic groups and cultures, African nations have clearly rejected the Westminster parliamentary model, in which a single vote of no confidence can bring down a government. They are continuing to search for distinctly "African" forms of governance and for a means of centralizing authority without resorting to dictatorship or destroying local initiative.

Generally in Africa, the organizational base of political parties has been in the urban areas. Few parties, even after the introduction of a one-party system, evolved into truly mass movements. Heads of government, once elected to office, tended to avoid further elections. On paper, party cadres were entrusted with a wide range of decision making. In reality, many leaders looked to their civil servants and to the military to instill national discipline and to implement programs. By the late 1970s, in nations in which political parties still existed at all, a growing number of people were refusing to pay their annual dues and to become involved.

In the decade after independence, many African nations developed government bureaucracies whose size was out of proportion to the country's resources. Senegal's problem was inherited from the colonial era when its capital, Dakar, was also capital of the massive West African Federation. Dahomey, on the other hand, enlarged its bureaucracy in order to give employment to the restless urban youth. In any case, the independence period has witnessed nearly everywhere the progressive bureaucratization of the government apparatus and an increased concentration of administrative responsibility in the hands of European-trained,

African civil servants who operate at the center of the political system. As we have seen, a large majority of the population has fallen outside the decision-making process. In the Ivory Coast, rural political apathy in the 1970s had been attributed to the almost total absence of village and town councils.

As bureaucracies have grown, so too has the incidence of corruption, bribery, graft, and nepotism. These tendencies, conceded by all government leaders, have been a major corrosive force in national life. Poverty in juxtaposition to great wealth, has proved to be one of the easiest lures to corrupt practices. Civil servants in many countries have entrenched only further the full range of colonial privileges. In nearly bankrupt Zaire, for example, civil servants live in the opulent Binza hillside section of Kinshasa while a few miles below in the *cité* (city), the masses exist in squalor. Corruption is especially great in the public corporations, in which funds are commonly misappropriated. But in most nations, it runs completely through the bureaucracy, from high-ranking ministers to the police and postal clerks. In Zaire and Nigeria, where it is blatant, there is also considerable nepotism by government functionaries. "Zaireanization" of the economy helped the families of party members. For example, the Société Generale d'Alimentation, a national food retail monopoly, became a Mobutu family enterprise and purchased goods from white-ruled Rhodesia and South Africa.

Corruption is recognized by most African heads of state as one of their most serious national problems, and they speak against it frequently. But words have rarely been matched by deeds. There has been a general reluctance to investigate corruption for fear that too much exposure would further erode public confidence in government. Nkrumah was one of the first to address himself to the problem in his famous "Dawn Broadcast" to the nation in 1961, but to no avail. Others, notably Nyerere, have established strict codes of ethics for their officials and have experienced moderate success. In 1967, Nyerere laid down the following principles:

1. Every TANU and Government leader must be either a peasant or a worker, and should in no way be associated with the practices of capitalism or feudalism
2. No TANU or Government leader should hold shares in any company
3. No TANU or Government leader should hold directorships in any privately-owned enterprise
4. No TANU or Government leader should receive two or more salaries
5. No TANU or Government leader should own houses which he rents to others.[14]

Unfortunately, these strictures have discouraged professional people with an instinct for commerce from government service. Consequently, many of the state enterprises are managed by people who lack the necessary skills.

[14] Ibid., p. 75.

Apologists for bribery argue that the African practice of "dashing" people for service performed predated the colonial era. There is considerable historical documentation to support this view. Others would contend that it breeds cynicism and hurts the poor and the powerless.

The roots of African political fragility lie in the origin of the modern nation-state, which was the creation of a small minority of European colonialists and Western-educated African elites, to which the traditional authorities were hostile and to which the masses, at first enthusiastic, were ultimately indifferent. As the avenues of legitimate opposition were closed off, the only means of change were through extraconstitutional acts. Only the military had the weapons to effect the overthrow of the old order.

LAW AND JUSTICE

The independence era witnessed a revival of interest in customary law and renewed efforts to fuse the former colonial "native courts" with those operating under European law. By the late 1960s Niger, Mali, and the Ivory Coast had abolished the separate status of customary courts and had created a unified court system. Ghana, Senegal, and Tanzania have empowered courts at all levels to deal with both customary and general law. Some countries have taken the multitude of ethnically based laws and fused them into a single corpus of customary law.

Changes in customary law have been greatest in the areas of property disputes, marriage and divorce, and inheritance. The Ivory Coast, with a significant Muslim population, took the radical step of abolishing polygamy, a pillar of Islamic social order but an impediment to family planning. Since African independence, local justice generally has returned to its traditional flexibility, which has enabled humane considerations to temper formal legal decisions.

On the negative side, the judiciary, independent in colonial times, has undergone considerable politicization. The colonial concept of an independent, impersonal judiciary has not withstood very well the strong political pressures to bend it to the will of the party in power. Throughout Africa, executive authority over the judiciary has increased. In Ghana, a constitutional amendment in 1964 gave the president (Nkrumah) the power to dismiss supreme court judges. In Zaire, the Judicial Council became an organ of the party (MPR), and is presided over by a deputy appointed by the president (Mobutu).

Constitutional clauses protecting the liberties of minorities also have been repealed. For example, in South Africa the constitutional clause guaranteeing the colored franchise in Cape province was repealed by the legislature in 1956. A new law removed the colored voters to a voting roll separate from the whites and gave them only limited, indirect representation in the national legislative bodies.

Civil liberties, especially habeas corpus, have been eroded through preventive detention. Ghana was the initiator in this area with the passage in 1958 of the Preventive Detention Act giving the government authority to detain a person for five years without any trial and without even being accused of a specific offense. South Africa, in its desire to preserve white supremacy, passed a similar bill in 1963. The General Law Amendment Act empowered police officers to arrest whomever they wished without a warrant and to detain them indefinitely without trial and without access to legal advisers. In 1969, Zambia's President Kaunda, hitherto known for his high respect for justice, amended the constitution to enable him to detain people up to one year without judicial review of their case. Kaunda's action seems to have broken a log jam, for within five years most African nations had instituted some form of preventive detention legislation.

Today, nearly every African nation has political detainees. Occasionally, a head of state will announce a general amnesty and free some political prisoners. Leaders of Africa, white as well as black, will argue that preventive detention is necessary in the early stages of nation-building in order to silence elements standing in the way of public order and obstructing the quest for national unity. Only history will tell whether in the long run, political independence advanced the cause of law and justice in Africa.

There is no question that sincere efforts have been made to achieve a marriage between modern statutory law and customary law. African legal experts are boldly tailoring modern rules of law, designed to promote rural economic development, to the fundamental values of traditional life and jurisprudence. Anthropologists continue to debate whether customary laws have much meaning when removed from the social context which interprets and supports them. Nevertheless, projects involving the recording, unification, and codification of customary laws continues and has met with much success in Tanzania, Kenya, Zambia, Malawi, and Botswana.

THE ROLE OF THE MILITARY

The military has been a major factor in African politics since the mid-1960s. The first military coup in independent Africa occurred in 1952 in Egypt. Togo led the way in sub-Saharan Africa with a military takeover in January 1963. For the next decade, Africa was plagued by continuous attempted coups, coups, counter-coups, and mutinies. Tanzania, Uganda, and Kenya were rocked by unsuccessful mutinies in 1964, and between November 1965 and November 1966, civilian regimes fell like kingpins in Zaire, Burundi, Central African Republic, Dahomey, Upper Volta, Ghana, and Nigeria. Mali followed in 1968. Still more coups rocked the continent in the early 1970s, notably in Niger, Chad, Uganda, and Ethiopia. By 1976, twenty out of forty-one states on the

African continent were ruled by military elements or by military-civilian coalitions. In less than two decades, Africa had experienced thirty-three military coups, eight in Dahomey (now Benin) alone. In the process, African armies had grown astronomically: Nigeria's from 8,000 to 221,000; Uganda's from 1,000 to 20,000; Ghana's from 7,000 to 15,000; and Zaire's from 6,200 to 43,400. Today, most African nations have armed forces and military budgets far out of proportion to defense needs. Total military spending in sub-Saharan Africa (excluding South Africa and Rhodesia) by 1977 had risen to an estimated $3.7 billion, almost four times the outlay three years earlier and forty times bigger since 1957, the commencement of the independence era. Military spending in South Africa alone has climbed to $1.9 billion and in Nigeria to $2.4 billion. Such expenditures have diverted precious national wealth from economic, social, and physical development to the military establishment. According to the prestigious International Institute for Strategic Studies in London, the number of black Africans under arms rose from 475,000 in 1975 to over 600,000 at the close of 1977. Nigeria supports the ninth largest standing army in the world. Since 1974, alone, military force has installed governments in Ethiopia, Angola, Mozambique, and Chad. This must be seen in light of the fact that before 1973, African nations south of the Sahara had gained their independence through constitutional negotiations, not through the barrel of a gun. Indeed, on the eve of independence, African armies were miniscule and were commanded mostly by European officers. Guerrilla force was unnecessary because the British, French, and Belgians were willing to decolonize, and at a rapid pace.

The above statistics strengthen the view of W.F. Gutteridge, an expert on the African military, that "military rule in Africa is now a norm rather than a deviant."[15] In 1976, only the Gambia, Swaziland, and Lesotho were without armies.

Africa's armies, which in colonial times were apolitical, took advantage of eroding citizen confidence in their civilian regimes and posed as the only force capable of fulfilling the original aims of the nationalists. Gutteridge, Professor Samuel Decalo, and others have offered a cavalcade of reasons why confidence in civilian regimes was so undermined that people were ready to accept the military alternative. They range from: financial extravagance and mismanagement of the civilian government, corruption, uncontrollable inflation and shortages in basic necessities due to import restrictions, rising youth unemployment, bureaucratic redtape and administrative paralysis, and un-fulfilled pre-independence promises of dramatic growth in the economy and in living standards. The historical record of most states affected by military coups validates these explanations.

Recently, military observers also have attributed coups to the internal dynamics of the officer corps, manifested through fears, discontentment, ambitions

[15] W.F. Gutteridge, *Military Regimes in Africa* (London: Methuen, 1975), p. 5.

of individual officers, and internal cleavages within the army ranks. Decalo suggests that, African armies have rarely been cohesive, nontribal, Westernized, or even complex organizational structures.[16]

Many military leaders, with an air of moral rectitude, have justified their coups by arguing that the regimes they replaced were corrupt. In most cases this was so. But there is evidence that the armies also were corrupt before coming to power. This was particularly true of the Ugandan army and its leader, Idi Amin. Few military forces once in power have been able to reduce corruption in the civil service. Nor have they been able to restore a semblance of political stability or public safety. Emperor Haile Selassie of Ethiopia was deposed in a military coup in 1974 after forty-six years of rule. Of the original leaders of the coup, less than half were alive six months later. Violent power struggles within the ruling military council, or Dergue, continued for the next three years and resulted in massive purgings both inside the Dergue and among dissidents in the civilian population. In November 1978, Amnesty International (a non-partisan independent international organization) reported that Ethiopia's government had resorted to large-scale killings of civilians and that ". . . repression of internal political opposition by the government's security forces has caused some thousands of deaths."[17]

The military in Africa also have criticized their civilian predecessors for their ethnic bias. In Uganda, Field Marshal and President Idi Amin liquidated the ethnic Acholi and Langi, whom he had earlier accused of dominating the ranks, and replaced them with members of his own group, the Kakwa. After the military coup in Burundi in 1966, Colonel Micombero, a Tutsi, launched a program of genocide against the Hutu.

Some armies have seized or held power to fulfil an ideological aim. For example, the establishment of a Marxist state was the goal of the military in Ethiopia, Togo, Guinea-Bissau, Mozambique, and Angola. More commonly, the military regimes were bereft of ideology. Most of their leaders were poorly educated, and lacked administrative expertise, and consequently have had to fall back on the existing civilian government cadres.

The arms race and the quest for military solutions to political problems have led to a revival of non-African intervention in continental affairs. Two liberation movements in southern Africa, the MPLA and FRELIMO, came to power with direct Soviet military assistance. Subsequently, the MPLA waged a civil war with the help of more than 13,000 Cuban troops. In 1977 in Ethiopia, the Marxist military regime invited Cuban and Soviet forces to repel the Somali invasion of the Ogaden and to suppress a secessionist movement in Eritrea. The Ethiopian

[16] Samuel Decalo, *Coups and Army Rule in Africa* (New Haven: Yale University Press, 1976), pp. 1–37.

[17] Human Rights Violations in Ethiopia, AFR 25/10/78 (London: Amnesty International, November 1978), p. 15.

regime, allied with the Soviets, was fighting a losing war with United States arms against Somalia, using Soviet weapons. For several years, Somalia had received Russian military aid. The tide turned in favor of the Ethiopians when they cut their links with the United States and accepted nearly $1 billion of Soviet equipment and some 12,000 Cuban troops. By 1978 the Soviet Union had become the largest foreign supplier of military aid to Africa.

France has also played a major direct military role on the continent. President Leon Mba of Gabon, overthrown in 1964, was quickly returned to power after the intervention of French troops. Starting in the mid-1960s France frequently intervened in a civil war in Chad, supporting the Christian black government against northern Muslim Arabs backed by Libyans with Soviet arms. In early 1977 France intervened in Zaire on the side of President Mobutu, whose U.S.-equipped army could not repulse the Soviet-supplied invasion of mineral-rich Shaba province by former Katanga mercenaries. French planes airlifted Moroccan troops to the Shaban front. The same year witnessed France flying Mirage jets for their U.S.-equipped Moroccan allies fighting Algerian-backed, Soviet-armed Polisario guerillas in the western Sahara.

Once in power, military regimes are as reluctant to step down as their civilian predecessors. Ghana returned to civilian rule in 1969 after more than three years of military rule. The military returned in 1972 when the Busia regime cut defense expenditures by ten percent. They have pledged to hand over power to an elected government in 1979.

Faced with mounting debts, economic stagnation, and rising popular discontent, particularly among young intellectuals, a few African nations have sought to reduce the size of their military establishment. It is a difficult political problem because in many states the army has become the nation's major employer, providing food, clothing, shelter, and training for the impoverished masses.

While the military regime in Nigeria evoked strong criticism in the local press, its proposal in 1977 to reduce the army's size by 100,000 men encountered widespread fear of further unemployment. The Supreme Military Council agreed to a return to civilian rule in 1979, though it reneged on a similar promise several years before. The only major nation in black Africa where military spending and armed forces have decreased is Zaire, a nation in technical bankruptcy. In January 1975 Mobutu announced to the nation, "I have decided that clothes and shoes must come before Mirages and tanks." "Soldiers must become producers."[18] Thus, Mobutu launched a verbal attack on the very army which had brought him to power a decade earlier. His efforts at partial demobilization reduced army morale and invited the invasion of Shaba which, without external aid, might have fallen.

By 1978, African history had come full circle. Some African nations had

---

[18] Address over radio in Kinshasa, Zaire, January 15, 1975.

returned to nineteenth-century imperialist policies, with Somalia invading Ethiopia and attempting to annex the Ogaden, with Libya sweeping down into Chad and annexing its northern regions, with Morocco and Mauretania partitioning the western Sahara without the consent of the local inhabitants, with Angola seizing oil-rich Cabinda after its people had declared their independence, with Uganda invading Tanzania and annexing a strip of its frontier, followed in 1979 by a Tanzanian invasion of a Uganda defended by Libyan soldiers. Western arms were again flowing into African countries, just as they had done in the 1870s, and again contributing to intra- and inter-state tensions and divisions. Internal military/civilian power struggles of the precolonial period had reappeared. As at the beginning of the European conquest in 1879, in 1979 the powerful leaders of black Africa were mainly the warriors. A century ago, the stage was set for Great Power rivalry on the African continent. Again, in 1978, Great Power rivalry, this time between the Soviet Union and the United States, was being played out—not in Europe where white lives would be at stake, but in black Africa. The actors may have changed, but the issues have remained the same: securing the sea routes to the East and acquiring raw materials from Africa itself.

By mid-1978, the continent was plagued by guerilla insurgencies in the western Sahara, Chad, Namibia, Zimbabwe, and Eritrea, and by boundary disputes between Togo and Ghana, Ethiopia and Somalia, and Kenya and Somalia. The potential for greater violence had increased since the halcyon days of the early 1960s. Great Power involvement has led to a growing polarization of the entire continent. Despite the rhetoric of nonalignment, a larger number of African nations have identified themselves with either the Eastern or Western bloc and have concluded military agreements.

chapter 8

Economic Horizons

THE AGRICULTURAL CRISIS

Agriculture in postindependence Africa continued to be the basis of livelihood
for most people, despite the continent's enormous real and potential wealth in
minerals. It was still the key sector of nearly all the economies. Since independence, peasants had greatly expanded the acreage and cultivation of cash crops,
more than doubling the production of all export crops. Nevertheless, subsistence
farming remained the primary feature of agriculture in most nations and pre-
capitalism continued to dominate the remote rural areas, particularly the more
arid zones. Sixty percent of the continent's arable land and seventy-five percent of its labor force in 1970 were still in subsistence production. Increasing
urbanization with its higher food consumption had begun to replace the old
subsistence crop production. By 1977 agriculture accounted for more than
thirty-six percent of the gross national product and sixty percent of the export
revenue of sub-Saharan Africa.

Production still rested mainly with peasant farmers working small scattered
plots individually or as extended-family units. Estate and plantation agriculture
and ranching continued to be concentrated in South Africa, Rhodesia, Namibia,
and the former colonies with large European settlements, notably Zaire, Angola,
Mozambique, Ivory Coast, and Kenya. By the early 1970s some nations, especially Ghana and Nigeria, had begun to encourage the expansion of large-scale
agriculture on government-owned or financed tracts.

Despite overall gains in agricultural output and export since 1960, food production for local consumption reached a historic crisis in the decade of the
seventies. By 1977, eighteen of the world's twenty-nine poorest nations were in
Africa and over the previous twelve years, food production per inhabitant had
declined in twenty-nine out of forty-seven African nations. This threatened to
spread to most of the others.

Historically, Africa has fed itself. Daily caloric intake may have been extremely low by modern Western standards and malnutrition was not uncommon. But massive deaths from starvation were infrequent. The major incidents of severe starvation in the nineteenth century were found in South Africa. Zulu expansionism in the 1830s, triggered by grain shortages, had dislocated thousands of Sotho-speaking people and forced many of them into cannibalism in order to survive. In 1856 the Xhosa destroyed their herds and crops in response to a vision received by a local prophetess which implied that such a sacrifice would cause the spirits to expel the encroaching Europeans. It was estimated that nearly a third of the population of 150,000 Xhosa starved to death as a result.

Today, many African nations are no longer self-sufficient in food, and the former colonies have found themselves increasingly dependent upon the West, particularly the United States, for their sustenance. Since the 1950s, food production has failed to keep pace with population growth and by the late 1970s, at least twenty percent of the population of sub-Saharan Africa was failing to meet basic caloric requirements. In some nations, twenty-five to forty percent of the children were suffering from malnutrition. The diet of most Africans has revealed a marked protein deficiency, lacking such body-building foods as milk, eggs, and meat. Staple foods in most of rural Africa continued to be protein poor yams and cassava. Consequently, kwashiorkor, or severe protein deficiency, has persisted in many rural areas.

Nearly everywhere in Africa the gap between food requirements and food supplies has increased. Given existing rates of population growth, a nation like Nigeria will double in population in a quarter-century. Yet in Nigeria, agricultural output is increasing at an annual rate of only two percent. In Africa, generally, the economically active population engaged in agriculture has not risen at a rate as fast as the population dependent on agricultural produce has. According to the Food and Agricultural Organization (FAO), food supplies and production must increase by 3.5 percent annually to meet the demands of the 1980s.

Because of escalating demands, food imports have been increasing by more than five percent annually. Food surpluses from advanced capitalist agriculture in the West as well as from South Africa were, by the early 1970s, being exported in growing quantities to tropical Africa. Zaire, for example, has come to depend almost solely upon the Continental Grain Company of New York for its grain imports and upon Botswana, Rhodesia, and South Africa for its meat. There has been a reluctance among many nations to impose stringent import controls for fear of popular discontent and for fear that they would produce a loss of foreign confidence in the economy.

Food shortages reached crisis proportions between 1972 and 1974 with a drought followed by massive starvation in Ethiopia and in seven Sahelian nations in West Africa. Even nations unaffected by prolonged drought have had severe and chronic food shortages, leading to high prices for staples and causing excessive pressure on wages, salaries, and on the balance of payments.

The explosive growth in food costs implies that the expansion of domestic food production has fallen behind effective demand. In almost circular fashion, the demand reflects the rise in real per-capita income since independence, at least among the urban wage-earners. Greater incomes in the boom years of the 1960s contributed to changes in food preferences. In many countries in the tropical zone, there was a tendency to substitute rice, maize, and wheat for indigenous root crops. In Zaire and Nigeria, for example, bread from imported wheat was produced by the late 1960s and began to push out locally grown manioc as a popular dietary item. Foreign rice had started to flow into Sierra Leone, Senegal, Tanzania, and Malagasy.

Scarce foreign exchange was spent on food imports—money which otherwise could have been used for importing capital equipment. The problem was exacerbated after 1973 by sharp increases in the cost of fuel, chemical fertilizers, and agricultural machinery. In 1965, a Tanzanian could buy a tractor from John Deere Inc. from the profits of 17.2 tons of sisal. The price of the same model in 1972 required 42 tons and in 1977 nearly 81 tons. In Africa, generally prices of major industrial imports have risen nearly three times faster than prices for most agricultural exports.

Local food production also has been hampered by a lack of government extension services and storage facilities, poorly developed marketing systems, and few secondary roads leading to main highways. Over the years, it has been amply demonstrated that farmers can produce a great deal more food when given incentives and technical know-how. One of the greatest restraints on agricultural productivity has been the low price-incentives to peasants. Many African governments deliberately have depressed prices of agricultural produce in order to satisfy the urban elites. In Ghana by 1977, prices for export crops were so low that a significant portion of crops were being smuggled across the borders into neighboring Ivory Coast and Togo where they fetched higher prices in a more valuable currency, the CFA franc. At the same time, local middlemen and "market mammies" paid low prices for foodstuffs and sold them at greatly inflated prices to consumers. In much of Africa, farmers were not paid enough for their crops, and many of their children were migrating to the urban areas where wages were higher, work was less burdensome, and amenities were superior.

Since the colonial era, the gap between rural and urban incomes has widened. In many nations, money incomes of farmers have decreased in real terms, contributing to a decline in rural purchasing power. Government appeals to people to return to the countryside have not been too successful, and large numbers of primary school graduates continue to gravitate toward the urban centers. As a result, rural areas are failing to retain young, educated people capable of modernizing that sector of the economy.

As in the colonial era, a disproportionate amount of government money and attention has gone into the promotion of industrial and exported crops, such as cotton, tobacco, sugar, coffee, cocoa, and tea. With the notable exception of

Senegal and the Ivory Coast, little support has been given to market gardening and fruit farming. In Africa, generally, the agricultural sectors of economies have been woefully neglected. In Nigeria's 1977–78 fiscal year, half of the recurrent expenditure was devoted to defense and police and only 1.05 percent to agriculture and rural development. While governments continued to concentrate on cash crops for overseas export, by 1973 people began going hungry for lack of rice and traditional cassava, millet, maize, and sweet potatoes which were no longer profitable for farmers to grow.

Ironically, Africa possesses the resources not only to feed itself but to become a net exporter to the world. In Nigeria and Zaire, for example, nearly eighty percent of the total arable land remained uncultivated in 1976. Some agronomists have suggested that great initial strides could be made if more attention were given to organic fertilizers, crop rotation, and to new plant varieties of wheat, rice, lysine-fortified corn, and sorghum.

From the early days of independence, some nations embarked upon ambitious programs to improve food crop production, particularly those nations lacking mineral resources. In 1967 Tanzania launched its policy of *ujamaa,* which called for the consolidation of the nation's widely scattered rural population into larger settlements. The Arusha Declaration of 1967 spelled out the theoretical parameters of ujamaa, a Swahili word meaning "familyhood." Tanzania's President Julius Nyerere reasoned that as long as rural families were thinly spread out, it would be economically and administratively impossible for them to be furnished with what he regarded as the prerequisites for economic and social progress: medical facilities, water for drinking and irrigation, educational institutions, and modern agricultural equipment. By concentrating the farmers into villages, it would be easier for the government to supply them with the materials and instruments needed for rural modernization. Over the next seven years, more than five million people, or one-third of the nation, were re-grouped into some four thousand cooperative, or ujamaa, villages. The ujamaa experiment was a new and more comprehensive departure in the gradual growth of the cooperative movement in Africa. It was communalistic and aimed to achieve self-reliance. All the fruits of community labor would be shared equally, and no surplus would accrue to any individual.

The cooperative movement originated in the colonial era as a capitalist instrument of colonial governments. After the 1920s in British and French West Africa, colonial administrations organized cash-crop producers into cooperatives and mutual aid or credit societies in order to improve standards of quality and to raise peasant production. After 1933, cooperative societies also were established in Tanganyika and by 1947, fifty-five African marketing societies were in existence there. The cooperative movement in producer, consumer, marketing, and credit functions grew rapidly throughout sub-Saharan Africa in the 1950s and 1960s. Cooperatives were seen then as the best way of directing large numbers of small producers towards market production. Many of the cooperatives were modeled after those operating so successfully in Scandinavia, Israel, Western Europe, the Peoples' Republic of China, and North America. Over the years, they gained a steadily increasing share of the marketing and processing of agricultural products. Governments accelerated the trend by furnishing credit and training programs, but at the same time they began to gain greater control over their marketing operations.

Cooperative movements have not been without problems. Nearly half of them have failed in that they could not realize sufficient profits to sustain or to expand their original membership. Some experts blamed the problems of cooperatives on their parastatal nature, particularly those cooperatives in Ghana, Zambia, and Tanzania. In Tanzania, especially, the government's central authoritarianism inspired resentment, weakened local incentive and morale, and hence adversely affected productivity. Excessive control from the central government in Dar es Salaam, the capital, along with interference from party bureaucrats, rather than supervision by trained agronomists, stifled local initiative. By 1975 the ujamaa program was no longer voluntary, and peasants were forcibly conscripted into it. Cooperatives were more successful in nations like Botswana, where they were not state-sponsored but private enterprises run by the local people themselves.

By the early 1970s, cooperatives were seen to be not the only answer to increased agricultural productivity. The Ghana government in 1972 launched a national program called Operation Feed Yourself. It was intended, in part, to encourage youth to engage in individual, small-scale farming. But the government pumped insufficient funds into the program and by 1977, Operation Feed Yourself had brought little relief from the country's chronic food shortage. In the previous year alone, consumer food prices rose an astounding eighty-eight percent, with few of the profits accruing to the local producers. Nigeria in 1976 launched a similar program, called Operation Feed the Nation, but it too was grossly underfunded. The people in both countries came to regard the programs more as public relations stunts than as serious efforts to improve food production and to reduce the crushing inflation in food costs.

In areas of European estate agriculture, notably in Kenya, government schemes were adopted for Africanizing the land and achieving a redistribution of assets. Beginning in late 1961—just before Kenya's independence—large agricultural enterprises were purchased by a Central Land Bank which in turn was financed by loans from Great Britain, the colonial power. More than two million acres were taken over for schemes entailing large government and cooperative farms, operated by individuals or private partnerships. Loans and grants were extended by the International Bank for Reconstruction and Development (IBRD), Great Britain, and West Germany to provide working capital for the new farmers. Many peasants became small-time rural capitalists, but in the early 1970s as land values rose and agricultural machinery became more costly, wealthy Nairobi-based African speculators began to buy up the small enterprises. Today, there is a growing trend toward absentee landlordism, and the peasants in some cases are finding themselves worse off than they were during the colonial era.

In Zaire, the process of confiscating European agricultural estates culminated in 1973 when the government abruptly nationalized European properties and established peasant cooperatives. It was intended that the urban unemployed would be drafted into working the new lands. However, the properties themselves were given to party loyalists, family members among the governing elites, and urban Africans prominent in business. The result was similar to the Kenya experience. The new owners operated the estates as absentee landlords and employed on-site managers in much the same exploitative manner as the former Europeans had. The estates were mismanaged, worker morale dropped, and productivity declined dramatically. Zaire's President Mobutu reacted to this in 1977 by repossessing the estates and placing them directly under central government control. In some cases, the former owners were invited back to serve as managers. Clearly, the overall effect of this land nationalization was not the transferral of land to peasants.

In Tanzania, the large European wheat-producing and dairy estates in the Mount Kilimanjaro area were abruptly nationalized in the early 1970s, and the white farmers quickly left the country, taking their knowledge of farming with them. The government lacked the expertise to operate them, and within months the nation had begun to suffer from severe food shortages.

Only in Ethiopia has there been a fundamental and sweeping land reform program. There, lands held in feudal style by local aristocrats and the Coptic Church hierarchy have been redistributed to the peasants, who formerly worked them under conditions of serfdom. Communist-bloc agronomists are providing them with a huge network of agricultural extension services.

In the short term, the Africanization of European agriculture has led to a decline in managerial efficiency and productivity. For example, in 1960 Tanzania's plantations and settler estates occupied only one percent of the land but produced more than half the country's agricultural exports. Today, the same area's output has dropped by more than a third. Some leaders in Africa have become convinced that the nationalization of agricultural lands must be accompanied by large infusions of government capital and technical assistance, especially to the peasants who suddenly find themselves with new responsibilities for which they are ill prepared. Many nations, notably Nigeria and Guinea, are now attempting to develop agriculture by encouraging state farming and imposing government direction on peasant farmers.

Since the early 1960s, governments have attempted to regulate economic development by publishing comprehensive and often overly ambitious plans. Too frequently, the economic development plans fail to take into account the impact on the environment. Most plans were drawn up by foreign consultants with little knowledge of local conditions. In the Ivory Coast, for example, lumber and lumber products have been the second most important export.

Under the country's development plan, the forests were being depleted faster than they could be replanted. In 1976 it was estimated that the nation's forest reserves would be exhausted within nine years. The rapidly diminishing forest and the accompanying depletion of the soil will have climatic effects. As the forest recedes, it is predicted, an ecological imbalance will be created. Without the protection of a forest canopy, rain will evaporate at an excessively rapid rate.

Ecological disruption of a similar nature has already occurred in the West African Sahel, along the Saharan desert fringe. Between 1947 and 1961 France and a succession of international agencies spent millions of dollars in the Sahel to dig deep wells and control rinderpest, a disease which kills cattle. The mortality rate of livestock dropped dramatically and herds multiplied in number. Eventually, the lands around the wells were overgrazed. Each year, more and more savanna grassland has disappeared as peasants have indiscriminately felled trees for leaves to feed their herds. The expansion of the cattle population also has made it more difficult to allow sufficient cropland to lie fallow. Nomadic cattlemen have resisted the enclosure of land and also have clung to the traditional system of stock management based on the short-term objective of maintaining alive as many animals as possible, regardless of the need for long-term conservation of land resources. Much land in Africa remains unenclosed or unfenced, and land conservation will require a social revolution in nomadic lifestyle. Clearly the erosion-producing practice of indiscriminate grazing and shifting cultivation must be replaced by programs in range-management and multicropping. Under the old practice of shifting cultivation, an area is worked for a few years until the soil loses its vitality, weeds invade, and crop yields fall. Land then is abandoned and a new parcel is cleared for cultivation. With crop rotation and multicropping, a farmer may protect himself better if a single crop fails, and also will achieve higher yields from a given parcel. One crop may restore to the soil what a previous one has removed.

Much of the aid for agricultural development has continued to be supplied by private and government sources from the former colonial power. This was especially true of French support of the French-speaking nations. Since the mid-1960s, international agencies have played a larger and larger role. One of the most effective bodies is the African Development Fund, a soft-loan agency established through the initiative of the African Development Bank with its seventeen, capital-exporting member nations from the Americas, Japan, the Middle East, and Western Europe. The fund extends loans to the poorer African countries, particularly for agricultural development schemes. Similar aid is extended by the World Bank and the United States government's Agency for International Development (AID). AID in the 1960s and 1970s focused its efforts on the small farmer and the rural poor in the areas of food production, rural development, and nutrition. In 1975 the United Nations established the permanent Committee on Food Aid Policies and Programs in hopes of improving coordination between bilateral and multilateral food aid programs.

Many agronomists believed in the 1970s that Africa's potential as a food producer had been seriously underestimated, and that the productive capacity of small farmers was unrealized by most governments. Africa contained the highest proportion of the earth's grazing area, along with river systems capable of generating relatively cheap hydroelectricity and providing water for irrigation. Yet in 1975, in most African nations, less than half of the potential food-producing land was under cultivation. When there was high unemployment, the agricultural sectors could have absorbed far more of a nation's labor force than they actually did.

MINING AND MANUFACTURING

Independence found nearly all the African nations with grossly underdeveloped industry. During the colonial era, manufacturing was neglected in all areas save those with large permanent European populations. Agricultural and mineral production was destined primarily for export, in raw form, to the metropolises in order to boost industrialization there and to provide employment for their own nationals. The colonies bought back the minerals and other goods as finished products, and usually at considerably higher prices than what they fetched

Owen dam and hydroelectric facility, outside Kampala, Uganda.

when originally leaving the continent. Most processing plants were built in Western Europe and North America, not in Africa. No wonder that Africans, once politically independent, demanded greater control over their own economies and gave priority in their development plans to industrial expansion. But economic self-determination has proved far more difficult to achieve than political independence. Economies have remained vulnerable to wildly fluctuating world prices for minerals and agricultural commodities, and that has led to severe balance of payments crises and the need to borrow extensively in international money markets.

In much of Africa, mining and manufacturing have expanded greatly since the advent of independence. Manufacturing still accounts for only a fraction of the gross national product of most nations and is usually concentrated in the areas of textiles, building materials, and the processing of fish, fruits, and other export crops. Both sectors were still under the management, if not the partial ownership, of foreign business interests. Nearly all of Africa's minerals, with the exception of South Africa, continued to be exported, usually in a raw or semi-processed state. Even in Marxist Angola, the major iron, oil, and diamond mining operations in 1977 were managed by Europeans. Angola's diamonds, the nation's third biggest export earner, were still mined by Diamang, a subsidiary of De Beers Consolidated Mines and by Anglo-American Corporation, both of South Africa. Oil was extracted exclusively by the Gulf Oil Corporation of the United States.

Africa has barely begun to reduce its dependence on the developed nations for manufactured goods and technology. Conversely, the industrialized nations have become more dependent on Africa for minerals. For example, for the United States, by 1976 more than thirty percent of its imports of chrome, diamonds, oil, platinum, mercury, manganese, and cobalt were from Africa. This growing dependency has stimulated multinational corporations, most of them U.S., British, West German, and Japanese-based, to penetrate African markets more deeply. It was not uncommon for some of these corporations to have gross earnings in excess of the gross national products of their host African nation.

Massive penetration of African markets by the noncolonial powers began after World War II. Driven by financial stringency and their indebtedness to the United States, the European colonial powers opened their overseas possessions to the relatively unrestricted inflow of foreign capital and a correspondingly unrestricted outflow of profits. Most of the new investment went into the mineral-extracting industries. After the mid-1960s, West Germany, Japan, and to a lesser extent other industrialized nations, began to invest in the development of many secondary manufacturing enterprises. Japan, particularly, became a major exporter of electronic equipment to Africa. Colonial firms, which hitherto had enjoyed near monopolies, responded to the expanding competition with varying degrees of success and failure.

THE PROCESS OF AFRICANIZATION

The growing presence and influence of the multinationals awakened Africans to the need for a concerted effort to indigenize, or Africanize, key foreign-owned businesses and to protect local enterprises from undue foreign competition. This inevitably has led to increasing government intervention in the private economic sector. Programs to replace foreigners with locals have taken different forms. Initially, some nations set up government-owned trading organizations to trade directly and to supply African wholesalers and retailers. Kenya was an early leader in 1965 when the Kenya National Trade Corporation (KNTC) was established to increase African participation in retail trade. In Tanzania, the Arusha Declaration of 1967 placed the major means of production under the control of parastatal bodies, such as the National Development Corporation, and established a state monopoly over commercial banking and insurance. The government also nationalized eight flour-milling companies and eight export-import firms, and bought majorities of stock in six industrial corporations. Zambia took similar, though less drastic, steps the following year with the launching of a program requiring a fifty-one percent government share in the nation's two giant copper mining companies, Anglo-American of South Africa and American Metal Climax, based in New York. By 1970, Zambia had set up two big state corporations, the Industrial Development Company (INDECO) and the Mining Development Company (MINDECO). INDECO became a government conglomerate or holding company, with interests in small-scale industrial development, transportation, and hotels. MINDECO was given control of the country's mining activities.

Nigeria embarked on an even more comprehensive program of Africanization in March 1972 by promulgating the Nigerian Enterprises Promotion Decree. It specified that twenty-two categories of businesses must be reserved exclusively for Nigerians. Under the decree, some sections of industry were required to have one hundred percent local participation, others sixty percent. The latter mainly affected such old colonial-era enterprises as the United African Company, CFAO-Nigeria, and the venerable John Holt Company. An amendment to the decree in 1977 called for sixty-percent local ownership of all banks and the nationalization of some large oil companies. Exxon, for example, became a state corporation called UNIPETROL.

In Zaire, nationalization of the extractive industries began in 1968 with the dissolution of the four major mining companies, including Union Minière du Haut-Katanga and Forminière. GECAMINES, an enormous state mining corporation, was created and given control over most of the mines. The pace of nationalization, or "Zaireanization" as it was called, was broadened after a decree in November 1973 that stipulated that large companies should be placed under state ownership and management, and that smaller firms, then held mainly by Greeks, Portuguese, and Belgians, would be handed over to individual

Zaireans. Two months later, Petro-Zaire was formed to oversee fuel distribution and to take over the property of the private, international petroleum distributors. The country was moving in the direction of state capitalism.

In Uganda, President Idi Amin in 1972 solved the problem of foreign ownership of business within the space of three months. Amin's policy of "restoring all business into the hands of black Ugandans" led to the abrupt redistribution of nearly four thousand, formerly Asian-owned enterprises and the expulsion of the entrepreneurs, some of whom were second-generation Ugandans of Indo-Pakistani descent. Their former businesses were turned over by the government to "deserving" individual black Ugandans. The larger Asian concerns, such as the Madhavi Industrial Group, large hotels, factories, and garages, were placed under direct government control.

Too often, precipitous nationalization has led to dramatic declines in economic activity. A major problem has been that foreign distributors have had long-established international links which ensured regular sources of supply of commodities. African newcomers have had difficulty in finding their own sources and in obtaining goods as cheaply. The result has been that many of the nationalized economies have encountered chronic shortages of basic commodities. All this became compounded by a lack of skilled, local manpower to operate the enterprises. The Asians, for example, tended to hire and train friends and relatives as managers and used the Africans as petty clerks and deliverymen.

Africanization of commerce did not necessarily result in greater benefits to the local consumers. Some African entrepreneurs were just as inclined to exploit their customers as were their foreign predecessors. Many enterprises were grossly mismanaged. In some cases, profits were spent on the conspicuous consumption of imported luxury goods. Growth did not always become more broadly based, and wealth did not always filter down to the masses. In Tanzania, the State Trading Corporation which had been established in 1967 to handle wholesale import and export trade and retailing, was managed inefficiently and in 1977 was split up into twenty-four smaller corporations. African governments have begun to recognize the problems inherent in Africanization and have made pragmatic modifications in their programs, often stretching them out over longer periods and placing different types of enterprises in different categories, depending on their importance to the economy and on the availability of local expertise.

The rate of nationalization and Africanization varies in different countries. In Ghana, Nigeria, Tanzania, Zambia, Mozambique, and Angola, the rate has been rapid. In others, particularly the Ivory Coast, it has been extremely slow. Since independence, the French community in the Ivory Coast has grown from approximately fifteen thousand to fifty thousand, and foreign technocrats and businessmen continue to hold the majority of well paid jobs. In some nations, notably Zambia, the parastatal corporations have adversely affected many flegling African enterprises, because the former have easier access to credit and monopolize trade with government agencies.

Africanization in some nations, most visibly Nigeria and Kenya, has resulted in the growth of an indigenous, capitalist, middle class which intensified disparities in wealth. By 1977 in Nigeria, one-half of one percent of the population controlled seventy-five percent of the wealth. In more socialist states, notably Tanzania and Mozambique, a conscious effort has been made to prevent the creation of an African capitalist middle class by extending the range of the government, or public, sector. In many cases, bureaucratic civil servants have not proved to be efficient economic managers.

TRADE, MARKETS, AND TRADERS

It has been said already that the postwar period witnessed an acceleration of trade and investment by noncolonial, industrialized Western powers, particularly the United States. After 1960, the Soviet Union and Communist-bloc countries, especially East Germany and Czechoslovakia, also entered African markets, though more slowly and more selectively. As a result of this, as well as of the economic recovery of the colonial powers, African trade has grown at an explosive and unprecedented rate: five percent a year in the 1950s, nine percent in the 1960s, and seventeen percent in the early 1970s. The volume of trade and investment of the United States in Africa has soared. In 1966, the United

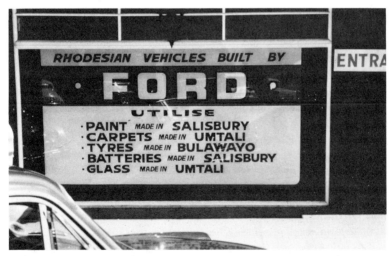

Automobile showroom, downtown Salisbury, Rhodesia, 1970. An illustration of Rhodesia's effort to achieve self-sufficiency in the face of international economic boycotts after the former British colony's illegal and unilaterial declaration of independence in 1965.

Market scene, the city of Ibadan, Nigeria. Due to lack of refrigeration, chickens are kept in baskets and sold alive.

States's direct investment in the continent amounted to $1.8 billion, in 1970 to $3.2 billion, and in 1975 to $4 billion. The United States's export growth was even more impressive, having swelled from $793 million in 1960 to a whopping $5.2 billion in 1976. Americans also were taking an increasing share of Africa's exports, especially oil from Nigeria after 1973. Exports from Africa to the United States grew from $534 million in 1960 to an astounding $12.6 billion sixteen years later. Much of this trade and investment was concentrated in the Republic of South Africa and Nigeria.

The establishment of the European Economic Community (EEC) in 1957, right before African independence, also helped to open the continent to greater and more diversified trade and investment. Initially, African and European products found unimpeded access to each other's markets. This was especially advantageous to Western Europe for it assured supplies of raw products for the six European EEC states instead of exclusively for the former colonial metropolises. After the French colonies became independent in the early 1960s, they maintained their trade connections with the EEC, even though France continued to dominate through its willingness to buy French-African commodities at prices above the world market value. The free-trade accord also gave the French-speaking states preferential entry for their products into the booming European economies and enabled them to reduce somewhat their dependence on France. In 1963, the first Yaoundé Convention was signed. This established a formal association between the EEC and eighteen, individual, French-speaking African states. Although French price supports were now withdrawn, Africa did not succeed in stabilizing the price of tropical products. A decade later, the French-dominated EEC Association Accord was widened to include a number of English-speaking states.

Under French President Charles de Gaulle and his successor Georges Pompidou, France continued to exert a powerful economic influence on its former colonies, especially Senegal, the Ivory Coast, and Gabon. With the death of Pompidou and the end of the Gaullist era, those relations lost a degree of intimacy, and links between France and francophone Africa became looser and more flexible. Throughout Africa various forms of bilateral metropolitan influence gradually have been replaced with multilateral relations extending beyond the former colonial zones of trade. Nevertheless, some of the former colonies have remained close to France. For example, in the Ivory Coast in 1976, French investments still accounted for eighty percent of total investments, and forty percent of the country's imports flowed in from the metropolis.

Through the 1960s and early 1970s, Africans were able to improve the terms of their trade with Western Europe. However, from the early 1970s the value of their exports either stagnated or declined, at a time when the cost of finished goods from the West soared. As we have seen, in some instances they were products manufactured overseas from raw materials of African origin.

Euro-African trade links became more institutionalized in February 1975. A convention of trade and cooperation between the nine-nation EEC and forty-six African, Caribbean, and Pacific (ACP) nations was signed in Lomé, Togo. Under the Lomé Convention, the majority of ACP manufactured goods and processed agricultural products were permitted to enter the EEC markets free of tariff or quota barriers. The accord also proposed a scheme, called STABEX, designed to stabilize raw commodity earnings by ensuring that a nation does not suffer a drop in such earnings through a price decline or natural disaster. STABEX, however, received only half-hearted support from the EEC, which feared it would weaken the free play of the market forces of supply and demand.

Though African nations have diversified their trade with overseas countries, political, ideological, and economic factors have prompted them to introduce obstacles to the freer movement of people, goods, and money among themselves. It is true that during the colonial era trade between the colonies of each European power was discouraged. Roads, railways, and other forms of transportation and communications often ended at the borders of each power's territorial possessions. On the other hand, the colonial powers forged large territorial domains out of hitherto closed and narrowly defined political and economic systems. Before the French broke up their huge federations of West and Equatorial Africa in 1957, trade flowed uninhibitedly across their administrative subdivisions. Likewise, in East Africa the British in 1961 created the East African Common Services Organization to facilitate trade and administration among Kenya, Uganda, and Tanganyika. This body matured into the East African Community in 1967. The East African Community, formed by the three former British possessions, was regarded at the time as a model for regional cooperation in Africa. In its heyday, the three independent nations had a common currency, an integrated fiscal system, a *de facto* common market, and jointly owned public corporations embracing the airways, railways, harbors, posts, and telecommunications. Just a decade later, the East African Community was dead, the victim of nationalism. Kenya, starting from a stronger economic position, was able to draw greater benefit from the shared services and market arrangements. In so doing it could expand its already superior economy at a faster rate. Tanzania, a far poorer and less developed country, suffered a chronic deficit in its trade with Kenya. The latter, with a relatively well developed manufacturing sector built up over colonial times by the white settlers, had products to sell to the Tanzanians. But Tanzania, with a largely agricultural base geared to crops needed in Europe, had little to offer Kenya. Each partner tended to place its own national interests above those of the community as a whole. Tanzania committed itself to forging a socialist/collectivistic economy, Kenya to a limited form of capitalist free enterprise, and Uganda, after Idi Amin's coup in 1971, to a fascist, military-based economy. Diplomatic relations among the three nations steadily deteriorated and in 1977, Kenya unilaterally dismantled the common services. Shortly afterwards, Tanzania breached the Treaty of East African Cooperation with regard to the common market by closing the border with Kenya. What makes the disintegration of the East African Community so significant is that its member-nations were probably better equipped, institutionally, for regional cooperation than any other group of nations on the continent.

Other attempts at economic integration have met a similar fate. The Union Africaine et Malagache (UAM) was formed by several French-speaking states in 1960 as a vehicle for economic cooperation. It set up a number of specialized agencies, including the Organisation Africaine et Malagache de Coopération Economique, the Union Africaine et Malagache de Postes et Télégraphes, and Air Afrique. The UAM dissolved itself four years later, a casualty of political-economic rivalry between the Ivory Coast and Senegal. Its successor, the Organisation Commune Africaine et Malagache (OCAM), established in 1965, was too political, and it also foundered on the rock of nationalism. A few regional economic groupings have fared somewhat better. The West African Economic Community, set up in 1974 by eight French-speaking states, has a fragile existence as does the Central African Economic and Customs Union. A more active grouping, the South African Customs Union, was formed in 1969 by South Africa, Botswana, Lesotho, and Swaziland. It was a child of the former colonial grouping of the British High Commission Territories and South Africa. All but South Africa are landlocked and must rely on South Africa's railways and ports for external trade.

One of the most significant efforts at economic regionalism since the close of the colonial era has been the fifteen-nation Economic Community of West African States (ECOWAS), founded in May 1975. Among its members are nine former French colonies and four former British possessions. ECOWAS aims to establish by 1990 a customs union similar to the European Common Market. There will be a common external tariff but no internal duties within the Community. Customs barriers will be lowered gradually until finally abolished. ECOWAS has been administered through an Executive Secretary, a Council of Heads of State, a Ministerial Conference, and commissions dealing with transportation, monetary problems, customs, and the like.

There always has been a very low level of inter-regional trade in West Africa, especially between English- and French-speaking states. In 1977 less than ten percent of total West African trade was within the region itself. At the same time there has been considerable smuggling across national frontiers. ECOWAS hopes to break down the fragmented patterns of trade.

The size and diversity of the ECOWAS grouping are impressive. The fifteen members represent a population exceeding 130 million with per capita incomes ranging from $712 annually in the Ivory Coast down to nearly $100 in Benin. Some members have expressed fears that Nigeria, with a population approaching seventy-five million, might attempt to dominate the community, much as Kenya did in the defunct East African Community. In 1977, Nigeria accounted for sixty-four percent of exports from the ECOWAS area and contributed one-third of the organization's budget. Nigeria has played a major role in sustaining ECOWAS since its inception. With relative industrial strength, some experts were predicting that Nigeria could emerge as an important producer of manufactured products for neighboring countries. This could further the dependency of the weaker ECOWAS states and place Nigeria in a status somewhat analogous to the industrialized nations of the West.

CURRENCIES AND MONETARY SYSTEMS

Most African nations, as recently as 1977, still were bound to the monetary systems and fiscal institutions inherited from the colonial era. However, they have gradually moved towards greater autonomy. In the former British possessions, each nation, though still in the sterling zone, has created its own Central Bank with a reserve system allowing it to issue its own currency and to make its own clearing arrangements. By contrast, nearly all the former French possessions have remained in the franc zone and have held to a system based on a precise monetary relationship with France. Most West African French-speaking states (Ivory Coast, Upper Volta, Niger, Benin, and Togo) participate in the West African Monetary Union (UMOA) and share a common Central Bank, the Banque Centrale des États de l'Afrique de l'Ouest. The equatorial African states of Cameroon, Central African Empire, Chad, Congo, and Gabon also have grouped themselves around their own Central Bank, the Banque des États de l'Afrique Centrale. Both institutions maintain most of their foreign exchange reserves at the French treasury in Paris. Under this arrangement, their currencies have parity with the French franc and can be converted into French francs at any time. If a member-state should have an external trade deficit, the French treasury would guarantee their foreign exchange commitments by offering low-interest loans. In return for that privilege, the French-speaking member-nations have allowed French firms and their expatriate employees to transfer their profits and salaries directly to France.

This linkage to the French monetary system has provided a compelling incentive for the Africans to continue their strong economic ties with their former colonial master. It has permitted French businessmen and civil servants to retain a large physical presence, and this in turn has retarded the process of Africanization. The relative stability and high value of the franc entices producers in weaker monetary systems to smuggle their goods out of their own countries into the franc zones. Nations with weaker currencies thus are deprived of a measure of trade revenue. For example, in the early 1970s much of Ghana's cocoa crop was smuggled into markets in neighboring Ivory Coast and Togo where it could be exchanged for a more valuable currency.

Over the years, monetary systems in the former British colonies have become weaker and more fragmented. A good illustration may be found in East Africa. When the East African Currency Board broke up, Kenya, Tanzania, and Uganda adopted their own currencies. Kenya's currency remained strong, while those of Tanzania and Uganda weakened. By 1977 Uganda's currency had lost almost all its convertibility.

Since their independence, African states have individually and collectively established their own banks to encourage the investment of public and private capital. In 1964 a large number of nations formed the African Development Bank, and within thirteen years its membership had grown to include forty-one nations on the continent. The bank created its own resources to grant or guarantee loans, to provide technical assistance, and to coordinate national social and economic development plans. From the beginning, the bank was plagued by insufficient funds, and it therefore sought to mobilize external resources by setting up two subsidiary institutions: the African Development Fund (ADF) in 1972 and the Société Internationale Financière pour les Investissements et le Développement en Afrique (SIFIDA). We must recall that the ADF, an Ivory Coast-based agency, includes seventeen capital-exporting nations in Europe, the Middle East, Japan, and the Americas. SIFIDA, a Swiss-based holding company, was set up in 1971. Its shareholders were companies from seventeen nations. By 1977 it had investments in twenty-two companies in ten African nations. SIFIDA mobilized international private capital for the promotion of private African enterprises.

Individual African nations have also founded their own development banks.

In Nigeria, such banks are regarded as the major instrument for industrial growth. The old banks of the colonial era, notably Barclay's and Standard Bank, still dominate the scene. But they must now face competition not only from the burgeoning indigenous banks but from American and other foreign financial institutions. In some cases in Africa, local banks are partially owned by overseas concerns.

The monetary systems of Africa and much of the noncommunist world have been influenced strongly by the International Monetary Fund (IMF), a United Nations agency founded in 1944. The IMF has functioned as a rule-making body of the world's monetary systems and as a lending agency to nations with balance of payments difficulties. The United States, with more than a third of the votes in IMF, has a controlling interest and thus is the decisive power. The overall effect of the IMF on Africa has been to ensure the domination of major capitalist monetary systems, particularly the U.S. dollar, in currency and foreign trade transactions. The IMF has been used as an instrument for imposing certain economic policies as a condition for loans. Marxists view the IMF as a neo-colonialist mechanism for safeguarding the financial interests of the leading capitalist countries. Others see it as an effective means of rescuing debt-ridden nations from default and for protecting the creditors.

Akin to the IMF is the World Bank, which makes development loans. It is one of the largest single sources of technological and financial assistance for the less developed countries. The World Bank was founded by the United States in the closing days of the Second World War to accelerate the reconstruction of Western Europe. The bank has a wide international membership outside the Soviet Union and the Communist-bloc countries. Having a measure of administrative autonomy from the United States government, its head always has been a U.S. citizen appointed by the president. The United States furnishes nearly a quarter of its operating capital. Since the early 1950s, it has turned its attention to the Third World. The World Bank has done much to facilitate the participation of private banking capital from the leading industrialized countries in the economies of the developing nations.

TAXATION AND REVENUE

Government revenues in the colonial period and afterwards were derived partly from direct taxes, notably on personal incomes and licenses. Indirect taxes such as import-export duties, excise taxes, and royalties on minerals extracted constituted the largest proportion of revenue, particularly in the mineral-rich nations of Zaire, Zambia, Gabon, and Angola. Budgetary expenditures usually fell into two categories: recurrent expenditures and capital expenditures. The former covered the everyday cost of government operations and the latter were used for development projects including new construction.

In the postcolonial era, expenditures in Africa tended to grow faster than revenues. The new nations embarked on ambitious and expensive development projects and in so doing greatly expanded the public sector of employment. In the prosperous years of the 1960s and early 1970s, government planners committed an increasingly larger percentage of annual budgets to capital expenditures with the expectation that growth rates would continue to rise. Public and private loans, mostly short-term and high interest-bearing, were easily secured from the industrialized nations. All went reasonably well until 1973 when an explosion in the cost of petroleum required drastic downward revisions in the economic plans of most nations. This event was precipitated by the Organization of Petroleum Exporting Countries (OPEC), a thirteen-nation, oil-pricing cartel dominated by Saudi Arabia and Iran. OPEC was founded in 1960 by the major oil exporting countries as an instrument for policy coordination among its members. By 1973 its membership included a number of African countries, including Nigeria and Gabon. Over the next two years, the organization succeeded in quadrupling the world price of petroleum. Nigeria, which had only begun to export oil in 1962, had within fifteen years become Africa's major oil producer and one of the world's largest. Nigeria, Algeria, and Libya by the mid-seventies accounted for ninety percent of the continent's oil output. Oil now determined those nations' economic growth rates. But for most African states, the rising price of oil became a major constraint on economic development and on efforts to lessen their dependence on the industrialized West. Sub-Saharan nations began to run up enormous external debts in order to pay for their oil imports. By 1975, debt-service payments as a percentage of exports constituted a heavy drain on their foreign exchange earnings. It should be recalled that the fourfold increase in world oil prices contributed to economic recession and inflation in the industrialized nations. Demand for African goods, particularly for such metals as copper, weakened substantially and the prices for metals fell dramatically. This was a disaster for countries like Zaire and Zambia, where copper mining accounted for nearly all of their export earnings.

This forced many African nations to turn to the IMF and other overseas institutions for compensatory financing to offset falling exports. The oil-price escalation was compounded by price rises in imported industrial equipment and chemical fertilizers, the latter being a necessary ingredient for agricultural productivity. Zaire is a classic case in point. Falling copper prices and internal mismanagement problems forced the nation in 1975 to fall behind on payments of both principal and interest to official creditors and of principal to private banks. Zaire's total foreign debt by October 1977 approached $3 billion, including $1.5 billion to official lenders in eleven nations and private loans guaranteed by such official institutions as the American-dominated Export-Import Bank. In effect the nation was in default. Creditor governments agreed to reschedule, over a ten-year period, eighty-five percent of the country's debt payments falling due in 1975-76 only. This was intended as a stop-gap measure, to tide the economy over until an upturn in copper prices. This did not happen and Zaire's debts continued to mount. By the close of 1977, the nation was unable to make payments on the principal owed in the previous fiscal year. Zaire's problems may seem extreme yet they are not unique. Many countries by the beginning of 1978 found themselves in a similar dilemma, with no apparent way out other than a big upturn in the economies of the industrialized nations.

This was not the first time that an African nation has been faced with the problem in which imports exceeded exports and government budgets fell out of balance. Under President Kwame Nkrumah, Ghana's total foreign debt climbed from $16.8 million in 1959 to a dizzy $526.9 million in 1964. At the time of his overthrow two years later, net external debt reached $853.5 million. One of Ghana's major problems, and indeed one that bedevils many African nations, was the relatively short repayment period, as loans were often made on a short-term basis. After considerable squabbling and hard bargaining, the nation's interest payments were rescheduled in 1974, with much of the debt amortized over an eighteen-year period.

As government deficits mounted in the 1970s, the gap widened between growth rates in current expenditure and in the material base of the economies. We have seen already that governments have tried to close the chasm by increasing the rate of taxation far beyond levels of the colonial era. This often has paralyzed the nation's savings capacity, preventing it from reaching the point of self-financing growth. By 1978 a significant number of African states were as far away from the goal of self-reliance as they had been a decade earlier. For many of them, development remained largely dependent on outside stimuli.

The oil crisis also underscored the growing inequality between the oil-producing African nations and those with little or no oil-producing or refining capacity. The affected nations were unable to persuade the OPEC cartel to sell oil at preferential prices. Tragically, many of the hardest hit countries were already the poorest and least developed and therefore the least able to carry the burden. Assistance to African nations with balance of payments problems due primarily to the higher cost of petroleum was, in 1977, provided by a multiplicity of agencies, mainly of Arab origin. Most prominent were the Arab-African Oil Assistance Fund, the Arab Loan Fund for Africa, the Arab Bank for Industrial and Agricultural Development in Africa, the Arab Investment Company, the Kuwait Fund, the Arab League Technical Assistance Fund, and the International Monetary Fund. In effect, the Arabs, after a hiatus of nearly a century, had resumed their active penetration of tropical African markets. Before the colonial era, the Arabs of North Africa and the Persian Gulf were the major foreign traders in sub-Saharan Africa.

TRANSPORTATION AND COMMUNICATIONS

Generally, African railroads, from the boom years of construction in the late nineteenth and early twentieth century, have been unprofitable, with the exception of those geared to mining operations. The continent's rail systems are, for the most part, a legacy from the colonial era. They usually were built within the framework of a single colonial possession and rarely crossed into the sphere of another. With the exception of South Africa, where mineral extractive industries became highly developed, few railway networks were economically viable. To complicate matters, Africa as recently as 1977 had no less than nine different rail gauges. Consequently, Africa's fragmented rail systems could not be joined. In the French colonies, one set of gauges were used and in the British, Portuguese, and Belgian colonies, another. Railroads

RAILWAYS OF AFRICA, 1979

have remained the carriers of the largest tonnages in Africa, primarily because they transport most of the mineral ores and heavy construction materials.

Many rail projects since the late nineteenth century were undertaken for political or strategic purposes: the British-built Uganda Railway from Mombasa to secure the upper Nile and Lake Victoria, the German-built Dar es Salaam to Lake Tanganyika line to hold the interior of German East Africa, and the French rail lines into the West African Sudan to supply troops quelling African resistors to French territorial expansion. These are but a few examples. Most postcolonial rail projects also have been the products of political and strategic goals. The longest rail line since the Second World War was the Chinese-built Tanzam Railway, which links Zambia with Tanzania's port of Dar es Salaam on the Indian Ocean. This 1,162 mile line, completed in 1975, was built primarily to free landlocked copper-rich Zambia from dependence on the rail system of white-ruled Rhodesia, Mozambique, and South Africa, and also to supply liberation armies seeking to overthrow those regimes. Similarly, the Botzam Railway from landlocked Botswana into Zambia was designed to diminish Botswana's reliance on South Africa's rails and harbors, and to give it a direct link with black-ruled Africa. By contrast, the trans-Gabon railroad in central Africa is being built to expedite the movement of iron, manganese, and other ores from the rich Gabon interior to the coast. Its construction is financed through loans from the African Development Bank, Algeria, France, Japan, and the United States Export-Import Bank.

Africa's railways steadily lost traffic to roads after the Second World War. Road transportation grew faster than rail, and many railway systems began to suffer from the competition, especially in Nigeria and East Africa. Road transportation was better because of its greater flexibility and lower construction cost. Today, Africans are concentrating on building local feeder roads to connect with national trunk arteries. Hitherto remote areas have been plugged into the burgeoning market economy.

Demands for trucks and automobiles have increased, and many of the larger African nations now boast of vehicular assembly plants set up as subsidiaries by overseas corporations. This has led to an uncontrollable surge in the volume of road traffic with the result that road beds are suffering enormous strain and damage. Highway mortality rates have skyrocketed, and cities, particularly Lagos, Nigeria, have chronic, paralyzing traffic jams.

Africans hope to stimulate inter-regional trade through the construction of a trans-Africa highway, now underway, which will link Kenya's port of Mombasa on the Indian Ocean with Nigeria's Atlantic port of Lagos. When completed in the 1980s, the road will stretch 4,000 miles and pass through six nations. It also will join a trans-Saharan artery from Algeria's Mediterranean port of Algiers to Lagos. These systems are destined to make Nigeria the hub of trans-African road transportation and will undoubtedly strengthen its position as the pre-eminent black power in tropical Africa.

Maritime transportation also grew noticeably in the postcolonial era. Several African states formed their own national and regional shipping lines, among the largest being Ghana's Black Star Line, the Nigerian National Shipping Line, and the now-defunct Eastern Africa National Shipping Line. With this development, foreign lines have adjusted to the economic realities and organized joint services with the new African lines. Elder Dempster Lines, the largest on the sea route from Britain to West Africa, teamed up with others on that route to form the U.K./West Africa Lines (UKWAL). By the early 1970s, the UKWAL Conference consisted of all the major shipping companies, including the Black Star Line, Nigerian National Shipping Line, the United Africa Company's Palm Line, and Elder Dempster. Unfortunately, the smaller shipping lines, many of them privately owned by Africans, have found it necessary to accept the freight increases and surcharges imposed by UKWAL and the other monopolistic shipping conferences.

Conferences are associations of mutually competitive lines operating along the same routes. Through legal compacts, they regulate competition among each other. Since 1972, trade between northern Europe and tropical Africa has been dominated by COWAC, the product of a merger of the huge France/West Africa and the Continental West Africa Conferences. Together, they cover nearly all the ports from Mauretania to Angola. Some UKWAL members belong to COWAC.

Japan and the Western nations exert considerable control over shipping through the conferences. However, in recent years the Communist countries have made impressive inroads. Since the late 1960s, Soviet state lines have greatly expanded their operations in East Africa, and in West Africa the Polish Ocean Lines have become active. At times, these lines successfully undersell the conferences and provide healthy competition.

In 1964 UKWAL introduced container shipping to West Africa and in so doing revolutionized freight-handling methods. By concentrating on containers, the large shipping companies are forcing the poorer nations either to invest heavily in infrastructure and capital-intensive port equipment or to lose a measure of ocean-going trade. On the other hand, mechanization of this nature replaces local longshoremen. Containerization illustrates how capital-intensive techniques risk driving out labor-intensive methods and throwing people out of work. In nations with low wages and high unemployment, labor-intensive devices may be more conducive to economic development. The shift to containers has given a competitive edge to those nations with facilities to handle them.

As maritime trade expanded in the 1960s, new ports were built and some old ones were modernized. Ghana's port of Accra had no harbor and ships were unloaded at sea and the goods brought in on wooden canoes. In the early sixties, a modern port was constructed at Tema, and Accra was quickly eclipsed. In volume, Durban, Dar es Salaam, Mombasa, and Lagos have become the busiest ports south of the Sahara. Most of the large ports are severely congested. At one time in Lagos in 1975 there were over four hundred vessels waiting to discharge cargoes.

In most African nations, air travel now has replaced other forms of transportation for long-distance international passengers. Air freight also is increasing rapidly its share of tonnage, especially in countries with underdeveloped road and railway networks. In airport development, Nigeria, Zaire, and South Africa lead all other nations on the continent.

In a few areas there is wasteful duplication of services and infrastructure. East Africa provides a good example. East African Airways was broken up in February 1977, after three decades of operation. Kenya, Uganda, and Tanzania then established their own national airlines, at considerably greater cost. Moreover, Tanzania recently completed the multimillion dollar Kilimanjaro International Airport, only a short distance from Kenya's well established and underutilized facilities.

Flight procedures are under international controls. The International Air Transport Association (IATA) ranks among the world's largest and most powerful airline associations. Airlines are bound by IATA's fare structures although, since 1975, several African carriers have violated them. In that year, twenty-one of the one-hundred-ten IATA members were flying African flags.

ICAO (International Civil Aviation Organization), established in 1947 as an agency of the United Nations, also performs regulatory functions and provides technical assistance to African civil aviation. The agency has done much to standardize air-traffic procedures throughout the world. Within Africa itself, the African Civil Aviation Commission was founded in 1969 as a loosely organized inter-governmental consultative body under the Organization of African Unity.

In 1958 there began a trend away from international or regional airlines and towards nationally supported carriers. That year also witnessed the break-up of the West African Airways Corporation, which since its inception in 1946 was operated by the colonial governments of the Gambia, Sierra Leone, Gold Coast (now Ghana), and Nigeria. By 1975, most of the independent African nations had their own airlines. We already have mentioned the collapse of East African Airways. Of equal significance was the demise of Air Afrique, an international line formed in 1961 by a dozen French-speaking nations. From 1976 to 1977 Cameroon and Gabon withdrew to form their own lines and others were expected to follow. Air Afrique has operated scheduled flights to Europe in association with the French corporation (UTA), and Air France. It also was connected with the American carrier, Pan-American, for transportation to the United States. Of the national airlines in sub-Saharan Africa, South African Airways and Ghana Airways were among the largest in 1977.

African airlines in the 1970s continued to face severe competition from European and United States carriers. One of the oldest European airlines in continuous operation in tropical Africa is Sabena/Belgian World Airlines, which first flew to Central Africa in 1925 and in 1977 was flying forty times a week to nearly all the major African cities. Many foreign airlines have provided financial and technical assistance for African carriers. For example, Trans World Airlines (TWA) and Pan-American have been closely linked with Ethiopian Airways and Air Zaire, respectively, and Alitalia with Zambia Airways.

Telegraph and telephone communications during the colonial era were as poorly coordinated as the transportation systems. Sub-Saharan port cities had begun to be linked to Europe by trans-oceanic telegraph cables in the 1880s, and by telephone from the early 1900s. Short-wave transmission had commenced by 1927 in South Africa. Most communication lines ran only between the colony and the metropolis, and consequently, a call placed in Nigeria to a town in French Niger a few miles across the border had to be routed via England, France, and Dakar, Senegal. Telegraph and telephone networks, most of which were operated by overseas corporations, did not begin to interconnect until the 1960s. Since then, with the advice of the Geneva-based International Telecommunications Union (ITU), African nations have been working toward the establishment of a continental telecommunications network. When finished in the late 1970s or early 1980s, the system will link African national networks together by microwave, telephone, telegraph, telex, and data transmission. It will no longer be necessary to go through a European-switching center for inter-African or overseas communication.

Space satellites also have given Africa a new dimension in communications. In the 1970s, nations began to install their own earth satellite stations which are linked to other nations through the United States-controlled, ninety-five-nation International Satellite Telecommunications Organization (INTELSAT). Nigeria, South Africa, and Zaire have made the most progress in satellite communication. Nigeria has set up a system of domestic satellite communications including radio and television broadcasting.

African nations inherited government broadcasting systems which after independence continued under state ownership and control. In South Africa, they always have been under the control of the South African Broadcasting Company (SABC), founded in 1936. Radio Bantu, on the air since 1940, is the largest component of the SABC and offers programs in seven African languages to more than 4.5 million adult listeners. The largest broadcasting system in black Africa is the Nigerian Broadcasting Corporation (NBC), which by 1975 had domestic and international service in four languages and could boast of five million radios and 85,000 television sets. Nearly all the television networks in Africa buy programs from European and American networks. Imported shows have undoubtedly acted as powerful acculturative mechanisms. No amount of colonial education commanded as much cultural influence over the African mind as have Western music and drama, transmitted via radio and television. At the same time, local programs also have crossed cultural frontiers and have contributed toward the establishment of a national, trans-ethnic, cultural and political consciousness.

Since colonial times, newspapers and periodicals also have opened people's minds to other cultures and have served as tools to educate and motivate. In colonial Africa, newspapers and journals were relatively independent from government, particularly in the British possessions but less so in the French, Belgian, and Portuguese colonies. Most firms were European-owned and managed, and not totally unsympathetic to the colonial regimes. However, before about 1948, local writers calling for black political self-determination were often suppressed or found it difficult to find a publisher.

Since independence, African governments have assumed a considerable degree of ownership and control, contributing to a decline in the number of dailies from over 250 in 1960 to under 140 in 1977.

Censorship became the rule in much of Africa in the 1970s as governments lost their toleration for criticism of their policies. Many African leaders criticized the press for being a divisive force at a time when building a national consensus on certain issues seemed essential. South Africa in 1963 established a Publications Control Board with powers of censorship over local and imported literature. Most newspapers were exempt and were left to discipline themselves. After the race riots of 1976, criticism of the government's policy of apartheid heightened, and the two major black newspapers, the *World* and *Weekly World* were banned and their editor imprisoned. By the start of 1979, white-ruled South Africa and Rhodesia had rigid press censorship, as did such nations as the Central African Empire, Uganda, Somalia, Ethiopia, Mozambique, Angola, Liberia and Zaire.

The freest presses in 1979 could be found in the Gambia, Ghana, Botswana, and Kenya. The last tolerates two independent privately owned English-language papers, the *Standard* (founded in 1902) and the *Daily Nation* (1957). Nigeria permits a high degree of domestic press freedom but has curbed foreign correspondents.

For news about the outside world, Africans are still dependent on foreign news services, principally Reuters, a private British agency, and Agence France Press, a semiofficial French concern. The American giants, the Associated Press (AP) and United Press International (UPI) have increased their coverage of Africa since independence. Some countries, notably Equatorial Guinea, have completely banned the Western press. Rhodesia in 1977 censored all reports filed by foreign correspondents. The Union of African Journalists, a rather weak organization, has been unable to pressure governments in Africa to relax restrictions on local as well as foreign journalists. Some nations have established their own press agencies. In 1974, the director of Agence Zaire press (AZap) stated that there should be no "hypocritical distinction between information and propaganda."[1] AZap exerts almost total control over Zaire's news media and suppresses criticism of government policies.

---

[1] Interview with author, August 2, 1974, in Kinshasa, Zaire.

LABOR AND LAND

The postindependence era has seen an acceleration in the trend towards permanent wage labor committed to industrial employment. The movement of people into the urban areas has reflected the swing from subsistence labor to wage labor. Governments in the more developed nations generally have continued to encourage the old colonial policy of maintaining a cheap migratory labor system.

In South Africa, migratory labor has remained a central feature of the economy. The less-developed peripheral states of Mozambique, Botswana, Swaziland, Lesotho, and Malawi still serve as labor reservoirs for South Africa's white farms and mines, even though mechanization has begun to reduce the rate of migratory employment. Indeed, mechanization in the agricultural sector has forced many Africans to leave the farms and seek employment in the commercial sectors of the white urban areas. Job opportunities there are limited and this has led to massive urban unemployment, especially among youth. By contrast, in the rural bantustans, a lack of mechanization and insufficient resources for soil conservation have stifled growth in food production and forced economically active people to travel long distances to find employment elsewhere. The dearth of workers in the black rural areas has led to economic stagnation and a weakening of the traditional spirit of self-reliance.

The social effects of migration have been even more devastating. The white regime actively discourages permanency among migratory workers in the urban areas by forbidding them to bring their families. Family life therefore is weakened because women and children are left behind. The migrants live as bachelors in crowded dormitories, free from the social constraints of family structures. The condition breeds prostitution, homosexuality, venereal disease, alcoholism, and violence.

Migratory labor is not unique to southern Africa. It continues in varying degrees in many regions. In West Africa, patterns of labor migration remain almost unchanged since the early decades of colonialism. Benin, Upper Volta, and Niger still depend on the coffee, cocoa, and peanut plantations of Ghana, Ivory Coast, and Nigeria to provide seasonal employment for many of their citizens. As a result the latter three nations, like South Africa, can command a strong voice in the domestic politics of those countries dependent so heavily on the earnings of their absentee citizens for public revenue. Over the decade or so since independence, many migrants have taken local spouses and become permanent residents in the nations of their employment. This in turn has resulted in a substantial shift in population, from the dry grassland rural interiors of East and West Africa to the growth centers of the forest and coastal zones. It has also led to a breakdown in tribal or ethnic loyalties and the strengthening of a national consciousness.

The economic recession of the 1970s created a surplus of laborers and forced many African governments to expel migrants from neighboring countries. In 1970, Ghana abruptly sent several thousand Nigerians packing. Amin of Uganda drove Kenyans across the border. As South Africa's mining production declined, tens of thousands of Mozambique workers were terminated.

A small percentage of workers prospered and joined the ranks of the nascent bourgeoisie, though most became part of the growing proletariat. With this trend towards proletarianism has come a greater sense of worker grievance and the desire for stronger labor organization.

We must recall that at first colonial governments resisted labor organization for fear it would lead to unacceptable rises in labor costs. Then, with the 1930s, the regimes tolerated labor unionization in hopes of bringing urban workers under greater government discipline and control. Labor unions had to register with colonial labor departments, and in the event such registration was revoked, the union would lose its legal standing.

After World War II, and the growing influence of labor parties on metropolitan governments, African trade unions were given greater freedom. In the 1950s, they played a significant role in the struggles for political independence. They seized the opportunity to mobilize the rapidly growing urban populations. In the final analysis, their overall impact on the quest for independence has not been decisive. Generally, the nationalist leadership has not been drawn from among the trade union ranks, but rather from the professional classes. Trade-union officials were second-level political leaders and therefore had less power and privilege. We should recall that there were a few exceptions, notably in Guinea, Ghana, and Kenya, where the trade-union movement was close to the political party because high union officials were also high officials in the party. Sekou Touré of Guinea was Secretary-General of the P.D.G. (Guinea Democratic Party) and head of the C.G.T. (General Confederation of Workers) union, and Tom Mboya of Kenya was a leader in both the K.F.L (Kenya Federation of Labor) and K.A.N.U. (Kenya African National Union). In the 1950s in the Gold Coast, the Convention Peoples Party (CPP) and the Trades Union Congress (TUC) worked together, the latter supporting calls for strikes. Most trade unions in Africa were too radical and militant for the nationalist leaders. In a few cases, nationalist parties competed with unions for the support of the masses.

Independence brought few real gains to the trade union movements. To the contrary, unions were brought under firmer government controls and were coerced into fighting for causes not usually relevant to the traditional union interests of higher wages, shorter working hours, and better working conditions. Government leaders exhorted laborers to work more and to make greater sacrifices. Unions were no longer allowed to function as instruments of political opposition. In 1976 more than fifteen major labor leaders lingered in jails as political prisoners.

In the early 1960s, T.A.N.U. (Tanganyika African National Union), Tanzania's official political party, started to gain control over the nation's trade union movement through its infiltration of the Central Tanganyika Federation of Labour. Once linked to T.A.N.U., the power of the federation was enhanced and soon overshadowed other movements. In Ghana, one of the first acts of the newly independent government in 1958 was to centralize power in the party-controlled TUC in order to prevent any union from remaining or becoming autonomous. In 1969, the Nigerian military government decreed an end to all lockouts and strikes.

As the biggest employer of labor, most governments are attempting to control the unions. In many nations, especially Nigeria, civil servants and municipal workers have become increasingly better organized and more militant in their demands. Many African unions, recoiling from the crushing spiral of inflation, have simply ignored prohibitions on strikes and have won concessions from their governments. Nevertheless, the power of trade unions is somewhat limited, particularly in smaller and poorer nations, because of the small size and low earning power of their membership. It should be remembered that most of the population of most African nations are still peasants. Union workers can afford to give only a small amount of their salary for union dues, and so strikes are often infrequent and of short duration.

In the colonial era, trade union movements were usually linked closely to their metropolitan counterparts. They, in turn, were affiliated with international movements. Since the 1950s, three international bodies have competed for influence over African unions: the International Federation of Christian Trade Unions (IFCTU), the British-dominated International Confederation of Free Trade Unions (ICFTU), and the Communist-dominated World Federation of Trade Unions (WFTU). African efforts to establish an autonomous trade union movement led to the formation in 1961 of the All-African Trade Union Federation (AATUF). It represented only a small percentage of workers, and the ICFTU soon gained ascendancy by securing for itself the affiliation of most African trade unions.

An even more influential force on the African labor scene was the fiercely anticommunist and New York-based African American Labor Center. The center was set up by the AFL-CIO under George Meany, and rapidly developed links with African labor movements. The All-African Trade Union Federation (AATUF) was weakened further in 1962 by the formation of the more moderate, pro-Western African Trade Union Confederation (ATUC). Forty-one unions joined the ATUC: Twenty-one were affiliated with the ICFTU, twelve affiliated with IFCTU, and the remaining had no ties to any international body. The confederation chose not to join any international union structure but to allow the individual national unions to affiliate with international organizations. As a result, many African trade unions continued their international connections. For example, in Nigeria in 1977, the largest union, the United Labour Congress (ULC), with 400,000 members, was affiliated with the ICFTU in Brussels, while the Nigerian Trades Union Congress with some 300,000 members is affiliated with the Moscow-based WFTU. Another attempt in Africa toward autonomy from the internationals was made in 1973 with the creation of the Organization of African Trade Union Unity (OATUU). Nonetheless, the internationals continued to exert a powerful influence throughout the continent.

Forced labor, so common in the colonial era, has almost disappeared in Africa. There are a few exceptions from time to time. In Equatorial Guinea in the mid-1970s, workers were assigned without pay to state-owned plantations on Ile Macias Nguema and to public works projects on the mainland. The effects of slavery are still felt in the economies and social structures of some nations. In parts of Nigeria, for example, there is still a stigma attached to descendants of slaves, and subtle barriers to their advancement persist.

In South Africa, white trade unions continued to dominate the economic scene. They were affiliated with either the ultra-conservative Trade Union Council of South Africa (TUCSA) or the Central Labour Organisation. A wave of strikes by black workers in 1972–73 resulted in some limited concessions by the Government. An amendment to the Industrial Conciliation Act (1956) permitted black workers to engage in strikes and lockouts under certain circumstances. Overall, black industrial wages have steadily risen in each subsequent year but lag far behind those of their white counterparts. The great majority of blacks still lived below the poverty line. The catalogue of occupations reserved exclusively for whites has been reduced, though job reservation was still a major obstacle to nonwhite economic advancement. In 1975, TUCSA decided to re-admit black unions, and the 23,000-strong National Union of Clothing Workers became affiliated. Black unions, still not recognized legally, have generally refused to affiliate with TUCSA because of its all-white leadership and its close government ties. South Africa's twenty-five black labor unions are small and fragmented, and most of their articulate leaders have been banned and silenced by the government. The majority of employers pay little serious attention to these unions. The government has attempted to further weaken and fragment nationwide union organization by encouraging individual plants to establish works committees consisting of joint worker/employer membership.

Land reform in sub-Saharan Africa in recent years has become an issue of even greater importance than labor organization. Since the inception of European rule, there has been a steady transformation in many countries from communal systems of land tenure to private, individual ownership. In the process, long and bitter legal disputes have ensued. Should lands of a deceased male be passed on matrilineally to his eldest sister's eldest son? Or should inheritance be patrilineal and go to his own son? Then again, should the lands revert to the chief who might sell them or distribute them to someone else? If you held a piece of valuable real estate in downtown Lagos, would you want it to remain with your immediate family? Or would you be willing to have it pass, traditionally, to a relative? Nearly everywhere, nations are seeking to reconcile traditional methods of land inheritance with the realities of modern life and its emphasis on capital accumulation.

Cash crops and population explosions have created these pressures for a redefinition of land tenures. Land has acquired a higher economic value, which makes people more desirous of buying and selling it. The shortage of cultivated land, most apparent in densely populated areas, has resulted in more privately owned land. Higher costs of fertilizers and farm equipment have forced farmers to seek loans. But the inability of an individual to own land in freehold makes it difficult in some nations for the farmer to use his land as collateral.

Land in most rural areas of tropical Africa is still held by chiefs, or by descent groups which sometimes act as a kind of land management agency whose profits are shared among its members. In areas of extensive cash-crop production, especially in the coffee and cocoa-growing regions, land is owned in freehold. In regions of pastoralism, people still generally adhere to a communal system.

It is becoming common today for governments of very poor countries to discourage or forbid the freehold system, especially if their lands have never had a high cash value or been privately owned by the local populace. In areas of former European settlement, it should be recalled that lands have been nationalized and in some cases redistributed to the local people on a communal basis. Three African leaders in particular have placed their nations on a course away from the private ownership of property: Samora Machel of Mozambique, Agostinho Neto of Angola, and Julius Nyerere of Tanzania. Their policies have discouraged landlordism and the concept of land as a marketable commodity. Individuals, and preferably groups, are given the right to use land productively but not to own it or to speculate on it for private financial gain. Ethiopia has probably gone farthest in attempts at land reform. We must recall that lands of the Coptic Church and the hereditary aristocracy, the majority of the best lands in the nation, have been confiscated and distributed directly to the peasants who formerly worked them under conditions approaching medieval European serfdom. In March 1975 the Ethiopian ruling military council (Dergue) inaugurated a program of sweeping land reform aimed at completely transfoming the nation's feudalistic land tenure system. By late 1977 there were 24,000 peasant associations embracing 6.7 million members. This suggested a high degree of peasant receptivity to the radical program. It remains to be seen if food production will substantially increase.

Land inequalities continued to persist in other areas of Africa. In Rhodesia in 1965, 28,197 whites owned some 34 million acres while 2.5 million blacks owned an equivalent amount, thereby giving a black/white ratio of acreages held of 89 to 1. In the black-ruled nation of Burundi, the small Tutsi ethnic group has controlled nearly all the most fertile lands and forced the majority Hutu people to work them under conditions of gross exploitation.

.

POPULATION, DISEASE, AND HEALTH

One of the most significant historical developments in tropical Africa over the last half-century has been the effective control of epidemics. The major thrust of public health work continues to be directed towards communicable disease control. The decades of the 1950s and 1960s saw an extensive and successful immunization campaign against smallpox, thanks to a massive vaccination program under the auspices of the World Health Organization (WHO) and the United States Agency for International Development (USAID). Over the last three decades, the World Health Organization has been in the forefront of health-related programs. WHO is an inter-governmental agency closely related to the United Nations. It has served as the major provider of medical personnel, health education, and research programs to assist nations in controlling diseases. WHO's vital work has been strengthened by the activities of UNICEF (United Nations Children's Fund) and the United Nations Development Program (UNDP).

Great strides also have been made in the eradication of leprosy and sleeping sickness; other diseases proved more difficult to treat and to prevent. Some have actually spread. Ironically, bilharzia has increased as a result of projects aimed at raising agricultural productivity, such as water management programs, irrigation, and hydroelectric dams. We must recall that bilharzia is a debilitating condition transmitted by snails in stagnant waters, and affects the bladder, kidneys, liver, and large intestine. The disease spread in the Sudan in the 1950s after construction of the Gezira irrigation scheme and its maze of canals. More recently, it spread along the quiet shores of lakes created by dams such as the one at Akosambo in Ghana which backed up the waters of the Volta River. River blindness also has been difficult to control. It is a disease caused by a worm transmitted by a fly. The worms multiply in the body and eventually invade the tissues of the eye, forming lesions and ultimately causing blindness or severe impairment of vision. Malaria remains the most widespread public health problem in tropical Africa. The majority of Africans at some time in their lives are affected by it. Rapid urbanization has placed tremendous strains on municipal water and sewer systems, many of which were laid out in colonial times when cities were a fraction of their present size. Urban congestion has led to a decline in standards of sanitation and a higher incidence of gastro-intestinal maladies and malaria.

Death and disease-reducing programs seldom have been balanced by birth-control programs. As recently as 1979, very few nations had organized effective family-planning services. This may be explained by the tenacity of traditional religious and social values favoring large families. It may also reflect the inability of governments to provide old-age benefits which might offset the need for children as economic security in later years. Economists blame resistance to family planning on a lack of labor-saving agricultural technology. In poor rural areas, a child is seen as a valuable unit of labor. Therefore, it remains a "Catch-22" dilemma. High population-growth rates have become a serious obstacle to real economic development because so much capital must be expended on meeting the needs of the exploding population: schools, hospitals, clinics, and the like. This problem is often difficult to explain, because sparsely populated regions are not necessarily free of population pressures. The determining factor lies in the carrying capacity of the land, and in sub-Saharan Africa much of the land today is over-grazed or not very fertile and vulnerable to soil erosion.

All this bring us to the point at which the problems of agriculture, industry, land, labor, and public health must be set within the context of population growth rates. In many African nations, the annual birth rate had reached 3.5% by 1977, making it possible for the continent's population to more than double within the next quarter-century. Africa's population in 1975 was estimated to stand at 401 million. By the year 2000, it is projected to rise to over 813 million. It is questionable if food production also can be more than doubled. Some agronomists predict massive famines in the decades to come. The drought in the West African Sahel and Ethiopia led to the starvation deaths of an estimated 250,000 people. Africa must find a way to feed itself, before it can find its way to real economic development.

chapter 9

Patterns of Culture

RELIGION IN TRANSITION

The independence period has been characterized by an accelerating growth in Islam. It has been estimated that for every one convert to Christianity, there are nine converts to Islam. By 1977, there were an estimated 109 million Muslims in Africa as opposed to approximately 98 million Christians. The religious brotherhoods, especially the Ahmadiyya, have helped to modernize Islam and to make it more relevant and responsive to the needs of contemporary Africans. Since 1960, Islam's African advance has been most rapid in West Africa, from Senegal to Nigeria's Lake Chad region. Nigeria in particular grew considerably after 1960. By 1976, it was estimated that 47 percent of the nation's population was Muslim compared to 34 percent Christian.

The proportion of Muslims to total population in 1977 ranged widely from country to country: from Mali where the population is 91 percent Muslim and 1 percent Christian, to South Africa where it is 2 percent Muslim and 73 percent Christian. Muslims constitututed a majority in Senegal, Mali, the Gambia, Niger, Chad, and Somalia, and an extremely influential minority (25-47 percent) in Nigeria, Ghana, Cameroun, Sierra Leone, Upper Volta, Central African Empire, and Tanzania.

After 1973, Muslims began to influence African foreign policy away from Israel and towards the oil-rich Middle East. King Hassan of Morocco, Idi Amin of Uganda, and Omar Bongo of Gabon made strong diplomatic overtures to Middle East states. After President Bongo converted to Islam in 1973, his nation became a major recipient of Arab aid. Some observers have argued that the oil price boom spurred Islamic conversions among some African elites. In 1977, Saudi Arabia gave Uganda and Niger financial support for the establishment of Muslim national universities.

In contrast to Islam, Christianity's growth has slowed, especially in the mission churches. The most significant postindependence trend has been in the rapid Africanization of the church hierarchies, particularly within the Roman Catholic Church in which before 1960 the clergy was overwhelmingly European. There also has been a substantial decline in white missionary endeavor and in overseas financial support. On the other hand, Christianity has become more ecumenical. The All-Africa Conference of Churches was established in 1959, and from its headquarters in Nairobi, it has dealt with ecumenical issues and matters of education, family life, refugees, famine relief,

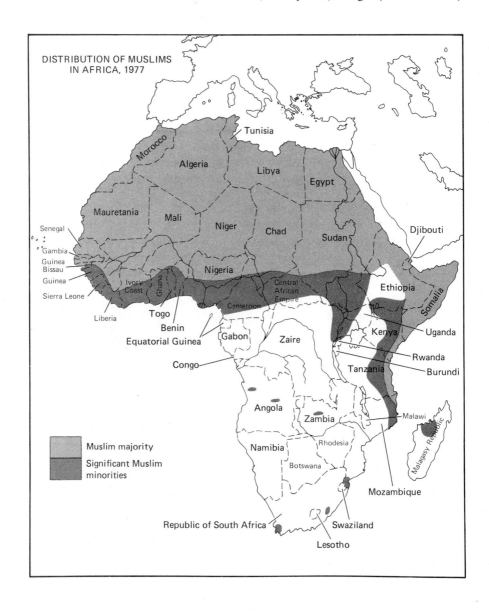

DISTRIBUTION OF MUSLIMS IN AFRICA, 1977

Muslim majority

Significant Muslim minorities

human rights, and others. Almost since its inception, the conference's effectiveness has been reduced by internal disputes. This came to a head in 1978 with the resignation of the controversial conference leader, the Reverend Canon Burgess Carr of Liberia.

The World Council of Churches has provided considerable assistance to Christian activities since its founding in 1948. This ecumenical body became increasingly politicized after the mid-1960s and strongly supported national

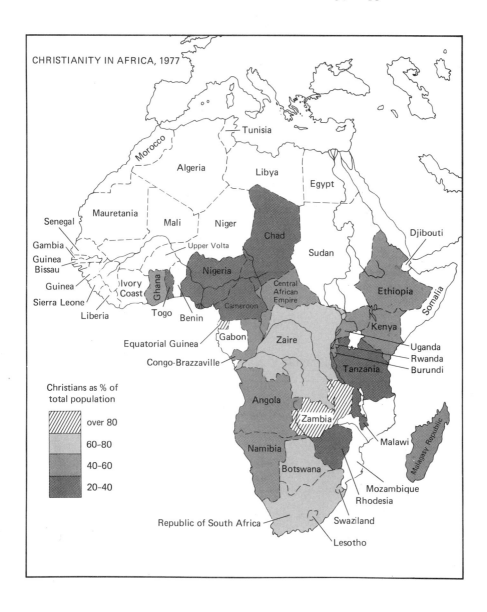

CHRISTIANITY IN AFRICA, 1977

Christians as % of
total population

over 80

60–80

40–60

20–40

Central mosque in the city of Kano, northern Nigeria.

liberation movements in southern Africa. In 1975 the World Council of Churches held its annual meeting in Nairobi and reaffirmed its commitment to seeking the elimination of racial discrimination on the continent.

Christianity became militantly reformist in South Africa and Zimbabwe (Rhodesia) in the 1960s and 1970s. Christian churches, once stereotyped as paternalistic agents of colonialism, began to challenge white supremacy. In Zimbabwe, Donal F. Lamont, a Roman Catholic bishop, attacked Rhodesia's conduct of the war against the black nationalist guerrillas and was arrested, imprisoned, and expelled. In South Africa, the Christian Institute, under its white Afrikaner leader, Reverend Beyers Naude, defended blacks and coloreds against the country's apartheid laws. The institute was banned in 1977.

In a growing number of African nations, Christianity has come under government attack. It has been weakened by severe church/state conflicts, particularly in Uganda, Zaire, South Africa, Malawi, Burundi, and Ethiopia. After independence, churches continued to assume a major responsibility for the operation, staffing, and curriculum of educational institutions. In a nation like Zaire, the Roman Catholic Church had operated a majority of the nation's schools since the early years of the twentieth century. Consequently, Christian denominations in many countries found themselves competing with governments over the shaping of its citizens' minds. The universalistic ideology of Christianity has been seen by some African leaders as an obstacle to nationalism, and many nations have sought to reduce the influence of religious organizations. Malawi's

President Kamuzu Banda labeled the Jehovah's Witnesses' refusal to join the nation's political party as treasonous. Since the early 1970s, several hundred Witnesses have been imprisoned and more than 30,000 driven into exile. In Zaire, President Mobutu regarded the powerful Roman Catholics as an obstacle to his policy of Authenticity. A decree in 1971 stipulated that only three religious bodies would be recognized by the state: the Roman Catholic Church, the Kimbanguist Church, and the Church of Christ in Zaire. All Protestant denominations had to merge into the latter body. The decree was aimed at halting the increasing multiplication of sects and bringing religion under closer government supervision. In 1972, Mobutu banned all religious youth movements and compelled all citizens to drop their Christian names in favor of African ones. Three years later, he outlawed the teaching of all religion in Zaire and demanded that religious instruction be replaced by courses in civic and political education. Shortly afterwards, Mobutu nationalized all the primary and secondary schools but was forced to repeal the move for lack of financial resources in the government treasury. Although two-thirds of Zaire's 23 million people are Christian, the date for Christmas was changed and dropped as a national holiday.

Uganda's President Amin, a Muslim, assassinated the nation's Anglican archbishop in 1977 for speaking out against Amin's violations of human rights. Amin in the early 1970s embarked on a policy of rapid Islamization in his nation where only 6 percent of the population is Muslim and some 60 percent is Christian. Decrees banning foreign aid to all religious denominations other than Islam have deprived the churches of much of their financial support. A Catholic archbishop in Guinea was imprisoned for life in 1970 for allegedly attempting to overthrow the nation's president, Sekou Touré. In Marxist Ethiopia, the extensive lands of the Coptic Christian Church were confiscated in 1975. This destroyed the economic power of the Church. Two years later, the government nationalized a radio station operated by the World Lutheran Federation. The station, called Radio Voice of the Gospel, broadcasted to a wide number of African nations from its studios in Addis Ababa, Ethiopia's capital.

Traditional African religions in some nations had begun by the 1970s to display a new vitality, as nationalist ideologies more and more asserted their Africanness in the face of the forces of Westernization. Both Islamic and Christian African clergy have showed a general willingness to accommodate. Religious services are held more often in the vernacular languages, and traditional musical instruments and melodies have replaced pianos and organs. The trend towards church separatism continued to gather momentum, and by 1970 there were an estimated 5,500 independent church sects embracing at least 30 percent of all Christian adherents. Kimbanguism had become the largest indigenous church in Zaire and possibly the largest in Africa.

Religious leaders had not found ways of controlling the growth of religious skepticism, agnosticism and the general trend towards secularization. Nevertheless, most Africans have remained basically religious. Atheism continues to be insignificant, even among the urban Westernized elites, despite the growth of Marxist thought. Indeed, some Marxist political leaders still practice Christianity.

EDUCATION

The postindependence period saw a rapid decline of missionary control over primary and secondary school education and the growth of secularization in curricula and staff. By 1970, the shift from church denominational to state control of the educational system was well advanced in many African countries. Governments assumed control over curricula and examinations and imposed courses of ideological content. No longer would final examinations be determined in Europe by Europeans. At the same time, African universities had begun to sever their links with equivalent institutions overseas. Formerly, the main models for their educational systems were drawn from the home country. Gradually they turned to the United States, Scandinavia, and Communist-bloc countries for inspiration and advice.

From the late 1960s, there was greater government supervision of the universities, in part to curb student opposition but also to make them more responsive to the developmental needs of the nation. Heads of government became titular chancellors, and subordinate rectors and vice-chancellors were typically government appointees. This was in contrast to the colonial era and the immediate postindependence period when African universities had a larger measure of autonomy than even their European counterparts. As academic faculties became Africanized and more dependent on government support, university independence eroded. After 1968, there were widespread student demonstrations on campuses throughout the continent. In Zaire, 211 students were shot in a clash with government police in 1969. In 1976, the Ethiopian regime killed 1,200 students in street fighting in Addis Ababa. In the same year, President Amin of Uganda seized Makerere University and infiltrated the student body and faculties with members of the security police. Student rioting followed the murder of a prominent third-year law student. In South Africa, government attempts to impose Afrikaans as the language of instruction in black schools touched off rioting in several African townships in 1976 and led to the death of more than 176 students and the imprisonment of hundreds more. By 1978, the government had banned most of the non-Afrikaner student organizations, including the black South African Students Movement in high schools and the South African Students Organization in universities. In South Africa and elsewhere, government heads had come to see education as an essential instrument for imposing a national ideology.

On the positive side, enormous quantitative gains had been made in education at all levels between 1960 and 1973. In Zaire, for example, the number of pupils in primary schools rose from 1.7 million in 1960 to 3.4 million in 1973, in secondary schools from 22,000 to 220,000, and at the university level from 20 in 1960 to 10,000 thirteen years later. In Kenya, the number of children in primary schools in 1977 totaled 3.3 million against less than one million at independence, while secondary school enrollment climbed almost tenfold. In the same general period, a growing percentage of national budgets were devoted to educational needs. It had reached 18.7 percent in Gabon by fiscal 1973. Before independence, all primary and secondary education in many colonies was on a fee basis. Afterwards, it became free and this largely accounted for the spectacular increases in enrollment, particularly at the primary school level.

Between 1960 and the early 1970s, educators concluded that the most critical shortages were in the area of secondary education, which had always lagged far behind. Consequently, it received considerable attention. Many secondary schools were built, faculties were expanded, and the proportion of school-age population in secondary schools increased.

The 1960s also was the period of trinational regional university systems. The University of East Africa came into being in 1963 and comprised Makerere College in Uganda, Nairobi University in Kenya, and the University of Dar es Salaam in Tanzania. Similarly, the University of Bostwana, Lesotho, and Swaziland, based in Lesotho, was established and supported by the three nations. These bold, cost-saving experiments were exceptions to the general trend towards national university systems, and by 1976 both tri-national experiments

Legon campus, University of Ghana.

Campus of the University of Dar es Salaam.

had become casualties of nationalist fervor. Within a few years of political independence, nearly every African nation had established its own university, often at the cost of wasteful duplication with neighboring states. Multinational communication on educational policies had not disappeared altogether. A meeting of the heads of African universities in 1963 led four years later to the formation of a loose body called the Association of African Universities.

Some African countries had begun in the early 1960s to re-examine the function of education, inevitably leading to disenchantment with the neocolonial paradigm of education. Curricula were henceforth based more on primary school agriculture and on nonacademic programs that would lead to productive employment. This "nonformal" education was manifested through extension services, adult education, and on-the-job training institutes. Many parents were reluctant to send their children to vocational programs instead of to schools with a formal academic structure.

Julius Nyerere of Tanzania provided much of the momentum behind attempts at the indigenization of education. His thoughts were contained in a booklet entitled *Education for Self-Reliance* (1967). Nyerere's thesis was that educational institutions have two functions in the reconstruction of society. One is social, in which students, particularly at secondary and university levels, learn attitudes and values appropriate to a rural, socialist society. Education, he argued, "has to foster the social goals of living together, and working together, for the common good. . . . Our education must therefore inculcate a sense of commitment to the total community and help the pupils to accept

Campus of Rand Afrikaans University outside Johannesburg, South Africa. It caters to whites, mainly Afrikaners.

the values appropriate to our kind of future, not those to our colonial past." Nyerere added that "this means that the educational system . . . must emphasize cooperative endeavour, not individual advancement; it must stress concepts of equality." He saw the second function of education as vocational, which must focus at the primary school level on which the greatest number of students are found. They must acquire modern agricultural skills and a respect for rural life. Nyerere called for a new emphasis on the precolonial notion of learning through practical work and sought to revive agricultural education, an area largely neglected during the colonial era.

Nyerere and other leaders also took measures to reduce the "attitudes of inequality, elitism, intellectual snobbery, and intense individualism" among the students in higher education. The Tanzanian president lamented that "education is such as to divorce its participants from the society it is supposed to be preparing them for."[1] He forced university students to work for a time in rural areas alongside farmers and required that they devote a certain number

[1] Julius K. Nyerere, *Freedom and Socialism,* pp. 267–68.

of years in national service after graduation. Nyerere echoed an earlier state-
ment by Ghana's late president, Nkrumah, that university education "must
always remain a living, thinking, and serving part of the community to which
it belongs."[2]

In the 1970s there was a shift in emphasis from secondary and university
education back to primary education and teacher training. There was an overall
change in direction, towards "developmental education," geared to national
economic and social development. The wealthier nations, notably Nigeria, introduced ambitious programs designed for free university and primary education.
There was also a movement in curricula away from the humanities. Educators
began to ask themselves whether education was meeting the problems of malnutrition, soil erosion, hygiene and the like. In response, educational systems in
the 1970s devoted more attention to training physicians, nurses, engineers,
agronomists, and primary school teachers.

Having an adequate number of academic personnel has always been a problem. In the 1960s, faculties were still staffed heavily by former colonialists,
particularly in what was French Africa. Nations benefited by volunteers from
the U.S. Peace Corps, the Canadian C.U.S.O. (Canadian Universities Students'
Organization), and other overseas agencies. Africanization of staffs greatly
accelerated in the mid-1970s and at the same time, there was rising opposition
to continuing a system of education closely tied, by syllabi and teachers, to the
standards set by former colonial overlords.

There was a growing tendency in the 1960s and 1970s for unemployment to
increase with the amount of formal education. Too many school drop-outs were
trained for nonagricultural jobs, and nations found themselves with the double
dilemma of a superabundance of students and an under-utilization of urban
manpower. Unemployment of primary-school drop-outs was hardly new. It
dated at least to the immediate post-World War II period and contributed to
the dissatisfaction leading to the struggle for national liberation. What was new
was its extent. In the early 1960s Nkrumah's Ghana tried to meet the problem
of unemployment among primary-school drop-outs by establishing "workers'
brigades" designed to provide vocational training and ideological orientation.
Similarly, Kenya developed "Harambee" (self-help) schools and village poly-
technics to "instill a national spirit" and teach practical job skills.

The worldwide economic recession beginning in about 1973 caused employment, especially in the urban areas, to fall dramatically behind the steady
increase in number of school drop-outs. Massive youth unemployment became
common in many African countries. Employers in both public and private
sectors, who in the 1950s and 1960s welcomed primary school graduates, had
begun to raise their sights. Even university graduates had difficulty in finding
jobs by the late 1970s. In 1978 the University of Nairobi estimated that of

[2] Kwame Nkrumah, *Axioms of Kwame Nkrumah*, p. 39.

their 1,800 graduates, a full 13 percent did not expect employment for at least three years. Part of the problem in many nations was the excessive attention given at the university level to the humanities and social sciences, and the comparative neglect of the natural and technical sciences. This distortion grew out of the late colonial era when most graduates went into the civil service for which a general education was preferred.

Educators argue that Africa has a long way to go in laying the solid foundations of an educational system at the primary and secondary school levels. Drop-out rates in Nigeria, for example, varied from 40 percent to 60 percent in the 1970s, and some nations, like Chad, had only a 6 percent literacy rate. Even Ghana, with one of the most developed educational infrastructures, had a literacy rate of only 25 percent in 1973.

Governments have paid lip-service to the concept of designing an educational system uniquely suited to national needs. Few nations have developed a coherent, indigenous educational philosophy and fewer still have radically restructured their educational programs. After the revolution, Marxist Mozambique established hundreds of "re-education camps," but they were mainly ideological in design. Tanzania and Nigeria were among the few nations in which there was real education reform. Unemployment among graduates at all educational levels has continued to soar, and the proportion of national budgets devoted to education began to decline after 1973 as more funds were earmarked for security and military requirements.

SOCIAL ORGANIZATION

Social stratification has increased since independence in nearly all African nations. The size of the Western-educated elite has grown enormously but is still extremely small and is confined mainly to the towns and cities. Education, income, and lifestyle have overtaken age and lineage affiliation as major criteria in determining social class. Behavior and status symbols of the former colonialists have been adopted by African elites as their own. They aspire to own chauffeur-driven limousines, large homes with domestic servants in segregated quarters of town, and the other perquisites of their colonial predecessors. Nevertheless, the traditional principles of social structure remain in force among the great majority of the population, even those living in urban areas.

In most nations, more than half of this new elite is employed in the public sectors. Many observers believe that the middle and upper-level civil servants have become less responsive to and more isolated from the population than their colonial and precolonial predecessors. Ukandi Damachi, speaking of his own nation, Nigeria, maintains that, "Relatively few members of this elite are conscious of their responsibility to lead their uneducated compatriots into the modern world."[3] He adds, "Most are preoccupied with solidifying their own position and in gaining the prerequisites of membership to an elite class . . ."[4] Other political scientists view Africa's civil servants as a parasitical elite group in that they consume up to three-quarters of the national budgets of most countries. Many of them also have been criticized for placing personal and ethnic relationships above bureaucratic standards of merit and efficiency.

Ironically, class contradictions and tensions escalated after Africans achieved their political freedom. The gap between rich and poor has widened since the early 1960s and has led to greater polarization of classes and an intensification of social and political violence and unrest. In Burundi, competition among the actual and potential members of the elite has engendered strong ethnic overtones. Numerous scholars have noted that this fierce competition between Hutu and Tusi for jobs resulted in greater rigidity in the nation's ethnic stratification and a deepening of Tutsi fears of eventual Hutu domination. After independence, the Hutu, who had been oppressed by the Tutsi for centuries, were frustrated at being denied a share of the elite status to which they felt entitled. In 1972 ethnic tensions burst into massive genocidal violence in which more than 150,000 Hutu, or 3.5 percent of the nation's total population, was exterminated. Less than a half-decade earlier, tens of thousands of Nigerian Igbos were slaughtered by other ethnic groups competing with them for elite positions.

Independence in Africa has brought considerable benefit to the African middle class, particularly to the managers of nationalized foreign businesses. But it has given little to the rural and urban masses. Indeed, the peasantry are generally more impoverished today than they were two decades ago. Relationships between townsmen and their kin in rural areas remain surprisingly strong, only intensifying the jealousies and disparities between the two. There is a deepening conflict between the minority of the population who have prospered and the vast majority who have not and whose standard of living has either stagnated or declined. In a few nations, particularly Kenya, Nigeria, and Gabon, rapid industrialization (and the oil boom in the latter two countries) has distorted wage differentials. In 1973, a laborer in Nigeria was paid a wage of only 5 percent of that of a middle-rank civil servant's salary. The gap widened further after the Udoji Commission in 1974 gave government employees an enormous increment in light of the explosive increase in oil revenues.

The African working class is still small, even though the number of wage laborers has grown since the early 1960s. Fewer than 15 percent of the populations of most nations could be considered proletariat, or dependent solely on wages for their subsistence.

---

[3] Ukandi G. Dimachi, *Nigerian Modernization* (New York: The Third Press), p. 37.
[4] Ibid.

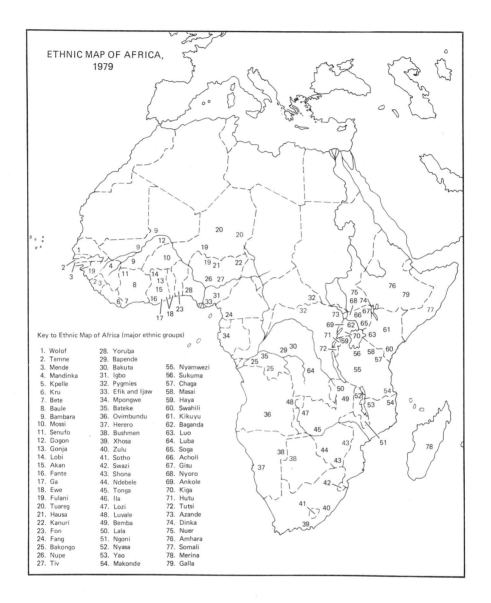

ETHNIC MAP OF AFRICA,
1979

Key to Ethnic Map of Africa (major ethnic groups)

1. Wolof	28. Yoruba		
2. Temne	29. Bapende		
3. Mende	30. Bakuta	55. Nyamwezi	
4. Mandinka	31. Igbo	56. Sukuma	
5. Kpelle	32. Pygmies	57. Chaga	
6. Kru	33. Efik and Ijaw	58. Masai	
7. Bete	34. Mpongwe	59. Haya	
8. Baule	35. Bateke	60. Swahili	
9. Bambara	36. Ovimbundu	61. Kikuyu	
10. Mossi	37. Herero	62. Baganda	
11. Senufo	38. Bushmen	63. Luo	
12. Dogon	39. Zulu	64. Luba	
13. Gonja	40. Sotho	65. Soga	
14. Lobi	41. Swazi	66. Acholi	
15. Akan	42. Shona	67. Gisu	
16. Fante	43. Ndebele	68. Nyoro	
17. Ga	44. Tonga	69. Ankole	
18. Ewe	45. Ila	70. Kiga	
19. Fulani	46. Lozi	71. Hutu	
20. Tuareg	47. Luvale	72. Tutsi	
21. Hausa	48. Bemba	73. Azande	
22. Kanuri	49. Lala	74. Dinka	
23. Fon	50. Ngoni	75. Nuer	
24. Fang	51. Nyasa	76. Amhara	
25. Bakongo	52. Yao	77. Somali	
26. Nupe	53. Makonde	78. Merina	
27. Tiv	54.	79. Galla	

Efforts are being made in Uganda, Ethiopia, Angola, Mozambique, and Tanzania to eliminate elitism and social stratification patterns. Nascent entrepreneurial middle classes have been undermined but at enormous cost to economic development and individual freedom. Civil servants and military cadres usually have filled the vacuum and have acquired elitist behavior similar to those groups whom they replaced.

URBANIZATION

One of the most significant and disturbing developments since independence in sub-Saharan Africa has been the uncontrollable acceleration of migration to the urban centers. Population statistics reveal the explosive growth:

Dakar: 1967, 374,700; 1976, 800,000
Abidjan: 1964, 257,500; 1976, 700,000 est.
Accra: 1960, 388,396; 1970, 564,300
Lagos: 1962, 450,000; 1977, 3,500,000 est.
Kinshasa: 1967, 901,250; 1974, 2,008,400
Dar es Salaam: 1962, 150,000; 1967, 353,000; 1976, 500,000
Luanda: 1960, 250,000; 1974, 498,000;
Johannesburg: 1972, 1,300,000 est.
Addis Ababa: 1960, 432,000; 1974, 1,083,000
Nairobi: 1962, 250,800; 1969, 510,000 est.; 1976, 840,000 est.
Libreville: 1960, 31,027; 1975, 251,400
Lusaka: 1960, 113,000; 1972, 265,000 est.

Generally, the capitals and provincial administrative centers have undergone a disproportionate amount of population growth. After independence, government ministries expanded in number and size; consulates and embassies appeared; international airports, hotels and conference centers were built; and

Street scene, Gwelo, Rhodesia, 1970.

Johannesburg skyline, 1976.

Harbor of Dar es Salaam, capital of Tanzania, 1970.

heads of state lavished enormous sums of money on their capitals, mainly for the sake of prestige. But African leaders have become as fearful as the former colonial authorities of population growth exceeding economic and infrastructural growth. Since the mid-1960s, most African cities have failed to keep pace. They are faced with paralyzing traffic congestion, power black-outs, pollution of municipal water, inadequate sewage treatment, unprecedented housing shortages, and deteriorating public amenities, especially parks and mass transportation. To compound matters, death rates have steadily declined and birth rates have soared. Some nations, notably Tanzania and Nairobi, have actively discouraged population growth in their capital cities. Dar es Salaam authorities have forcibly expelled the urban unemployed, and Nairobi officials have ruthlessly bulldozed away the shanty-towns on the city's perimeter. The South African government passed a series of laws after 1963 transferring influx control from municipal bodies to labor bureau, making it more difficult for unemployed blacks to remain in urban areas. South Africa's laws are obviously reprehensible because they discriminate on the basis of race.

Large cities everywhere are populated more and more by marginal masses of unskilled, underemployed workers. The proportion of rural migrants able to find permanent employment in the cities has steadily declined. The urban areas are breeding more alienation, poverty, crime, and "anomie," the latter being a state of confusion over values and ethics often making deviant behavior more acceptable. While Africa's large towns and cities are developing a foundation of permanent, or second- and third-generation resident, there has been a general

Soweto, a sprawling black ghetto township of more than a million residents located on the periphery of Johannesburg, South Africa.

An example of racially segregated public facilities in the Republic of South Africa.

weakening of family ties. The traditional concept of the extended, interdependent family has assumed less importance among urbanites.

The unemployed and underemployed cannot afford to buy or rent the type of housing constructed by the public and private sectors. Consequently, squatter settlements have mushroomed on the peripheries of major cities and towns. By 1975, nearly 42 percent of Dar es Salaam's population lived in squatter settlements and about 33 percent and 39 percent in Lusaka and Dakar. By 1978, Soweto in South Africa had a population exceeding 850,000 with more than 16,000 families on a waiting list to obtain houses. As a result, men often leave their families behind in the rural homelands. In many parts of Africa, men outnumber women in the urban areas and women outnumber the men in the countryside. In Dakar, the ratio in 1977 was 139 men to 100 women, and 80 percent of all males were between the ages of 15 and 40.

Many cities have now begun to add manufacturing to their administrative and commercial functions. Among the leading manufacturing cities are Nairobi, Salisbury, Johannesburg, Port Elizabeth, Cape Town, and Lusaka. A few nations have begun to construct new capital cities, partly to attract people away from the old ones. Tanzania is planning to move their capital to Dodoma in a remote rural area in the center of the nation. Nigeria is building a new capital near Abuja in the sparsely populated middle belt. Malawi has moved its capital from Blantyre to the new city of Lilongwe.

Though the majority of Africans continue to live in small villages, the proportion of people in towns with populations over 20,000 has climbed rapidly. By 1973 in South Africa it had reached 48 percent; in Zambia, 30 percent; in

Zaire, 26 percent; and in Nigeria, 20 percent. Some nations have remained over-whelmingly rural, the extremes being Ruanda and Burundi, whose rural popula-tions exceeded 97 percent of the total citizenry.

More positively, African cities (places of 100,000 or more inhabitants) are becoming increasingly modern and cosmopolitan. More than ever before, they are radiating culture to the countryside. Urbanites also are gaining greater control over their municipal affairs, even in South Africa where the government has grudgingly begun to recognize the reality of a permanent, black residential population. Urbanologists argue that the only way to stem the flow of rural-urban migration is to improve employment opportunities and municipal services in the rural areas. Clearly, there must be considerably more public and private investment outside the urban centers. In the past, rural villages have scarcely benefited from the earnings of the countryside.

Urban life and urbanization, for better or worse, have become increasingly important to the development of modern African civilization. Unlike the United States and Western Europe, cities in Africa are in vogue, and the present rate of urbanization is both very recent and almost unprecedented in world history. The percentage of total population in sub-Saharan Africa (excluding South Africa) classified as "urban" rose from 7.8 percent in 1950 to 11.3 percent a decade later to nearly 20 percent in 1978. Sub-Saharan Africa is seen by nearly all indices to be urbanizing more rapidly than any other region of the world. This may not be surprising, because it was one of the least urbanized areas before this century. Africa's rate of urbanization may be slightly less than that of the Peoples' Republic of China, but the growth of its urban population (in numbers of people) is unparalleled.

Barring some great catastrophe or radical reversal of social ideology, Africa by the year 2000 will probably be as urbanized as even the most advanced Western industrialized nations are today.

THE ARTISTIC RENAISSANCE

African culture since independence has entered a period of renaissance. This is especially true of art. External influences from Muslim North Africa, the Middle East and India, and from Christian Europe have helped for centuries to shape African art. But because of termites, fungi, and mosses, art objects have had short life spans. Each generation of artists has had to create its own art. Thus, African art always has been in a state of transition and transformation. It always has been receptive to new materials, techniques, and forms and through local genius, these have been adapted to the contemporary African condition. Since indepen-dence, the rate of external penetration has greatly accelerated, and the variety of art forms and the amount of experimentation have multiplied.

Western-trained artists are turning to Asia, Oceania, and the West as well as to their own continent for inspiration. Many of them do not see themselves as

Modern Makonde sculpture, with abstract
zoomorphic forms. Found in Tanzania and
northern Moazambique. (Photo: Lascell
studios)

"tribal" or ethnic artists, and their work is of a cosmopolitan, eclectic nature intended largely for overseas patrons who can afford their high prices. People trained in the old guilds, or folk-artists without any formal training, continue to be inspired primarily by the traditional, indigenous motifs and techniques. Even some of them have evolved new forms. Makonde sculptors living along the Tanzanian/Mozambique frontier have rich naturalistic traditions to draw upon in their development of new, highly abstract, and impressionistic forms. The communal spiritual roots of traditional Makonde art have been replaced by a modern secular individualism. Some critics argue that modern Makonde sculpture reveals seeds of an artistic renaissance in East Africa. It is an outstanding example of the continuity and change in African art.

New forms of indigenous African art are appearing in numerous parts of Africa, usually in and around experimental centers. The contemporary art movement in Nigeria sprang up in the early 1960s around Oshogbo and in the ancient city of Ife, the cradle of Yoruba civilization. In 1962, an art school was established under the inspiration of Ulli Beier and Suzanne Wenger at the Mbari Mbayo artists' club in Oshogbo. Since then, the Mbari school has trained a large percentage of Nigeria's finest contemporary artists, among them the painters Jimoh Buraimoh and Twins Seven Seven (Taiwo Olaniyi). Twins Seven Seven is one of Nigeria's "Renaissance men." He is known nationally as a drummer and dancer, and internationally as a canvas and sculpture painter. Like many contemporary African artists, his motifs are often taken from scenes and characters from ancient myths and legends. Since 1961, there has been considerable experimentation in the art department of the University of Nigeria, Ibadan campus. Enormous credit for preserving and advancing culture in Ghana must go to Kofi Antubam, former head of the arts and crafts department of Achimota School and a member of the Arts Council of Ghana and the Ghana Society of Artists. The Institute of African Studies at the University of Ghana, Legon campus, since the early 1960s has been a major center for cultural experimentation and innovation. Many of the nation's cultural leaders are graduates of Legon. In Tanzania and Kenya, Rebecca and Elimo Njau founded the Kibo Art Gallery and workshop in the foothills of Mount Kilimanjaro and the Paa-Ya-Paa Gallery in downtown Nairobi. The two centers in the late 1960s and early 1970s had an enormous impact on the direction of contemporary East African art and awakened in the East African people and governments a keen interest in promoting the arts in general.

Ironically, Africa's artistic renaissance has found its greatest flowering in the Republic of South Africa, one of the unhappiest and most racially strife-torn countries. The most prominent centers to gain national and international recognition since the early 1960s are: the Ndaleni Art School, the Evangelical Lutheran Church Art and Craft Centre at Rorke's Drift, the art department of Fort Hare University, and the Polly Street Art Centre in Johannesburg. Cecil Skotnes, as a leader of the Polly Street Centre, has made a profound impact on the growth of contemporary South African art. Other highly influential artists emerging in the 1960s and 1970s include Azaria Mbatha, a graphics instructor at Rorke's Drift; Sidney Kumalo, an instructor in sculpture at the Polly Street Centre; and the sculptor/painter Eric Ngcobo. Peter Magubane has become one of South Africa's leading photographers through his internationally acclaimed photo essays depicting the miseries of black life under apartheid.

An increasing number of black South African artists have recently won national and international recognition. Much of their work focuses on the human face and figure and is done mainly in watercolor and gouache painting, wooden sculpture, and, more recently, graphics. Apartheid fortunately has not been effective in stultifying the African quest for artistic self-identity and the expression of self and country through its works. Artists have freely exhibited in the prestigious Durban Art Gallery, at the Republican Arts Festival, and elsewhere in South Africa and overseas. In addition, folk art has begun to emerge in the black urban ghettos, called "township art," and providing an often devastatingly visual narrative of urban life in the segregated and poverty-ridden black townships. There is much brutal realism in their work and a vivid revelation of racial and ethnic conflict and oppression.

The doyens of South African art, whose works were executed before the ferment and "new realism" of the 1970s, included the late oil painters, Maggie

Laubser and Irma Stern, whose use of vivid colors has influenced the generation of the late 1960s and 1970s.

Artistic experimentation in French-speaking West Africa is concentrated in the Department of Negro Plastic Arts, founded in the School of Arts at Dakar in 1962. Tapestry is one of Senegal's most creative recent contributions to contemporary African art, its center being at the National Tapestry Factory at Thies. Zaire also has paid considerable attention to the arts. Many brilliant artists have come out of the Academy of Fine Arts in Kinshasa. In 1973, Zaire was host to the Third Congress of the International Association of Art Critics.

A growing number of African governments have taken Nigeria's lead in establishing laws and agencies for the collection and preservation of its best traditional and contemporary modern art, and to prevent it from falling into the hands of foreign art speculators. Laws in Nigeria to protect antiquities have been on the books since 1939, even though they were not strictly enforced until the decade after independence. In 1970 Zaire established the Institute of the National Museums of Zaire and organized scores of musicological, archeological, and art-collecting missions in every region of the nation. Within five years, more than 50,000 objects were collected and placed in the several museums built since independence. For the study of Zaire's art, the National Institute also has established photographic archives and a documentation center that is almost unrivaled on the continent.

Some traditional African art has been corrupted by commercialism, particularly wood carving. In the major urban centers, cooperative carvers' societies turn out copies of original pieces in varying degrees of quality. This "airport art," as it is called, caters to casual foreign tourists, expatriates, and the urbanized African middle class that often cannot afford to buy original works. There is no question that art is thriving in modern Africa. The traditional artists and craftsmen who worked for African royal families and ritual leaders are rapidly declining in number. But a new generation of creative people has emerged and has begun to lead the continent in exciting new directions.

MUSIC IN TRANSITION

The pace of experimentation and innovation in music does not rival art, but it has accelerated since about 1970. In the early 1960s there was a blending of bebop and the old African highlife. In 1966, Western soul music of the Americans James Brown, Chubby Checker, and Ray Charles was introduced along with the pop music of the American Jimmy Hendrix and others. In fact, black American music began to have an enormous influence on the direction of modern African music.

The first soul band in West Africa, "The Heartbeats" of Sierra Leone, introduced soul and pop music to Ghana and Nigeria between 1966 and 1968. In

French-speaking Africa, variations of the "Congo" jazz music and "Brazilian" music have continued to dominate the record parlors and nightclubs. Kinshasa in the 1960s became the center of modern music in French-speaking Africa and has some of the best jazz nightclubs on the continent.

The 1970s was a decade of adapting Western music and synthesizing it into distinctly African rhythms. Afro-beat, which became enormously popular in East and West Africa in the seventies, was pioneered by the Nigerian, Fela Ransome-Kuti. It represents a fusion of African and Afro-American music. Many college bands have sprung up across the continent, and their leaders have composed extremely creative variations of Afro-beat. Fela's music is loaded with political comment, much like the protest music of the preindependence period and the Oriki music of precolonial times. Through song, nuance, and gesture, he attacks bureaucratic waste and corruption, and praises pan-Africanism and Nkrumahist ideas. Fela and his musicians consequently have been harrassed by the Nigerian government, and since 1976 their activities have been severely circumscribed. In South Africa, many outstanding musicians, composers, and singers have gone into exile, among them Miriam Makeba, Dollar Brand, and the famous trumpet player, Hugh Masekela. Nevertheless, a kind of protest "ragtime" and pennywhistle blues continues to be heard in the beer gardens and *shebeens* (speak-easys) of the black townships.

In much of modern Africa, attempts are being made to return to such standards as vibrations rather than conventional signs like the musical note or the alphabetical letter. Thus, there is a certain continuity in the African musical world, but African youth have begun to turn away from classical African music. Inexpensive transistor radios have brought Afro-beat and other modern beats to even the most remote villages. Traditional African music is quickly losing its functional, socio-religious, and symbolic meanings. Some efforts have been made to use traditional instruments in playing contemporary music, most successfully by Richard Bank of Zoetele in Cameroun. The lure of the electronic guitar and other Western instruments everywhere persists. There has been a small though robust revival of classical African music, strongly encouraged by the governments of Ghana, Mali, Guinea, and a few others. The singer Fanta Sacko's "Musique du Mali" gained wide recognition and in Guinea, Kouyate Sory Kandia has cut several records of classical African music using such traditional instruments as the balafon, kora and bolon (a type of xylophone). Mustapha Tette Addy, a Ghanaian master drummer trained in the "old school," has enjoyed modest popularity.

DANCE, DRAMA, AND CINEMATOGRAPHY

Music, dance and drama continue to influence each other, but to a lesser extent than in the precolonial period. West Africa, particularly Nigeria, has been the scene of the greatest theatrical activity south of the Sahara. The Ibadan

Arts Theatre in Nigeria opened just before independence and is responsible for numerous fine productions. Of equal quality is the Duro Ladipo National Theatre. In 1962, Duro Ladipo founded the Mbari Mbaya Club in Oshogbo partly as a theater workshop and exhibition center. Ladipo has emphasized the use of oral tradition and employs Yoruba myths, legends, and history to build his dramas. His play *Oba Kòso,* for example, is based on the legend of Shango. As in precolonial times, the audience in modern African dramatic productions is encouraged to react by participating through the language of oral tradition.

Modern Nigerian drama was launched in about 1962 with John Pepper Clark's *Song of a Goat.* His play *Ozidi* (1966) is a shortened version of a series of traditional Ijaw plays that used to take seven days to perform. Wole Soyinka became the foremost Nigerian Playwright with his plays, *The Trials of Brother Jethro* and *The Swamp Dwellers* (1963). His *A Dance of the Forests* (1963) is a satire of contemporary Nigerian society. Overseas, Soyinka's best known play is *Kongi's Harvest* (1967), a bitter attack on power and corruption in a West African nation.

In Ghana, Efua Sutherland, whose work is associated with the Ghana Writers' Workshop, has completed more than six major plays. Since independence, many nations have begun to finance and promote drama and dance, and many national dramatic societies and folk dance and ballet companies have appeared since Guinea took the early lead in 1959. Through the impetus of the government and the Institute of African Studies at the University of Ghana, Legon campus, the Dance Company of Ghana was founded in the 1960s. It has gone on overseas tours and has had critical acclaim everywhere. Students at the Institute's School of Dance are required to study labanotation, a graphic system of recording body movements. They also must study traditional dance in local villages through personal observation. Ghana's dance company and the university students creatively blend modern and traditional choreographics and music. At times, dancers also must sing and play musical instruments during a performance, much as their traditional predecessors were required to do in precolonial times.

Until the late 1960s, East Africa had lagged behind West Africa in the development of modern dance and drama. Under the leadership of Rebecca Njau, Kenya's first female playwright, a few fine productions have been staged at the Kibo Art Gallery in Tanzania. In Uganda, the National Theatre in Kampala was the scene in the late 1960s of outstanding dramatic and musical productions. But under the dictator Idi Amin, a few of its most creative people have been exterminated or driven into exile.

The theater in South Africa also has been inhibited by government restrictions, though to a lesser extent. Much powerful drama has been written and produced in recent years. In the early 1970s, John Kani and Winston Ntshona produced and acted in *Sizwe Banzi Is Dead* and *The Island* which were scathing indictments of apartheid and won high acclaim in London and New York. *Sizwe* was unparalleled by any presentation yet witnessed in South African black theater. At the Box Theatre at the University of Witwatersrand, Makwedini Mtsaka's *Not His Pride* was well received in 1975. Much fine black drama has come out of the Ikhwezi Players who are based outside of Grahamstown. Equally active is the University of Pretoria's drama department which stages a huge quantity of dramas each year, many in the Afrikaans language. The smash musical hit, *Ipi 'N Tombia,* contains songs written by Bertha Egnos and Gail Lakier combining traditional musical themes with contemporary African-township jive.

Like art, black South African drama today is preoccupied with themes of racial injustice and oppression. They have been brought out with enormous force and poignancy by one of South Africa's foremost playwrights, Athol Fugard, formerly with the famed Cape Town Theatre. His play, *The Blood Knot,* first was performed in 1962 in Johannesburg. Fugard won international recognition in 1976 for his play, *Boesman and Lena.* Though the theater in South Africa is under continuous government attack, it manages to remain alive.

African cinema has become, in the independence period, an entirely new cultural dimension. The Carthage Film Festival, first held in 1966 in Tunis, was the springboard for the development of an indigenous black African cinema. The Federation of Pan-African Film Producers (founded in 1969) became the major organization for African cinematographers.

In the 1960s and 1970s, Senegal and South Africa were the most important and prolific film producers south of the Sahara. Filmmaking in white South Africa dates back to the period before the Second World War, but few films ever gained recognition outside the country. In the late 1960s, the Senegalese, Sembène Ousmane, became the foremost black filmwriter and cinematographer. With the opening in 1969 of Ousmane's film *Mandabi* in Dakar, black African filmmaking began to reach beyond the elite audiences of international film festivals to the local masses. Ousmane, a Marxist, is concerned with social transformation and regards film as the most effective cultural medium for molding ideas and popular attitudes. He is bitterly critical of neocolonialism and places much of the blame on his fellow Africans, who too often have placed private gain above civic principle. Ousmane's film, *Xala,* deals with the alleged impotence of many of Africa's contemporary political leaders.

Dakar emerged in the 1960s as the film capital of black Africa, thanks largely to the leadership of Ousmane. By 1970, other centers emerged in Niger, Ivory Coast, Nigeria, and Ghana. In that year, Upper Volta sponsored the First African Film Festival, the first in black Africa. In Nigeria, Francis Oladele established the Calpenny-Nigeria Plans Ltd., which began to produce films based on the highly successful novels of Chinua Achebe. The South African, Nana Mahomo, founded the Morena Film Company and produced a series of documentaries on the effects of apartheid on the black populations. His devastating films, *End of a Dialogue* and *Last Grave at Dimbaza,* had to be shot secretly on location in South Africa.

Indigenous cinema in Africa is growing quantitatively and qualitatively. Its speed had been slowed by an increasing incidence of government censorship, and because the distribution of films remains largely in foreign hands. In West Africa, Lebanese interests have owned many theaters and prefer to show less expensive, third-rate productions from India, Japan, Spain, and the United States. In addition, filmmaking is expensive, and few Africans can afford the investment in necessary equipment.

THE LITERARY ARTS

Sub-Saharan Africa continues to make steady advances in the literary arts. The postindependence generation of writers has begun to reevaluate the objectives and deeds of their nations' ruling classes and the political, social, and economic structures through which the elites operate. Many of the novels and poems since the late 1960s reveal an alienation of the intellectual from his political society. They also indicate a disillusionment with the promises of independence. Because of this, they are viewed by their governments as a dangerous source of embarrassment and a stimulus to popular discontent. Consequently, an increasing number of African writers have been exposed to government censorship, harassment, and imprisonment. Writers imprisoned in the 1970s include the Ghanaian Kofi Awoonor, the Nigerian Wole Soyinka, the Kenyan Ngugi wa Thiong'o, the white South African Afrikaner, Breyten Breytenbach, and Wally Serote of the Black Consciousness Movement in South Africa. Others have reacted by turning inward, towards introspection and more universalistic and metaphysical themes.

In Nigeria, the Igbos and Yoruba in particular, continue to dominate the literary scene in English-speaking Africa. Amos Tutuola and his contemporaries, like the artists and dramatists, have drawn heavily on oral literary traditions, especially proverbs, for inspiration. Their short stories strongly resemble precolonial West African didactic tales of moral and ethical content.

By 1965 the Nigerian Chinua Achebe had become Africa's foremost fiction writer. Since independence, Achebe has written three major novels, *No Longer at Ease* (1960), *Arrow of God* (1964), *A Man of the People* (1966), and a fine collection of short stories. They are widely read in Africa and have a large audience in Europe and North America. Achebe's works have been translated into more than seven languages, and he is probably the world's best known African writer. His global fame is shared by a few other Nigerian novelists, including Cyrian Ekwensi, a prolific writer who published six novels between 1954 and 1969, the most notable being *Jaqua Nana, People of the City,* and *Burning Grass.* Achebe, Ekwensi, and other African novelists initially concerned themselves with the legacy of colonialism, particularly the ambiguities of values and the continuing conflict between tradition and modernism.

East Africa got off to a somewhat later start in literature. Initially, European settlers wrote most of the novels, poems, and plays. But by the mid-1960s, the region had begun to produce a number of fine African writers: the Ugandan Okot p'Bitek who wrote *Song of a Prisoner* (1971); the Kenyan Grace Ogot author of *The Promised Land* (1966); and the Ugandan Eneriko Seruma author of *The Experience* (1970). p'Bitek's thirteen-part poem *Song of Lawino* (1966), originally written in the Acholi language, established him as one of the leading poets of Africa. It expresses the need for Africans to retain their traditions and customs and not to rush headlong into Western culture. The poem is tender, yet full of subtle bitter irony and satire. It is a kind of dramatic soliloquy. p'Bitek, like other African writers, addresses himself to the problem of the clash of cultures: African versus Western and rural versus urban. Recent African literature suggests that while Africans are pursuing Western values, they still feel a strong need for the traditional way of life.

Between 1968 and 1977 there was a literary revival in South Africa, mainly of poetry. Mafika Mbuli, Oswald Mtshali, and Adam Small have taken the lead. Small, of mixed racial ancestry, is considered one of the best poets to write in the Afrikaans language, and his *Black Bronze Beautiful* (1975) has won critical acclaim. Previously, writers were made up mainly of essayists, fiction writers, and autobiographers. Many of them followed the musicians and dramatists into exile in the early and mid-1960s, notably: Alex La Guma, Dennis Brutus, Ezekiel Mphahlele, Sydney Clouts, Roy Campbell, and William Plomer. Among the Afrikaner poets who have chosen to leave include Elisabeth Eybers, Olga Kirsch, and Barend Toerien. Others have stayed behind, notably the world-famous novelists Alan Paton, best known for his *Cry, the Beloved Country* (1948), and Nadine Gordimer who wrote *A Guest of Honor* (1971). South Africa's long and rich literary traditions have been stifled considerably by the Publications and Entertainments Bill (1963) which empowers the government to prosecute writers for works threatening public security. The *Sestiger* movement has faded and its board was taken over by the more conservative Voortrekker Press. The erosion of this autonomy in writing brought protests from English-speaking as well as Afrikaans-speaking writers, and from blacks as well as whites. Those who have remained in South Africa, feel increasingly isolated intellectually from the rest of the world. Despite the growing repression, black writers in South Africa turned out a surprising number of excellent pieces in the "thaw" of 1968-1977.

The literary movement in French-speaking Africa remains vital but has not kept pace with other regions. Since 1960, négritude has lost much of its influence as an intellectual and political force. English-speaking intellectuals, particularly Wole Soyinka and Ezekiel Mphahlele, believe it is undignified to draw attention to what is already obvious: one's blackness. "Must a tiger proclaim his tigritude?"[5] chides Soyinka. English-speaking Africans hold that négritude is

---

[5] Gerald Moore and Ulli Beier, eds., *Modern Poetry from Africa* (Baltimore: Penguin Books, 1963), p. 15.

irrelevant to them, for they argue that their African character and experience always will be reflected in their writings. They also find négritude inappropriate because under indirect rule, the British, unlike the French, did not consciously attempt to culturally assimilate Africans. Consequently, intellectuals in British Africa felt less threatened by losing their identity and thus were less inclined to be preoccupied in their writing with proclaiming their blackness or Africanness. Now that French-speaking Africans may freely determine the extent of French cultural penetration, they too have lost a degree of enthusiasm for the négritude theme. Négritude has not died completely and perhaps will remain on the scene as long as Léopold Senghor, one of its major proponents, remains intellectually active. The younger French-speaking writers, especially the Senegalese Malick Fall and Cheik Ndao, are turning to other themes. A new spirit of innovation in the use of French as a literary language is everywhere evident. The old ortho-doxy is passing as a growing number of intellectuals graduate from universities in Africa itself rather than in France.

Much credit for the growth of written literature must go to the commercial publishing houses and university presses which have expanded in size and num-ber since the advent of political independence. Heinemann's "African Writers Series," one of the greatest achievements of contemporary publishing on Africa, began in 1962. Within a decade they could boast of publishing 150 titles by African novelists, poets, and political writers. Though based in London, it has offices in Nairobi, Lusaka, and Ibadan. Penguin Books Ltd. has also published a considerable quantity of African fiction in its "Modern Classics" series. The venerable Oxford University Press has produced the "Oxford Library of African Literature" and maintains major branches in Nairobi, Accra, Salisbury, and Cape Town. The Longman Group Ltd. of London has also been an active pub-lisher of books by and about Africans. Hachette is the most important French publisher in Africa and serves many prominent French-speaking writers.

There are scores of small, local presses across the continent; some of them are subsidiaries of or are financed by foreign publishing houses. In Zimbabwe, the Mambo Press Ltd. has been among the more active ones. Thanks to the East African Publishing House, with offices in Nairobi and Dar es Salaam, English-language literature from East Africa has had robust growth. The East African Literature Bureau and the Tanzania Publishing House (1966) also have been active. In South Africa, AD. Donker Ltd. and Ravan Press, both of Johan-nesburg, have courageously published controversial works by black authors. Among the university presses, the Universities of Nigeria and Ghana have out-standing records of publishing high quality literature and text books. African literature has been introduced to wide American audiences, largely through the efforts of Bernth Lindfors and the Nigerian, Joseph Okpaku. Professor Lindfors is editor of the journal *Research in African Literatures,* founded in 1970 at the University of Texas, Austin campus. Joseph Okpaku is founder of The Third Press in New York City and has published and edited a number of works, including *New African Literature and the Arts* (three volumes). Double-day & Co. of New York has published the major works of Chinua Achebe and in so doing has further awakened Americans to contemporary African literature.

Generally, African culture has grown in international stature since indepen-dence. The old traditions are still very much alive and continue to inspire and enrich the new. They provide an essential continuity. The interaction of the two, as well as the interrelatedness of African and Afro-American culture, have been manifested most vividly through two highly successful international cul-tural festivals. In 1966, Senegal was host to the First Festival of the Negro Arts, held in Dakar. Nigeria in January 1977 hosted the Second World Black and African Festival of Arts and Culture (FESTAC). Within a short decade, impres-sive strides have been made in bringing the talents of blacks in Africa and in the diaspora into a dynamic synergism. Africa is in a state of constant change, but in no other realm has there been as much experimentation and innovation as in culture. In culture, Africa remains refreshingly and uniquely African. Africans have had difficulty in achieving political unity, and pan-Africanism as a political movement has not been realized. Nor has a new, uniquely African political or economic order emerged. Perhaps these problems must be resolved by future generations. The enormous success of African culture must inevitably serve as a source of inspiration to the major political, social, and economic thinkers. Since classical antiquity, African culture has enriched both Africans and people living in foreign lands. Indeed, it is the continent's greatest con-tribution to the world.

Selected Bibliography

GENERAL

African Encyclopedia. London: Oxford University Press, 1974.

HUGHES, ANTHONY J., ed., *Africa Report.* New York: African-American Institute, 1959 to the present.

LEGUM, COLIN, ed., *Africa Contemporary Record: Annual Survey and Documents.* New York: Africana Publishing Co., Inc., 1975 to the present.

McEVEDY, COLIN, AND JONES, RICHARD. *Atlas of World Population History.* Harmondsworth: Penguin Books Ltd., 1978.

Nigeria Handbook: 1973. Lagos: Ministry of Information, 1974.

SYNGE, RICHARD, ed., *Africa Guide: 1978.* Essex, England: Africa Guide Co., 1977.

UWECHUE, RALPH, ed., *Africa: An International Business, Economic and Political Monthly.* London: Africa Journal Ltd., 1971 to the present.

GOVERNMENT

ADE AJAYI, J.F., AND CROWDER, MICHAEL, eds., *History of West Africa,* volume II, New York: Columbia University Press, 1973.

AFIGBO, A.E. "The Indigenous Political Systems of the Igbo," *Tarikh,* 4, no. 2 (1972), 1–13.

APTER, DAVID. *Ghana in Transition.* Princeton: Princeton University Press, 1963.

——. *The Political Kingdom in Uganda.* Princeton: Princeton University Press, 1967.

ATANDA, J.A. "Indirect Rule in Yorubaland," *Tarikh,* 3, no. 3 (1970), 16–29.

BENNETT, GEORGE. *Kenya: A Political History: Colonial Period.* London: Oxford University Press, 1963.

BIOBAKU, S.O., ed., *Sources of Yoruba History,* London: Oxford University Press, 1973.

BOZEMAN, ADDA B. *Conflict in Africa.* Princeton: Princeton University Press, 1976.

BRETTON, HENRY L. *Power and Politics in Africa.* Chicago: Aldine Publishing Co., 1973.

CHILCOTE, RONALD. *Portuguese Africa.* Englewood Cliffs, N.J.: Prentice-Hall, Inc., 1967.

CROWDER, MICHAEL. *West Africa under Colonial Rule,* Evanston, III.: Northwestern University Press, 1968.

——. "The Adminisration of French West Africa," *Tarikh,* 2, no. 4 (1969), 59–72.

DECALO, SAMUEL. *Coups and Army Rule in Africa.* New Haven: Yale University Press, 1976.

DORO, MARION E., AND STULTZ, NEWELL M., eds., *Governing in Black Africa: Perspectives on New States.* Englewood Cliffs, N.J.: Prentice-Hall, Inc., 1970.

DUFFY, JAMES. *Portugal in Africa.* Baltimore: Penguin Books, Inc., 1963.

FORDE, DARYLL, AND KABERRY, PHYLLIS M., eds., *West African Kingdoms in the Nineteenth Century.* London: Oxford University Press, 1967.

FORTES, M., AND EVANS-PRITCHARD, E.E., eds., *African Political Systems.* London: Oxford University Press, 1970.

GANN, L.H., AND DUIGNAN, PETER, eds., *Colonialism in Africa 1870–1960,* volume II, London: Cambridge University Press, 1970.

GEISS, IMANUEL. *The Pan-African Movement.* New York: Africana Publishing Co., 1974.

GREEN, M.M. *Ibo Village Affairs.* London: Frank Cass & Co. Ltd., 1964.

GRUNDY, KENNETH. *Guerrilla Struggle in Africa.* New York: Grossman Publishers, 1971.

GUTTERIDGE, W.F. *Military Regimes in Africa.* London: Methuen & Co. Ltd., 1975.

HODGKIN, THOMAS. *Nationalism in Colonial Africa.* New York: New York University Press, 1956.

HORRELL, MURIEL, ed., *Legislation and Race Relations.* Johannesburg: South African Institute of Race Relations, 1971.

HULL, RICHARD W. *Munyakare, African Civilization before the Batuuree.* New York, John Wiley and Sons, Co., 1972.

Human Rights Violations in Ethiopia, AFR 25/10/78. London: Amnesty International., 1978.

JOHNSON, SAMUEL. *The History of the Yorubas.* London: Routledge & Kegan Paul Ltd., 1969.

JORDAN, ROBERT S. *Government and Power in West Africa.* New York: Africana Publishing Co., 1969.

KEPPEL-JONES, A. *South Africa.* London: Hutchinson & Co., 1975.

LAST, MURRAY. *The Sokoto Caliphate.* New York: Humanities Press, 1967.

LEGUM, COLIN. *Pan-Africanism.* New York: Praeger Publishers, Inc., 1962.

MAITLAND-JONES, J.F. *Politics in Africa: The Former British Territories.* New York: W.W. Norton & Co., 1973.

MARQUARD, LEO. *The Peoples and Policies of South Africa.* New York: Oxford University Press, 1969.

MINOGUE, MARTIN, AND MOLLOY, JUDITH, eds., *African Aims and Attitudes. London:* Cambridge University Press, 1974.

OGOT, B.A., AND KIERNAN, J.A., eds., *Zamani: A Survey of East African History.* New York: Humanities Press, 1968.

OLORUNSOLA, V.A., ed., *The Politics of Cultural Sub-Nationalism in Africa.* Garden City, N.Y.: Doubleday & Co., 1972.

OPOLOT, JAMES. *Criminal Justice and Nation-Building in Africa.* Washington, D.C.: University Press of America, 1976.

OWEN, ROGER, AND SUTCLIFFE, BOB, eds., *Studies in the Theory of Imperialism.* London: Longman Group Ltd., 1972.

POST, KEN. *The New States of West Africa.* Baltimore: Penguin Books Inc., 1968.

RANGER, T.O., ed., *Aspects of Central African History.* London: Heinemann Educational Books Ltd., 1968.

RATHBONE, R., "World War I and Africa," *Journal of African History,* 19, no. 1 (1978), 1-11.

ROBERTS, A., ed., *Tanzania Before 1900.* Dar es Salaam: East African Publishing House, 1968.

ROSCOE, J. *The Baganda.* London: Macmillan Ltd., 1911.

ROTBERG, ROBERT I., ed., *Rebellion in Black Africa.* New York: Oxford University Press, 1971.

RUBIN, LESLIE, AND WEINSTEIN, BRIAN. *Introduction to African Politics* (2nd ed.) New York: Praeger Publishers, Inc., 1977.

SEIDMAN, ROBERT B. *Research in African Law and the Process of Change.* Los Angeles: University of California Press, 1967.

SMITH, R.S. *Kingdoms of the Yoruba.* London: Methuen & Co. Ltd., 1969.

THOMPSON, V.B. *Africa and Unity: The Evolution of Pan-Africanism.* London: Longman Group, Ltd., 1971.

UKPABI, SAMUEL C. *Military Involvement in African Politics.* New York: Conch Publishers, Inc., 1972.

VERHELST, THIERRY. *Safeguarding African Customary Law.* Berkeley: University of California Press, 1968.

WALLERSTEIN, IMMANUEL. *Africa: The Politics of Independence.* New York: Alfred A. Knopf, Inc., 1961.

——. *Africa: The Politics of Unity.* New York: Alfred A. Knopf, Inc., 1967.

WALKER, ERIC A. *A History of Southern Africa.* London: Longman Group, Ltd., 1972.

WELCH, CLAUDE E. "The Dilemma of Military Withdrawal from Politics," *African Studies Review,* 17, no. 1 (April 1974), 213-29.

WILSON, H.S., ed., *Origins of West African Nationalism.* London: Macmillan, 1969.

WILSON, MONICA, AND THOMPSON, LEONARD, eds., *The Oxford History of South Africa, Volume II: 1870-1966.* New York: Oxford University Press, 1971.

YOUNG, CRAWFORD. *Politics in the Congo.* Princeton: Princeton University Press, 1965.

THE ECONOMY

AMIN, SAMIR. *Neo-Colonialism in West Africa.* Harmondsworth: Penguin Books, Ltd., 1973.

ARIKPO, OKOI. *The Development of Modern Nigeria.* Baltimore: Penguin Books Inc., 1967.

ARNOLD, GUY. *Modern Nigeria.* London: Longman Group Ltd., 1977.

ARRIGHI, G. *The Political Economy of Rhodesia.* The Hague: Nihoff Publishers, 1967.

BERRY, L., ed., *Tanzania in Maps.* New York: Africana Publishing Corp., 1972.

BRETT, E.A. *Colonialism and Underdevelopment in East Africa: 1919-1939.* New York: Nok Publications, 1973.

COHEN, ROBIN. *Labour and Politics in Nigeria.* London: Heinemann Ltd., 1974.

COLLINS, ROBERT O., ed., *Problems in the History of Colonial Africa: 1860-1960.* Englewood Cliffs, N.J.: Prentice-Hall, Inc., 1970.

DAAKU, K.Y. "Aspects of Precolonial Akan Economy," *International Journal of African Historical Studies,* 5, no. 2 (1972), 24–53.

DAMACHI, U.G. *Nigerian Modernization: The Colonial Legacy.* New York: The Third Press, 1972.

——, AND SEIBEL, H.D., eds., *Social Change and Economic Development in Nigeria.* New York: Praeger Publishers, Inc., 1973.

DAVENPORT, T.R.H. *The Right to the Land.* Cape Town: David Philip Publisher, Ltd., 1974.

DAVIES, P.N. *The Trade Makers: Elder Dempster in West Africa, 1852–1972.* London: Oxford University Press, 1973.

DAVIS, KINGSLEY. *World Urbanization 1950–1970,* volume II. Berkeley: University of California Press., 1972.

DEKIEWIET, C.W. *A History of South Africa: Social and Economic.* London: Oxford University Press, 1966.

DIKE, K.O. *Trade and Politics in the Niger Delta, 1830–1895.* London: Oxford University Press, 1956.

DUMONT, RENÉ. *False Start in Africa.* London: Sphere Books, Ltd., 1966.

EKUNDARE, R.O. *An Economic History of Nigeria, 1860–1960.* London: Frank Cass & Co., 1973.

FLINT, J.L. *Sir George Goldie and the Making of Nigeria.* London: Oxford University Press, 1960.

FORDHAM, PAUL. *The Geography of African Affairs.* Baltimore: Penguin Books, Inc., 1965.

GRAY, RICHARD, AND BIRMINGHAM, DAVID., eds., *Pre-Colonial African Trade.* London: Oxford University Press, 1970.

GREEN, L.P., AND FAIR, T.J. *Development in Africa.* Johannesburg: University of Witwatersrand Press, 1965.

GUTKIND, PETER, C.W. AND WALLERSTEIN, I., eds., *The Political Economy of Contemporary Africa.* Beverly Hills, Calif.: Sage Publications, Inc., 1976.

HALLETT, ROBIN. *People and Progress in West Africa.* London: Pergamon Press, Inc., 1966.

HARLOW, VINCENT, ed., *History of East Africa,* volumes II and III, London: Oxford University Press, 1967.

HEPPLE, ALEX. *South Africa: A Political and Economic History.* New York: Praeger Publishers, Inc., 1968.

HERSKOVITS, M.J., AND HARWITZ, M., eds., *Economic Transition in Africa.* Evanston, Ill.: Northwestern University Press, 1964.

HOPKINS, A.G. *An Economic History of West Africa.* London: Longman Group Ltd., 1973.

——. "Imperial Business in Africa: Part I," *Journal of African History,* 17, no. 1 (1976), 29–49.

——. "Imperial Business in Africa: Part II," *Journal of African History,*17, no. 2 (1976), 267–91.

HOUGHTON, HOBART D., AND DAGET, J., eds., *Source Materials on the South African Economy* 1860–1970, 3 volumes. Cape Town: Oxford University Press, 1972.

KAMARK, A.M. *The Economics of African Development.* New York: Praeger Publishers, Inc., 1967.

KAY, G.B., ed., *The Political Economy of Colonialism: Documents 1900–1960.* London: Cambridge University Press, 1972.

KAY, GEORGE. *Rhodesia: A Human Geography.* London: University of London Press, 1970.

KIMAMBO, I.N., AND TEMU, A.J., eds., *A History of Tanzania.* Dar es Salaam: East African Publishing House, 1969.

KIMBLE, G.H.T. *Tropical Africa,* volume I. Garden City, N.Y.: Doubleday & Co., Inc., 1962.

LIVINGSTONE, I., AND ORD, H.W. *Introduction to Economics for East Africa.* London: Heinemann, 1968.

McLOUGHLIN, PETER F.M., ed., *African Food Production Systems.* Baltimore: Johns Hopkins University Press, 1970.

McPHEE, ALLAN. *The Economic Revolution in British West Africa.* London: Routledge Kegan Paul Ltd., 1926.

MORGAN, W.B., AND PUGH, J.D. *West Africa.* London: Methuen & Co. Ltd., 1973.

MUNRO, J. FORBES. *Africa and the International Economy 1800-1960.* London: J.M. Dent & Sons., 1976.

NAFZIGER, E. WAYNE. *African Capitalism.* Stanford, Calif.: Hoover Institution, 1977.

NKRUMAH, KWAME. *Neo-Colonialism.* New York: International Publishers, 1965.

OMOSINI, O., "The Gold Coast Land Question: 1894-1900," *International Journal of African Historical Studies,* 7, no. 2 (1974), 18-30.

PEDLER, F.J. *Economic Geography of West Africa.* London: Longmans Green Ltd., 1955.

PHILLIPS, EARL, "State Regulation and Economic Initiative: The South African Case to 1960," *International Journal of African Historical Studies,* 7, no. 2 (1974), 56-91.

ROBSON, PETER. *Economic Integration in Africa.* Evanston, Ill.: Northwestern University Press, 1968.

RODNEY, WALTER. *How Europe Underdeveloped Africa.* Dar es Salaam: Tanzania Publishing House, 1972.

ROUX, EDWARD. *Time Longer than Rope.* Madison: University of Wisconsin Press, 1966.

RWEYMAMU, A., ed., *Nation-Building in Tanzania.* Dar es Salaam: East Africa Publishing House, 1970.

SUNDSTROM, L. *The Exchange Economy of Precolonial Tropical Africa.* London: Tudor Press, 1974.

SURET-CANALE, JEAN. *French Colonialism in Tropical Africa.* Budapest: Isto Press, 1971.

THOMAS, M.F., "Environment and Land Use in Africa," *African Environment,* I, no. 3 (October 1975), 91-101.

THOMPSON, LEONARD M., AND BUTLER, JEFFREY, eds., *Change in Contemporary South Africa.* Berkeley: University of California Press, 1975.

VAKHRUSHEV, VASILY. *Neo-colonialism: Methods and Manoeuvres.* Moscow: Progress Publishers, 1973.

VAN ZWANENBERG, R.M.A. *An Economic History of Kenya and Uganda, 1800-1970.* London: Crest Press, 1976.

WARD, W.E.F., AND WHITE, L.W. *East Africa: A Century of Change 1870-1970.* New York: Africana Publishing, 1972.

WHETHAM, E.H., AND CURRIE, J.I., eds., *Readings in the Applied Economics of Africa,* 2 volumes. London: Cambridge University Press, 1967.

WICKINS, P.L., "The One Big Union Movement among Black Workers in South Africa." *International Journal of African Historical Studies,* 7. no. 3 (1975), 391-417.

WILSON, FRANCIS. *Labour in the South African Gold Mines, 1911-1969. London:* Cambridge University Press, 1972.

——. *Migrant Labour in South Africa.* Johannesburg: Spro-Cas, 1972.

WILSON, H.S. *The Imperial Experience in Sub-Saharan Africa since 1870.* London: Cambridge University Press, 1978.

RELIGION AND CULTURE

ABRAHAMS, LIONEL, AND SAUNDERS, WALTER, eds., *Quarry '76.* Johannesburg: A.D. Donker, 1976.

ABRAHAMS, PETER. *Mine Boy.* New York: The Macmillan Company, 1970.

ACHEBE, CHINUA. *A Man of the People.* Garden City, N.Y.: Doubleday & Co., 1966.

——. *Things Fall Apart.* New York: Fawcett World Library, 1970.

——. *Arrow of God.* Garden City, N.Y.: Doubleday & Co., 1969.

ADEDEJI, J.A. "Oral Tradition and the Contemporary Theatre in Nigeria," *Research in African Literatures,* 2, no. 2 (Fall 1971), 134-50.

"African Music Today" (record). New York: Afri-Art Guild Publishing, 1974.

ALEXANDER, F.L. *South African Graphic Art and Its Techniques.* Cape Town: Human & Rousseau, 1974.

"Apartheid: Its Effects on Education, Science, Culture and Information." Paris: United Nations Educational, Scientific and Cultural Organization, 1968.

ASARE, BEDIAKO. *Rebel.* Nairobi: Heinemann Educational Books Ltd., 1969.

AWOONOR, KOFI, AND ADALI-MORTTY, G., eds., *Messages: Poems from Ghana.* Ibadan: Heinemann Educational Books Ltd., 1971.

AYANDELE, E.A. *The Missionary Impact on Modern Nigeria 1842-1914.* London: Longman Group Ltd., 1966.

BALANDIER, GEORGES. "Messianism and Nationalism in Black Africa," in *Perspectives on the African Past,* ed. Martin A. Klein and G. Wesley Johnson. Boston: Little, Brown & Co., 1972.

BASCOM, WILLIAM. *African Art.* New York: W.W. Norton & Co., 1973.

BASCOM, W.R., AND HERSKOVITS, M.J., eds., *Continuity and Change in African Cultures.* Chicago: University of Chicago Press, 1959.

BATTLE, VINCENT, AND LYONS, CHARLES H., eds., *Essays in the History of African Education.* New York: Teachers College Press, 1970.

BEIER, ULLI. *Three Nigerian Plays.* London: Longmans, Green Ltd., 1967.

——, AND MOORE, GERALD, eds., *Modern Poetry from Africa.* Baltimore: Penguin Books, Inc., 1963.

p'BITEK, OKOT. *Song of Ocol.* Nairobi: East African Publishing House, 1970.

——. *Song of a Prisoner.* New York: The Third Press, 1971.

——. *Song of Lawino.* Nairobi: Heinemann Educational Books Ltd., 1966.

BRENCH, A.C. *The Novelists' Inheritance in French Africa.* London: Oxford University Press, 1967.

CARTEY, WILFRED, ed., *Whispers from a Continent: The Literature of Contemporary Black Africa.* New York: Random House, Inc., 1969.

CARTEY, WILFRED, AND KILSON, MARTIN, eds., *The Africa Reader: Colonial Africa.* New York: Random House, Inc., 1970.

CLIGNET, R., AND FOSTER, P.J., "French and British Colonial Education in Africa," in *Perspectives on the African Past,* ed. Martin A. Klein and G. Wesley Johnson. Boston: Little, Brown and Company, 1972.

COLEMAN, JAMES S., ed., *Education and Political Development.* Princeton: Princeton University Press, 1965.

"Colloquium on Negro Art," Dakar: Presence Africaine, 1968.

CONTON, WILLIAM. *The African.* New York: Signet, 1960.

COOK, DAVID, AND LEE, MILES, eds., *Short East African Plays in English.* Nairobi: Heinemann Educational Books Ltd., 1968.

COOK, MERCER, AND HENDERSON, S.E., eds., *The Militant Black Writer in Africa and the United States.* Madison: University of Wisconsin Press, 1969.

COPE, JACK, AND UYS, KRIGE, eds., *The Penguin Book of South African Verse.* London: Penguin Books Ltd., 1968.

CORNET, JOSEPH. *Art from Zaire.* New York: African-American Institute, 1975.

COWAN, L. GRAY, O'CONNELL, JAMES, AND SCANLON, DAVID G., eds., *Education and Nation-Building in Africa.* New York: Frederick A. Praeger Inc., 1966.

DAVIDSON, BASIL. *The African Slave Trade.* Boston: Atlantic-Little, Brown & Co., 1961.

——. *The African Genius.* Boston: Atlantic-Little, Brown & Co., 1969.

DE JAGER, E.J. *Contemporary African Art in South Africa.* Cape Town: C. Struik, Ltd., 1973.

DIETZ, B.W., AND OLATUNJI, M. *Musical Instruments of Africa.* New York: John Day Inc., 1965.

DODD, W.A. *Education for Self-Reliance in Tanzania.* New York: Teachers College Press, 1969.

EGUDU, ROMANUS, AND NWOGA, DONATUS. *Igbo Traditional Verse.* Ibadan: Heinemann Educational Books Ltd., 1973.

EKWENSI, CYPRIAN. *Jagua Nana.* New York: Fawcett World Library, 1961.

FELDMANN, SUSAN, ed., *African Myths and Tales.* New York: Dell Publishing Co., Inc., 1970.

FORDE, DARYLL, ed., *African Worlds.* London: Oxford University Press, 1968.

FRASER, DOUGLAS. *Village Planning in the Primitive World.* New York: George Braziller Inc., 1968.

GARDI, RENÉ. *Indigenous African Architecture.* New York: Van Nostrand Reinhold Company, 1973.

HODGKIN, THOMAS. *Nationalism in Colonial Africa.* New York: New York University Press, 1957.

HORRELL, MURIEL, ed., *Legislation and Race Relations.* Johannesburg: South African Institute of Race Relations, 1971.

HUGHES, LANGSTON, ed., *Poems from Black Africa.* Bloomington: Indiana University Press, 1963.

HULL, RICHARD W. *African Cities and Towns before the European Conquest.* New York: W.W. Norton & Co., 1976.

JONES, EMRYS. *Towns and Cities.* London: Oxford University Press, 1966.

KACHINGWE, AUBREY. *No Easy Task.* Ibadan: Heinemann Educational Books Ltd., 1966.

KANDIA, KOUYATE. "L'Epopee du Mandingue" (record). Conakry: Edition Syliphone, 1972.

KANE, HAMIDOU. *Ambiguous Adventure.* New York: The Macmillan Company, 1969.

KILLAM, G.D. *The Novels of Chinua Achebe.* New York: Africana Publishing Corporation, 1969.

KNAPPERT, JAN. *Myths and Legends of the Congo.* London: Heinemann Educational Books Ltd., 1971.

KRITZECK, J., AND LEWIS, W.H., eds., *Islam in Africa.* New York: Van Nostrand Reinhold Company, 1969.

KROG, E.W., ed., *African Literature in Rhodesia.* Salisbury: Mambo Press, 1966.

KULTERMANN, UDO. *New Directions in African Architecture.* New York: George Braziller Inc., 1969.

LA GUMA, ALEX, ed., *Apartheid: A Collection of Writings.* New York: International Publishers, 1971.

LARSON, CHARLES R. *More Modern African Stories.* Glasgow, Scotland: Fontana, 1975.

LEROUX, ETIENNE. *To a Dubious Salvation.* London: Penguin Books Ltd., 1972.

LEUZINGER, ELSY. *Africa: The Art of the Negro Peoples.* New York: McGraw-Hill Book Company Inc., 1960.

LEWIS, I.M., ed., *Islam in Tropical Africa.* London: Oxford University Press, 1966.

LITTLE, KENNETH. *African Women in Towns.* London: Cambridge University Press, 1973.

LITTO, F.M. *Plays from Black Africa.* New York: Hill and Wang, 1968.

LLOYD, P.C. *Africa in Social Change.* Harmondsworth: Penguin, 1967.

——, AND MABOGUNJE, A.L. *The City of Ibadan.* London: Cambridge University Press, 1967.

MABOGUNJE, AKIN L. *Urbanization in Nigeria.* New York: Africana Publishing Co., 1968.

MAIR, LUCY. *African Societies.* London: Cambridge University Press, 1974.

MAKEBA, MIRIAM. "The Voice of Africa." New York: Radio Corp. of America, 1964.

MBITI, JOHN S. *African Religions and Philosophy.* New York: Frederick A. Praeger Inc., 1969.

MERRIAM, ALAN P. *African Music on L.P.* Evanston, Ill.: Northwestern University Press, 1965.

MICHELMAN, FREDERIC. "The Beginnings of French-African Fiction," *Research in African Literatures,* 2, no. 1 (1971), 5–18.

MIERS, SUZANNE, AND KOPYTOFF, IGOR, eds. *Slavery in Africa.* Madison: University of Wisconsin Press, 1977.

MOORE, CARMAN. "Ghana's Dance Company," *African Report,* (March, 1970), 30–3.

MPHAHLELE, EZEKIEL, ed., *African Writing Today.* Baltimore: Penguin Books Inc., 1967.

"Mustapha Tettey Addy-Master Drummer from Ghana" (record). London: Tangent Records, 1973.

NATHAN, FERNAND, ed., *La Poesie traditionelle.* Paris: Classiques du Monde, 1971.

NEWMAN, THELMA R. *Contemporary African Arts and Crafts.* New York: Crown, Inc., 1974.

NWOGA, DONATUS, ed., *West African Verse.* London: Longmans, Green and Co. Ltd., 1967.

OGOT, GRACE. *The Promised Land.* Nairobi: East African Publishing House, 1966.

OJO, G.J. *Yoruba Culture.* London: University of London Press, 1966.

——. *Yoruba Palaces.* London: University of London Press, 1966.

OKAM, HILARY, ed., "Traditional and Contemporary African Literature," *Yale French Studies,* no. 53 (1976).

OKPAKU, JOSEPH. *New African Literature and the Arts,* 3 volumes. New York: The Third Press, 1973.

OLIVER, PAUL, ed., *Shelter in Africa.* New York: Praeger Publishers, Inc., 1971.

OLIVER, ROLAND. *The Missionary Factor in East Africa.* London: Oxford University Press, 1965.

PARRINDER, GEOFFREY. *Religion in Africa.* Baltimore: Penguin Books, Inc., 1969.

——. *African Mythology.* London: The Hamlyn Publishing Group Ltd., 1967.

PEIL, MARGARET. *Consensus and Conflict in African Societies.* London: Longman Group, Ltd., 1977.

POVEY, JOHN, ed., *African Arts,* 7–12 (December 1970-December 1978).

RATTRAY, R.S. *Ashanti Proverbs.* London: Oxford University Press, 1916.

ROYSTON, ROBERT, ed., *To Whom It May Concern: An Anthology of Black South African Poetry.* Johannesburg: AD. Donker, 1973.

RUBADIRI, DAVID. *No Bride Price.* Nairobi: East African Publishing House, 1967.

SACKO, FANTA. "Musique du Mali" (record). Bamako: Ministry of Information, 1970.

SAMKANGE, STANLAKE. *On Trial for My Country.* Nairobi: Heinemann Educational Books, Ltd., 1969.

SEPLAMA, SIPHO, ed., *Sketsh, South Africa's Magazine for Theatre and Entertainment,* (Summer, 1975) Vol. 2.

SERUMA, ENERIKO. *The Experience.* Nairobi: East African Publishing House, 1970.

SIMMS, RUTH. *Urbanization in West Africa.* Evanston, Ill.: Northwestern University Press, 1965.

SIMONS, H.J., AND R.E. *Class and Color in South Africa 1850-1950.* Harmondsworth: Penguin Books Ltd., 1969.

SKINNER, NEIL. *Hausa Tales and Traditions,* volume I. New York: Africana Publishing Corporation, 1970.

SMALL, ADAM. *Black, Bronze, Beautiful.* Johannesburg: AD. Donker, 1975.

SOYINKA, WOLE. *The Lion and the Jewel.* Ibadan: Oxford University Press, 1970.

——, ed., *Poems of Black Africa.* New York: Hill and Wang, 1975.

STOUT, J. ANTHONY. *Modern Makonde Sculpture.* Nairobi: Kibo Art Gallery, 1966.

TEMPELS, PLACIDE. *Bantu Philosophy.* Paris: Pan-African Press, 1969.

TRIMINGHAM, J.S. *The Influence of Islam upon Africa.* New York: Frederick A. Praeger Inc., 1968.

TUCKER, MARTIN, ed., *Africa in Modern Literature.* New York: Frederick Ungar Publishing Co., 1967.

UCKO, P.J., ed., *Man, Settlement and Urbanism.* London: Duckworth, 1972.

VAN DEN BERGHE, PIERRE. *South Africa: A Study in Conflict.* Los Angeles: University of California Press, 1967.

VAN DER MERWE, H., compiler, *Looking at the Afrikaner Today.* Cape Town: Tafelberg, 1975.

WEBSTER, J.B. "Independent Christians," *Tarikh,* 3, no. 1 (1969), 56–82.

——. "Syncretism," *Tarikh,* 2, no. 1 (1967), 1–4.

WEEKS, SHELDON. *Divergence in Educational Development: Kenya and Uganda.* New York: Teachers College Press, 1967.

WHITELEY, W.H., compiler, *A Selection of African Prose* (written). London: Oxford University Press, 1964.

——, compiler, *A Selection of African Prose* (oral). London: Oxford University Press, 1964.

WILLETT, FRANK. *African Art.* New York: Praeger Publishers, Inc., 1971.

Index